Life
at the
Bottom

Books By John Langone:

VITAL SIGNS: The Way We Die in America
LIFE AT THE BOTTOM: The People of Antarctica

For Children:
DEATH IS A NOUN: A View of the End of Life
GOODBYE TO BEDLAM:
Understanding Mental Illness and Retardation
BOMBED, BUZZED, SMASHED, OR . . . SOBER?
A Book about Alcohol

Life at the Bottom

The People of Antarctica

JOHN LANGONE

Little, Brown and Company — Boston – Toronto

FIRST EDITION

T07/77

Second Printing

The author is grateful to the following publishers for permission to quote from previously copyrighted materials:

J. B. Lippincott, for excerpts from *The Heart of the Antarctic* by Ernest H. Shackleton.

Dodd, Mead & Company, and McGraw-Hill Ryerson Limited, for lines from "The Heart of the Sourdough" and "The Call of the Wild" from *Collected Poems of Robert Service*.

Constable & Company, Ltd., for excerpts from *The Worst Journey in the World* by Apsley Cherry-Garrard.

LIBRARY OF CONGRESS CATALOGING IN PUBLICATION DATA

Langone, John, 1929–
   Life at the bottom.
    1. Antarctic regions. I. Title.
  G860.L36   919.8   77-1540
  ISBN 0-316-15426-3

Designed by Susan Windheim

*Published simultaneously in Canada
by Little, Brown & Company (Canada) Limited*

PRINTED IN THE UNITED STATES OF AMERICA

For Dolores

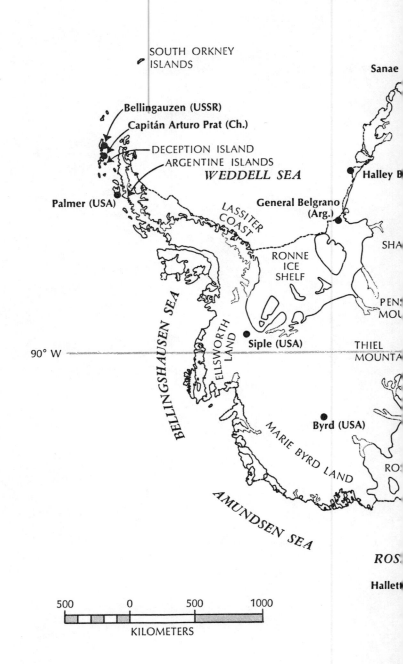

SOUTH ORKNEY
ISLANDS

Sanae

Bellingauzen (USSR)

Capitán Arturo Prat (Ch.)

DECEPTION ISLAND
ARGENTINE ISLANDS

WEDDELL SEA

Halley B

General Belgrano
(Arg.)

Palmer (USA)

LASSITER
COAST

SHA

RONNE
ICE
SHELF

PEN:
MO

BELLINGSHAUSEN SEA

ELLSWORTH
LAND

Siple (USA)

THIEL
MOUNTA

90° W

Byrd (USA)

MARIE BYRD LAND

RO:

AMUNDSEN SEA

ROS

Hallet

| 500 | 0 | 500 | 1000 |

KILOMETERS

ANTARCTICA Sele

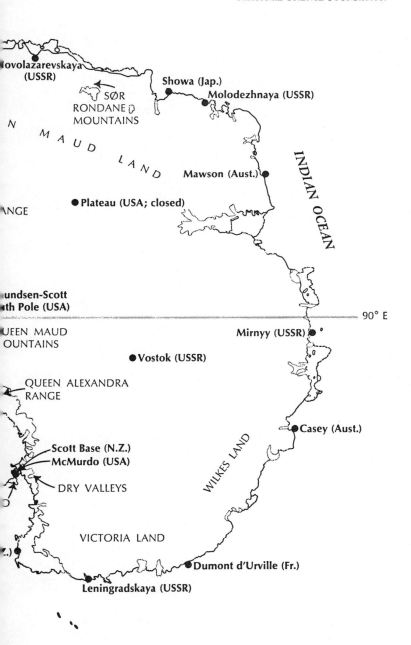

Novolazarevskaya (USSR)

SØR RONDANE MOUNTAINS

Showa (Jap.)

Molodezhnaya (USSR)

N

MAUD LAND

Mawson (Aust.)

INDIAN OCEAN

RANGE

●Plateau (USA; closed)

Amundsen-Scott South Pole (USA)

90° E

QUEEN MAUD MOUNTAINS

Mirnyy (USSR)●

●Vostok (USSR)

QUEEN ALEXANDRA RANGE

Casey (Aust.)

Scott Base (N.Z.)
McMurdo (USA)

DRY VALLEYS

WILKES LAND

D

VICTORIA LAND

Dumont d'Urville (Fr.)

Leningradskaya (USSR)

ions and Physical Features

Acknowledgments

In writing this book, I relied heavily on my own notes taken while in Antarctica, on taped interviews, on secondary sources, and on recollection. Some names have been changed to spare their owners embarrassment, and I have altered certain events and their place in time to suit my purposes, one of which was to make the narrative as interesting as possible. A few of the characters presented herein are composites.

Among those to whom I am most indebted are Guy G. Guthridge, Director of the Polar Information Service of the National Science Foundation; Walter Dodd of NSF's Public Information Office; Capt. Alfred N. Fowler, USN, former Commander of Antarctic Support Activities, Davisville, Rhode Island; EO2 Victor "Moose" Marino, the "Mayor of McMurdo"; UTC James Wallace; and CM1 Jimmie Evans.

My special thanks to Herman R. Friis, Director of the Center for Polar Archives of the National Archives and Records Service; and the late Robert J. Buettner, Project Manager, Antarctic Support Services, Holmes & Narver, Inc.

The *Antarctic Journal* of the United States was an invaluable source of reference, as were the Houghton Library of Rare Books at Harvard University and the library of the Boston *Herald American*.

My gratitude, finally, to my able editor, William Phillips.

While I am grateful to all who have assisted me, my thanks should not imply that each agrees with this book's point of

ix

view. I alone am responsible for that and for any errors contained herein.

JOHN LANGONE
Hingham, Massachusetts
June 1976

Come, my friends,
'Tis not too late to seek a newer world.
Push off, and sitting well in order smite
The sounding furrows; for my purpose holds
To sail beyond the sunset, and the baths
Of all the western stars, until I die.

—ALFRED, LORD TENNYSON

Life
at the
Bottom

1

I have an old globe at home on my study desk, and it is perched on a brass rod fixed to a three-legged stand like a ball twirled on a juggler's finger. The rod is about a half-inch in diameter, and it is set directly into the South Pole, covering it as though the mapmaker couldn't have cared less about the spot's significance or, what is more likely, given the age of the sphere, didn't know all that much about the place he must have seen as godforsaken. Everything else on the globe, even the area around the North Pole, is marked clearly and neatly with black type, and in various colors. Antarctica is but a hazy outline, all white, with this brass screw piercing it. No place names, no topographic features, though it is the size of the United States and Mexico combined, with mountains, valleys, plateaus, and lakes, 5½ million square miles in all, just lines of longitude converging under a screw.

When I was selected to go there, my knowledge of Antarctica was as sketchy as that of most Americans. Robert Falcon Scott's ill-fated race against Roald Amundsen to be the first at the South Pole was a long time ago, 1912, and they belonged to British and Norwegian schoolboys anyway. Richard Evelyn Byrd's Antarctic public relations machine ground to a halt with the outbreak of World War II, and those of us who were teenagers during those years, cut off from the admiral's explorations, had to turn to the more violent idols thrust upon us by the Office of War Information.

I had never burned from adolescence to visit Antarctica. It

would be nice to be able to say that I had and that it was a dream fulfilled, as did several others I was to meet later on. Antarctica was, for me, simply one of the seven continents, always the last one I'd mention, mispronounced or misspelled, whenever a grammar school teacher asked me to list them. I knew it was covered with ice and snow, and that it was hidden under the brass screw.

Years later, I read Poe's *Narrative of Arthur Gordon Pym*, about a New England kid who stows away on a whaler, and there's mutiny and cannibalism, and at the conclusion he's drifting toward the South Pole in a canoe, and this huge white figure looms out of the mist and so on. Then I was into H. P. Lovecraft, mostly because he liked Poe, too. He picked up on the Antarctic theme, and wrote *At the Mountains of Madness*, an eldritch dimension of horror on the ice, as the book jacket told my wide eyes. The barren windswept interior of Antarctica was lifeless, or so the expedition from Miskatonic University thought until they found the strange fossils of unheard-of creatures and the mind-blasting terror of the City of the Old Ones. It finally took a recording of Ralph Vaughan Williams's Sinfonia Antartica, with its woodwinds and brass, bells and wind machine portraying the Antarctic chill and the blizzard that defeated Scott in his march across the frozen ghostland, to correct the impressions with which the jaundiced geographers, Poe and Lovecraft, infected me. But that was after I had been to Antarctica, and I am thankful for that. Had I heard the music before the visit, as suggestive as it is of the bleakness of the polar region, it would have whetted my interest, but I would have been denied the immense and incomparable pleasure of recognition, of remembering. Playing it now that the trip is over is like running through my own family photograph album, not someone else's.

Getting to Antarctica, unless you have been invited and

have business there, is virtually impossible, and that criterion rules out most people. One cruise ship makes an occasional stop, catering to those who have had everything else for Christmas, and that's usually at the tip of the Antarctic Peninsula, which juts up to meet Tierra del Fuego. The Navy personnel there call it the banana belt because its average temperature is 26 degrees Fahrenheit, with 23 inches of precipitation a year.

In contrast, the interior, where professional tourists never go, is what gives Antarctica the distinction of being the coldest, windiest continent in the world, with temperatures that have plunged to 126.9 degrees below zero, a world record, and fierce katabatic winds roaring down from the high ice plateaus toward the sea at up to 200 miles an hour.

I wanted to go, after talking to a competing journalist who had been there, because I wanted to see the show, too, because those of us in this business have insatiable egos and terrible insecurities, and we like to deal in superlatives and news that deviates from the norm, the bigger the deviation the bigger the news. What better place than Antarctica and the South Pole to get all of that together — highest, driest, windiest, coldest — to be one of the relative handful of people who have ever set foot that far south, braving the frozen wastes and all that. It was the ultimate trip; why, it would be like going to the moon, almost.

I also wanted to get away for a while, too, from rewriting my own clips — some already brittle-brown from only a few years in the manila morgue envelopes — in an effort to come up with a "fresh" approach to an article about the effects of a heat wave on urban dwellers, or a cold wave. I had done stories like that over ten summers and ten winters, and it had got so that I didn't even need the clips anymore except for a glance at the leads so I wouldn't repeat them exactly.

And I wanted to get away from the solid gold sounds

slamming out of AM radio and my kids' rooms at six in the morning, from nine to five and home at six, supper at seven. I was also a hard person to buy for at Christmas.

But those are not reasons enough when you write to the National Science Foundation, which is responsible for funding and managing all U.S. activities on Antarctica. You got to sling a little bull, my competing journalist who had been there told me. They eat that right up; it's like writing a grant proposal, or a campaign speech. A little promise about plenty of space and a big headline display, you want to help better educate the public about the most successful program of international research in the history of science, stuff like that. Main thing is to hit the applied science, that's the key word, *application*. The basic stuff, forget it. You've got to apply it. Just like the scientist does when he puts in for his grant. They're just not going to give it to him anymore if he can't tell them what he's doing may — with a capital M — help, in finding a cure for something or other, or it's going to have global implications for weather.

So I applied in the summer, one of a hundred or so journalists who do, and I must have slung it better than the other applicants. In September, I got a call from the office of the chief of information of NSF, Jack Renirie, and he told me, pausing dramatically after he breathed my name into the phone, "Hang onto your goosebumps, you're going to the ice." Wow, I said, my stomach suddenly thrilling and weak. There'd be an official letter in a few days and he'd see me later. I hung up, and my office mate came over, and I told him excitedly, "I'm going to the South Pole." He looked at me with pity and said, "What did you do to deserve that? The Navy sent me up to Kiska during the war and what a pisshole that was."

I called one of my summer shrink contacts, who doubled as

6

a winter shrink when we did the effects of prolonged cold on the psyche, and told him I might be needing him when I got back. He told me about a physician friend of his who spent six months there, and had to take some instruction in how to perform surgery on himself. He got so nervous about it all that he had his appendix and gallbladder removed before he went down.

It all moved along quickly. The first letter that came was from H. Guyford Stever, director of the National Science Foundation, inviting me, on behalf of the departments of State and Defense and the NSF, to observe the U.S. Antarctic Research Program (USARP) and the U.S. Navy support effort during the forthcoming field season. "I think," concluded Stever, "that you will find your visit to Antarctica stimulating and productive of information of great interest to the public. Good luck!"

Then a letter from Jack Renirie, congratulations on my selection and sure that I would find plenty of material for a variety of articles during my stay. They'll reserve a seat for me aboard an Air Force C-141 Starlifter, departing Quonset Point Naval Air Station, Rhode Island. It'll be 48 hours to Christchurch, New Zealand, with en route stops at Hickam Air Force Base in Honolulu, and Pago Pago, American Samoa. A night in Christchurch on the way down and on the way back at my expense. "Every effort, while you are on the continent of Antarctica, will be made to fly you to the South Pole station and other points, subject, of course, to the whimsy of the Antarctic weather!" There's a briefing held at Skyland in Virginia prior to departure, all cold weather clothing necessary for comfortable existence will be issued at Christchurch by representatives of the Foundation's Office of Polar Programs. Baggage weight allowance of 100 pounds per visitor, please fill out the attached personal information form

7

and the clothing size form and return it immediately in the envelope provided. Please do not get this envelope confused with the one for your physical examination form.

And another one from Renirie a few days later, necessary tidbits, he says they are: USARP doesn't issue indoor clothing, so bring jeans or wool pants, wool shirts, shorts, T-shirts, handkerchiefs, and a towel or two. Stamps and stationery, in short supply on the ice in the Antarctic spring and summer when we will be there. He includes some materials to provide some background about Antarctica and Antarcticans. "Some of it might even be productive of a story or two!"

I went to see my physician for the required examination and handed him a two-page, single-spaced memorandum, Physical Qualifications for Antarctic Visitors. It said, "The bearer of this memorandum and appended forms is preparing for a trip to Antarctica in the near future. While there he may be engaged in physical activity at altitudes of 9,000 to 11,500 feet, may experience temperatures as low as minus fifty degrees Fahrenheit and may make flights in unpressurized aircraft. Meals are irregular and it is common to go without sleep for long periods. Such stressful environmental conditions and extreme remoteness from major medical facilities make it mandatory that he be in good physical condition and free from any disability which could imperil his health, restrict his activities or create a burden for others in Antarctica." The memo invited his particular attention to the examinee's apparent physical age, endocrine disturbances, any condition which tends to compromise cutaneous circulation and sensation, herniation of vertebral disc, reduced vital capacity, vascular diseases, unrepaired hernias, active peptic ulcers, history of hepatitis, and he's to put the whole business onto forms SF89 and SF93.

My doctor shook his head and asked me how long I'd be gone, and I said no more than a month. He shook his head again and told me he'd been to Alaska and he never had to go through this business. He didn't like putting his name to that kind of stuff, government bureaucracy. Can you imagine what it'll be like if national health insurance comes in? But he finally asked me how I felt, pretty good? I said yes, so he put that down and he asked me if I had any of those things on the form, and I told him no, except for the disc operation a few years ago. He said, well, how is it now? I said, fine. So he put that down, and marked everything else okay.

2

Skyland

Mid-September, and five buses take us slowly through an early morning mist into the subdued greenery of the Shenandoah Mountains of Virginia. There are some 250 of us heading to Skyland Lodge for an orientation session for field personnel participating in USARP. Sponsored by the National Science Foundation and arranged by Holmes & Narver, Inc., the giant West Coast–based firm of contractors that, along with the U.S. Navy, handles a huge proportion of the scientific support and construction activities on the continent, such predeployment meetings are held annually to familiarize investigators with the overall program, the history of Antarctic research, survival techniques, and international cooperation, and to enable them to meet their colleagues and senior administrative personnel. "It's a total immersion thing," says an NSF official. "Skyland is miles away from anything, no phones in the rooms, three meals a day in the dining hall, no swimming pools, no movies except ours."

The group appears to be considerably younger than the scientists one usually encounters on stateside projects. Most of them are from west of the Mississippi. When I comment on the ages to a senior scientist sitting next to me, he says, with a slight edge, "Pardon me, but a lot of them aren't scientists, you know. The *real* scientists do go to the ice, of course, and some have gone back many times and will go again to continue their work. But a lot of them find it difficult to get away regularly; they've got deans sometimes who figure they're just out indulging themselves in the playground of the midnight sun. So what they do is send their students down to count the penguins and band the skua gulls and tend the stations they've set up in seasons past. We're not like the Russians." He frowns.

"They keep their polar experts in Antarctica year after year, middle-aged men who have made the ice a career. I'll bet that ninety percent of the people on these buses are on a first-time trip south, and furthermore, I'll even go so far as to say that they're not all going for science, no sir. Don't kid yourself. Science is just the vehicle, the ticket to get to the most improbable place on earth. They're going because they want a thrill, a holiday, and they get really upset when they can't get on a flight from McMurdo to visit the South Pole Station. That's the tipoff about how serious they are."

He says the ones he really doesn't care much for are those who use the Antarctic because it is the Antarctic, personal gain versus doing the job, the guy who figures he can make it big with some esoteric research that he could never do stateside, and it is a good place, maybe, he admits, for people with limited capability at home.

His last remark stirs two or three people sitting nearby, and one says, well, to be honest the funding got away from ice crystal physics so he switched to acoustics without missing a beat, thank God, and another says he got into cirrus clouds after all the work got done in some other kind of cloud I do not catch, and all the problems got solved and there was this Jap pain in the ass who was acing everyone out of the game, someone should have put sugar in his gas tank, slow him down.

One of the women on the bus asks how many are wintering over this time, and four or five hands go up rather quickly, for it is always winter-overs versus summer crews, the pecking order of the Antarctic. Though numbers vary from year to year, depending on the availability of research funds and the set of the economic thermostat, Antarctica might have a total summer population as high as 3,000, including representatives of all the nations with research activities there. Some 2,000 U.S. support personnel and 200 scientists spend the relatively pleasant period from mid-September to February working in a somewhat eerie 24 hours of sunlight. But when the last plane leaves the continent in February (daylight at the South Pole begins September 21 and ends March 21) only a handful will winter over, possibly some 20 scientists and 200 or fewer support people, all trying to cope with the desolation, the boredom, and the seemingly perpetual night, emerging from their shacks and, as is the case at the old Pole Station, from under-ice rooms, at infrequent intervals to tend to their experiments and apparatus. The few who stay the winter, the longest period of isolation for Americans on earth, are virtually out of touch with the outside world for six months, with no mail, radio contact subject to the weather and the earth's magnetic field, no fresh food, no one new to talk to.

The hands of the winter-overs tend to be clustered at the back of the bus, and their owners are aware that they are members of an elite corps looked upon as "the loon platoon" by those who have wintered over and hated it, and with much envy and admiration by those who have either been declared unfit for such rigorous duty or who have never applied because they knew it was not for them. The social order on the continent — apart from the obvious lines that separate junior scientists, senior scientists, technicians, civilian construction and maintenance personnel, and the military with its own caste system of officers, enlisted men, pilots, and shiphandlers — ascends from personnel who spend only the summer season, to those who winter over at McMurdo Station on Ross Island, the U.S. Antarctic Headquarters, to the smaller and more select group that winters over at the South Pole itself. For it is the Pole, though discovered, that remains Mecca to the visitor to Antarctica. Few who go to the continent, however, will ever make the difficult pilgrimage because of severe space limitations on the few planes that run the McMurdo shuttle only during the daylight months and only when weather permits.

The men on the bus who have announced they will winter over appear to enjoy their exalted position, although in a somewhat quieter way than the rest, who are heading south for only the summer season. Two or three will winter at Pole, and they are even more subdued than the McMurdo winterovers. All have been psychiatrically screened, a difficult process that is not always successful.

We arrive at Skyland and line up for our shared room assignments in the rustic lodges set deep in the wooded hilltop overlooking the valley. I draw a hulking Polish exchange scientist for a roommate. He's just returned from a wintering hitch at McMurdo for a debriefing and he says little, even less when he finds out I'm a journalist. He strips down to bright red wrestler's briefs, falls onto a bed, apologizes that he found it difficult to sleep in Antarctica, and does so immediately, snoring loudly.

I take out my authorization from the NSF Office of Polar Programs, which tells me that I must adhere to certain restrictions: "You must not interview during scheduled sessions. This generally leaves only meal times and late evenings. You may not file news stories on the orientation program itself. You will arrange and pay for your own accommodations at Skyland. We shall provide your meals free of charge."

Later, we all gather at the convention hall for the opening

of four days of lectures, slide shows, informal meetings on the lawn, and meals in the dining hall. Welcoming address by an ex-Navy officer turned NSF official. He talks a little bit about the research activities, saying this year's will focus more on the west Antarctica area, where the big ice shelves and the exposed rock are. Obviously, money is a restraint, he says, noting that it takes a lot of support to make the work safe and effective. Five to one: ratio of support to science dollar. He tells us about the natural resources, pointing out that no one is taking anything out of the ground, yet. But, of course, he admits, any kind of geology and mapwork leads to such things, and he laughs. The question of exploitation of resources is to be decided by the treaty nations, someday, he doesn't know just when because every time they meet it's on the agenda but there's been no decision yet, and that treaty, signed in 1959, runs out in 1995. Commercial development is sure to come, though.

Outside on the grass during a break, we meet Dr. Carl Thompson, a crowd-pleasing old Antarctic hand, a geologist who traveled with Byrd, and he's a repository of Antarctic lore, which he releases in carefully timed, intentionally over-dramatic bursts. He gives us a crash course on things we might like to know and will obviously forget. He talks about Sir Hubert Wilkins, an Australian, who with Carl B. Eielson, an American, thank God, made the first flight over the continent in 1928. And then Byrd, who in 1926 was the first man to fly over the North Pole and who became the first to do the same thing over the South Pole, in 1929, and how well he remembers that, as though it were yesterday. The headlines announcing that the flight was free from mishap. News elates Hoover. Commander Byrd is conqueror of two ends of earth. Thompson has his eyes closed and he's sitting motionless against a tree. He quotes verbatim, out of the air: "My calculations indicate that we have reached the vicinity of the

South Pole. Flying high for a survey. Byrd." That was it, he says, opening his eyes, that was all there was to it. "But dear, sweet Lord, what a feat, what a feat, soaring to the Pole and back, not knowing what sudden Antarctic blizzards would buffet his frail craft, the fiercest winds on this God-made earth, nonstop they are, and to put down would have meant death in the icy wasteland. You can have your moon-men, there is no comparison, none whatsoever. Those flights into space were as easy as riding a train on a track, they were that simple." He remembers the roaring welcome they gave Byrd in New Zealand, his sturdy ship, the *City of New York*, plainly showing the ravages of wind and ice, the merciless battering it sustained on its homeward voyage through the ice pack, the weather-lined faces of the commander and his gallant men. Hardy and fit, though, they were as they stepped ashore at Dunedin, to the scream of ships' whistles and sirens and the joyous shouts of the marvelous, marvelous people of New Zealand.

Somebody interrupts to ask him about the other three people who were on the plane that made the historic flight, the pilot, for one, Bernt Balchen, why doesn't someone give him a little credit, too? Thompson is nudged slightly off stride. "Good men," he says, "all of them, Harry June, the copilot; Ash McKinley, the aerial photog; and Balchen, too, even though he found it necessary to libel the memory of his commander only recently with that preposterous charge that Byrd lied when he claimed to have been the first to fly over the North Pole. What a terrible thing to do, attack a man not capable of defending himself, my Lord." Dr. Thompson shakes his head. Somebody says, yeah, he heard about that, wasn't it that Balchen said Byrd couldn't have made it to the Pole and back in the time he claimed under the tough weather conditions, that the plane wasn't capable of doing that? "Terrible, terrible," says Thompson, "a defamation, good Lord, the Presidents, Hoover and FDR, very bipartisan, not to mention the *National Geographic,* recognized the admiral's feat, and that should be enough to lay it all to rest."

Dr. Thompson pulls himself together and is back on course, over the South Pole again, *South,* he emphasizes, saying that Admiral Byrd *modestly,* and he emphasizes that word, credited his crewmen for the success of that flight, and he shoots a glance at the person who raised the initial question.

"More than the flight over the Pole," he goes on, "was the discovery of hundreds of miles of new territory, such as Marie Byrd Land, named after his wonderful wife, God rest her. The Edsel Ford Range, the Rockefeller Mountains," he adds, noting with a smile that names like that don't hurt when you're fund-raising to mount an expedition. He veers off into other place names. Ruppert Coast, Hearst Island, the Lowell Thomas Mountains, Rothschild Island, and Sulzberger and Mobiloil Bay, and are we getting the picture?

"Of course, even though money is an unfortunate necessity, there are other names that don't smack of the long green, the nineteen composers, for example, the Bach Ice Shelf, Beethoven Peninsula, the Grieg and Liszt Mountains, the Handel and Mozart Glaciers, the Mendelssohn and Schubert Inlets, not to mention a group of small isles named for the great Russian, Mikhail Ivanovich Glinka, and last but not least, the Verdi, and that has a strong ring, doesn't it? But there are also the really stirring names, the ones that send a chill up your very spine, Mount Terror, Cape Disappointment, the Neumayer Escarpment, the Blunt Nunatak — that's a lone hill or mountain of exposed rock sticking up above the surrounding ice — Exasperation Inlet, Warning Glacier, the Nordenskjold Ice Tongue — that's a projection of floating ice sculpted by wind and current — the Moore Embankment, Four Ladies Bank — that was discovered in

1937 by an expedition under the Norski whaling tycoon Lars Christensen, who named it after the ladies of his party — the Dufek Massif — that's a strong name, fitting a strong man, that old Bohunk, George. Whirlwind Inlet and Roberts Ice Piedmont — that's valley glacier feeding into lowland ice areas."

Dr. Thompson goes on to say that the U.S. Board of Geographic Names, for anyone who is interested, states in its rules covering such things that there are three categories of names in the Antarctic. First order, such as regions, seas, coasts, mountain ranges, plateaus, and large glaciers. Second order, peninsulas, prominent mountains, capes, islands, gulfs, large bays, straits, and passages. Third order, nunataks, cliffs, anchorages, shoals, camps, and sites. "But," he cautions, "even though there's a lot still waiting for names out there, you can't name points of interest after just anyone, no sir, and the U.S. Board has something to say about that." Under inappropriate names, he says, are such things as the names of products, sled dogs, or pets.

Back in the hall we hear from Commander Larson, who talks about the Navy's logistics operations, and he invites everyone to bring all their problems to him. "Used to be a saying in the Navy," he says, "take your troubles to Jesus, the chaplain's gone ashore. That doesn't hold true on the ice. I'm the chaplain, the man to see when you're in trouble. Got an exotic chemical you want? I'll try to deliver it. But it takes time, so limit your requests. Want to build a fish hut? Please, please, don't order enough wood to build the John Hancock up in Boston." He's onto safety. Antarctic travel is still difficult and treacherous. Blizzards come up fast, last for days, winds so strong they'll lift huge blocks of ice and toss them around like stones, pull stuff right out of your hands and shake the heaviest piece of gear rolling. He warns of crevasses ranging from a few inches wide to gaping, 100 feet deep, snow over them to form a bridge, and he scares hell out of everybody with a story about getting caught in a field of crevasses in the middle of a whiteout, that Antarctic phenomenon in which light reflects between snow and clouds until all shadows and horizon disappear, confusing directions. It's like walking around inside a pillow case. "So watch it," he says, "if you see anything that doesn't look safe, tell me; don't die with the secret. I don't want the job of notifying your next of kin."

Next is a State Department official who discusses the Antarctic Treaty. Ten nations have year-round operations on the continent. There's an unprecedented provision in the treaty that allows for inspection, and it's a model for outer space, the seabed, and any nuclear test ban. Nuclear explosions are prohibited. There are bilateral arrangements for the exchange of scientific personnel. "All, however, is not honey and roses," says the official. "Apart from the development and exploitation of natural resources, there's a little matter of territorial claims, not to mention the confused legal picture relative to jurisdiction in civil and criminal cases. Antarctica is the only continent with no indigenous population, and man's contact with it has been very short indeed. Much of it was explored by the British. Therefore, in 1908, the British were the first to assert a claim. Many countries make claims to pie-shaped segments, all converging at the South Pole, which is run by the United States. Three claims overlap. Two areas have never been claimed, and these are *terra nullius*. The validity of all claims is subject to question in the international arena. The U.S. position is that we reserve our territorial rights without defining what they might be. We recognize no claim and make none. The Soviets have taken the same position, though for a long time they claimed Antarctica because of some early voyages."

Someone asks if this jurisdictional business means he could commit murder on the ice and get away with it. Everyone laughs, and the question goes unanswered. Shots were fired over Antarctica, the State Department man tells us. In 1952, the Argentine Navy let fly a couple shots across the bow, so to speak, of some British scientists trying to set up a weather station in a contested area. A few days later, the Royal Navy sent an armed frigate down and they got an apology. "There is no unanimity about what action would be taken if someone not a signatory decided to do some research there. The Romanians walked in one day and asked to be let in. No one really knows why, except the Romanians." The whole business is tricky, requires deft handling, he says. Back in the thirties, Hitler sent Dr. Alfred Ritscher down on the ice to establish a German claim, named scores of mountains and inlets after Nazis, claimed some 600,000 square miles. Later, Hitler occupied Norway and got Quisling to claim all of Antarctica because of Amundsen's discovery of the South Pole.

Next day, it is on to Before You Leave for Antarctica. Predeployment processing, contractor facilities, cargo and excess baggage, clothing. Colonel Javery, Air Force, describes the Starlifter that will take us. "Agony Airlines," he calls it, "the only ride in town, and the food is horrid, so eat before you board, if you can." For those of us leaving from the East Coast, it's 2,040 nautical miles to Travis Base on the West Coast. Us sailor types should know that a nautical mile equals 1.15 statute miles. Travis to Hickam Field, Hawaii, 2,124 miles. Hickam to Pago Pago, and we probably won't see it or the grass skirts because it'll be early, in the A.M. That's 2,263 miles. Pago to Christchurch, that's Chee Chee, 1,974, and then more than 2,000 more to the ice. "Bring money. At U.S. stations, on the research ships and in the field, there's no charge for meals if you're an NSF grantee. On Navy and Coast Guard ships, it's three to five dollars a day, one thirty-five on the Starlifter. Wine charges if you're traveling with foreign expeditions. Smallpox shots required. Buses will take us to the plane. Bright scientific types like this crowd won't have any trouble because it doesn't look like any other bus on the pad; it's got a large USN painted on the side. No weapons, not even nail-clippers; those go into stowed cargo. No porn." Someone wants to know about *Playboy* mag, and he says, "Are you kidding? That's money, baby, the Russians will give you their station for a copy." No narcotics. Grass? No. Make sure we order any packing ice we need well in advance, and he tells about the dead penguin that didn't stay frozen because some ding-dong didn't have enough freeze. "That was a trip that old Agony won't forget."

Javery is followed by a lecturer on Antarctic clothing. "It's been tested and evaluated under actual and simulated polar conditions. Make sure it fits properly. The doctor will talk about some of what could happen later. The parkas are still going through a development phase, and they're costly, so don't get any ideas about hanging onto them when you leave the ice. The price has gone up fifty-seven percent over what it was a year ago. They've got to be turned in because the wolf and wolverine fur inside is no longer available and has to be reclaimed. Don't cut off those USARP emblems as souvenirs, either. You'll be issued one when the tour's over. There are trophy hunters at McMurdo, in the mess hall, who'll slit that insignia off in a wink, so wear it. Stealing a parka, of course, is a heinous crime, the worst offense you can commit on the ice, and when you get there you'll understand why."

After lunch, a fast slide show and map tour of Antarctica, its geography, climate, and other peculiarities. No treeline to mark the edge of the continent. there are no trees, period.

All but four and a half percent is buried under ancient ice and snow. Ninety-five percent of the world's permanent ice is there, seven million cubic miles of it, some of it two to three miles deep, compressed in layers on the landmass beneath. If it all melted, the oceans would probably rise two hundred feet. You could say goodbye to Cape Cod.

Antarctica is the highest of the continents, an average elevation of 7,500 feet. The coldest and the driest, with annual precipitation at Pole the equivalent of less than two inches of water. (Phoenix gets 7.2 inches, New York City 42 inches.) Almost no fresh water, only small streams of meltwater from glaciers. The ice pack surrounding the continent is dense with plankton, and there is more living matter per acre in the area than anywhere else on earth. There is an active volcano, Mount Erebus, not far from McMurdo, 12,000 feet high and smoking. Six months of daylight, six months of darkness. Daylight at Pole begins on September 21 and ends March 21. Periods of continuous daylight or darkness decrease as you get away from either Pole until a line is reached 23½ degrees from the Pole, where there is only one summer day with no sunset, one winter day without sunrise. It is confusing, the lecturer admits, but remember that in the Southern Hemisphere this line is the Antarctic Circle. Summer in Antarctica begins December 22, winter on June 22. When it's summer in the Antarctic, it's winter in the Arctic, and never the twain shall meet. Point to remember. The Antarctic is a continent surrounded by three oceans, the Arctic is an ice ocean surrounded by three continents. Temperature in the Antarctic is, on the average, 35 degrees colder than in the Arctic.

Someone talks about communications, and advises that everybody learn how to use a radio. Class E or Echo messages are personal ones, the speaker points out, and are transmitted free over Navy circuits. Only certain subjects are acceptable, like matters of life and death and serious illness. Or birth announcements in the immediate family. Christmas greetings. No trivial, indecent, or frivolous messages, no duns or business solicitations. Hamgrams, for personal communications, are transmitted via the ham radio network. Limit 25 words. Each U.S. station has a ham. Amateur radio equipment at the stations can establish unofficial direct voice contact with stateside people.

In the evening, it's a special presentation by Dr. Thompson. It's billed as a crowd-rouser by those who've heard it before. It consists of a slide show, featuring Thompson all over Antarctica, at the bottom of crevasses, on top of Erebus, inside a helicopter, manhauling a sledge. He delivers rapid-fire, in constant motion before the screen, striding back and forth across the stage, snapping the cord of his hand-held mike like a tiger's tail at the right moment, interrupting his monologue now and then to read dramatic messages, he calls them, from a dozen or so books, slips of blue paper sticking out of the pages he has marked for ready reference. "Ah yes, gentlemen, and ladies, I did see one or two of you distaffers out there, did I not?" he says. "We had a little brush with starvation here in this shot, nothing serious. There I am, cooking a bit of hoosh over a fire I had to build with my rubber boots for fuel." He says he recalls the moment as though it were yesterday. He calls for a slide, and there he is, picking his way across the crumbling sea ice. "I was twenty-two pounds lighter when I got back from this little outing, let me tell you, and I still shiver when I think of it." He says he wondered then if it was all worthwhile. "Of course it was," he answers. Slide. "Ah yes, there I am, caught in a raging blizzard not far from where the marvelous Robert Falcon Scott perished in a similar blow. I wondered if I would make it." He leans into an imaginary gale. "I did, but only after plodding and thrusting and driving through the white desert through swirling snow hurled as though from a sandblaster into my face, through sastrugi, the heel of one foot never placed beyond the toe of the other. Oh God, thank you for the steel tempered in those Vermont winters of my youth." And he is there again, out of breath onstage but calm and smiling in the slides that follow, stripped naked to the waist and standing nonchalantly in a snowfield, peeking out of a frosted sleeping bag, hugging a frosted husky, sitting on the ice in bathing trunks, surrounded by penguins, erect on skis, parka hood doffed, before an American flag at the Pole, beard crusted with ice. "The best act in town, kids," he says, "me."

He invokes Scott and Sir Ernest Shackleton, bent over in their traces, pulling their sledges, treading uncharted snow-lands on their own muscle and blood alone. Holding an open book in one extended hand, he intones, "For scientific leadership, give me Scott. But when you are in a hopeless situation, when there seems no way out, get down on your knees and pray for Shackleton." His voice is in stage whisper now. "They were the greatest, the greatest. We shall never see their likes again, so eat your hearts out, Neil and Buzz." Someone wants to know why he doesn't mention Amundsen, he discovered the goddam Pole, didn't he? "A good dog-driver," snaps Dr. Thompson. He pauses, and before picking up another book, he adds, "He did what he set out to do, but it sure as hell wasn't for science."

Dr. Thompson winds up. "Yes, he was the greatest, Scott, a man who is synonymous with the South Pole, whose pioneer work made all the later successes possible, and don't you forget it. We need him today, we need a reawakening in these soft, permissive days, these times of the antihero."

He pauses, reflects a moment. "Writers, you know, don't really write at all. They rewrite and rewrite some more until they have what they want. But not Scott. His last diaries — I urge you to read them, ladies and gentlemen — written with frozen, dying fingers in a tent in a blizzard, are a masterwork, a tour de force, not a rewrite job but one draft because that is all he had time for. Mortal spirit against the forces of nature, his life ebbing and flowing out of his pen." And someone in front of me mutters, "Pencil, you dud."

The next day it is preventive medicine and survival. Lieutenant Ranazzi of the Navy's medical corps begins by saying there have been relatively few medical problems in Antarctica. There are some things he wants us to know, though, about carbon monoxide poisoning, frostbite, personal hygiene, snow blindness, hypothermia, dehydration, and high altitude acclimation. This snow blindness can be a bitch, he says, so prevent it, wear your glasses when you're outside, simple, period, no problem. If you don't, you'll have pain, and it's intense, the scratchiness is unbearable, and you'll wish you wore your glasses, and so will Lieutenant Ranazzi. You can also get it on overcast days because of the high level of ultraviolet light. Treatment is simple. Go to a dark place, or wear a blindfold.

Frostbite is tipped off by a sudden blanching of the skin, so if your buddy starts to go white you know he's getting it. Please, please don't lay snow on it. That's a goddamn old wives' tale. Place a warm hand over the affected spot until it starts to hurt. Warm your hands under your armpits. Frostbitten feet, you shove them under your partner's clothes. Windchill. Your body continually loses and produces heat. From the waist up you're warmer, from the waist down, colder. Remember that when you're stacking beer cases down there. Too close to the floor, they might freeze up. The ones stacked in the middle are just right to drink. There's a fifty-degree differential between floor and ceiling.

He devotes much of his briefing to carbon monoxide poisoning, which, he says, hasn't been watched as carefully as

24

it might have been. In the past, we haven't realized its potential. Many of the buildings and vehicles are poorly ventilated, so we'll perhaps notice that your friend is a little more irritable than he has been, says his eyes burn, got a headache and he's just damned hard to get along with. We're going to say, gee it's sad, the ice has finally got to my old buddy. That's a good possibility, but before we pass it off as work for the shrinks we do a little investigative work, and don't rule out carbon monoxide. For all anyone knows, some of the vehicle accidents on the ice happened because a man wasn't as alert as he should have been because he had a high level of carbon monoxide in his blood. Interesting story about Admiral Byrd. During his second expedition, he set up an advance weather base in a prefab shack more than a hundred miles south of Little America. To protect the hut against wind and cold, it was set in a pit dug into the ice shelf, its roof only two feet above the surface, with the trapdoor in it. Byrd stayed in that one room alone from March 28 through August 10 of 1934, keeping a careful record of the weather. No man had ever wintered so far south. About six weeks after the start of his isolation, the admiral noticed that he was unable to concentrate, words ran together while he read, his eyes hurt, and he had headaches. He discovered that the stovepipe joints of his caboose-style stove were loose and the pipe was clogged with ice and snow. He repaired the pipe temporarily and felt better, but there was another source of carbon monoxide, a leaking generator exhaust. Byrd periodically lost consciousness and for a while was unable to hold down food. He continued his work as best he could, struggling up and down the ladder to get data for his weather records. He managed to maintain radio contacts with his base three times a week, concealing his situation. But they got suspicious of his erratic messages and sent a rescue party, found him hollow-cheeked and haggard.

A word about aircraft safety. Look, says the lieutenant, we're going to land at Willie Field on the ice and we're going to step off that plane and be surrounded by a strange and unsurpassed beauty. We're going to become excited and exhilarated. Thinking about all the wonderful things we're going to do down there, we're going to turn right around and walk, whammo, into an airplane propeller, and people down there are going to see us walking into it and they're going to scream and holler, but we won't hear it because the noise of the engines is deafening and our heads're all covered in fur. They'll all sit around later over a beer and say, what a tragedy. Same thing near the helos. Those blades dip four feet and that's enough to catch you right here, if you're standing tall, and Lieutenant Ranazzi gives himself a karate chop just above the eyes.

It goes on for two more days, the focus toward the end on the specific scientific projects so that, we are told, each grantee will have an opportunity to learn about another discipline and develop techniques of coordination. "The Antarctic program," says the speaker we don't see because we're out on the lawn, "has been distinguished by its interdisciplinary research, and the scientific disciplines are recognizing their dependence on each other in a truly symbiotic sense. Antarctica is a melting pot of scientific brainpower, a fertile seminar." A young man in jeans, purple track shoes, and a sweatshirt with Fletcher School of Law and Diplomacy printed on the chest, is leaning against the soft-drink machine, muttering, "Oh what pap. What the hell is symbiotic about zooplankton and plate tectonics, anyway?" He's just your average weatherman, he says. He's been to Antarctica several times, studying the winds and temperature profile just over the snow surface, and when I ask him what for, he laughs and says, "Well, the public probably couldn't care less but it has to do with absorption and reflection of solar radiation and energy exchange at the point where snow and air meet." He says he's generally enjoyed the experience, which has helped him professionally, but he's through with it after this season because now he's grown up he has got to go to work. He says it's not one big happy laboratory down on the ice, and he takes a noisy swig on a Coke. "It's all egoism," he adds, "everybody doing only what'll produce the greatest good for themselves." The scientists, he says, usually just sit around and chuckle at the press guys who visit because of the way they're followed around by NSF, like on some Intourist junket in the Soviet. "Getting back to this thing, though, about nobody walking alone on the ice," he says. "If they do team it, it's out of sheer necessity. The egoist sometimes has to take care of his neighbor, because it's a means of furthering his own end; it's the best way to go." No, he says, there are no true altruists on the ice, or anywhere else for that matter. And Captain Scott, the hero of the Antarctic? Why, he asks, do I think he didn't try harder to get home? I didn't know that he hadn't, I tell him. "Because he was a loser," says the weatherman. "He wasn't doing it for old John Bull, show them that Englishmen could die in their tracks. He killed himself out there, maybe even took the morphine they carried, because he couldn't face the music. It was his reputation he was saving. Egoism."

Depressed, I am back in my room. I thumb through a book on the Antarctic and there is an introduction by Apsley Cherry-Garrard, who was with Scott. I read it and wonder who is kidding me, Cherry or the weatherman in purple track shoes:

"Courage, or ambition, or love of notoriety may take you to the Antarctic, or any other uncomfortable place in the world, but it won't take you far inside without being found out; it's courage; and unselfishness; and helping one another; and sound condition; and willingness to put in every ounce you have; and clean living; and good temper; and tact; and good judgment; and faith. And the greatest of these is faith, especially a faith that what you are doing is of use. It's the idea which carries men on."

3

November 8, late afternoon, and we roar off a runway at Quonset Point Naval Air Station in a driving rain and high wind, seated six abreast, facing a heap of lashed cargo creaking and straining in the midsection of the giant Starlifter, headed for an icy springtime. Our backs are to the nose, and the pilots sit high above and behind us, occasionally visible, all zippers and blue nylon, through a hatch at the top of a ladder. There are no windows where we sit, in the front row of eight in standard commercial airline seats that have been specially set into tracks for this trip, and no women. The only light comes from the harsh wide overheads that make it look like five in the morning in a cold-water flat, and from the few portholes in the cargo area aft, one vast cavern stacked high with metal-banded crates, skis, bundles of clothing, everything chained or roped to the deck and bulkheads. The noise of the jet engines is absolutely deafening. Except for the padded seats and the clothing, there is nothing soft-looking inside, it is iron-ass military, gray cold metal everywhere, no scarlet carpeting, no designer plastic panels to camouflage the configuration and the bulk of the fuselage, no supermarket music to dull the takeoff.

This plane is a truckhorse, and it hauls it all, mail, food, fuel, equipment, and people when it has to. A black loadmaster in green coveralls and an armful of sergeant's stripes whispers to me later on after he sneaks a drink or two from my bottle of brandy in his coffee cup. He doesn't mind, no sir, converting this here box into a hospital, like they do when they bring the guys that got hit out of Nam. But it's this VIP thing, yes sir, trying to make the VIPs comfortable on their way to the ice, that can be a bitch. Fuckin' seats, he says. Could use that space, eight rows, or all that shit sittin' back there in the warehouse. Got to come back for it, you know, that's another trip he hadn't planned, wanting to lay over for a little R and R in Oahu. Fuckin' civilians, he sneers, his mother was one, too, he hates to admit. The press is okay, though, sir, he says, and I don't know whether he's serious or he likes the brandy. They're okay, he says, you can talk to them guys, usually working stiffs like him unless you get some pretty TV face looks like a faggot or some columnist gives you his name and waits for you to fall over in a hydrologic fit, he calls it. I'm afraid he'll ask to see the travel authorization in my pocket from the Commander, U.S. Naval Support Force, Antarctica, AUTHORIZATION TO TAKE PASSAGE IN NAVAL SHIPS AND DEEPFREEZE MILITARY AIRCRAFT. Because there's also with it the note that we travel with the DVs (Distinguished Visitors), defined as "persons military in the grade of O-6 and above and comparable rank officers of foreign nations, civilians in the grade of GS-15 and above, and distinguished personnel designated DVs by the NSF or by the Support Force Commander." That's important because it means you get to board the aircraft first, followed by other officers, followed by senior enlisted personnel, followed by "all other" Deep Freeze passengers, followed by "space available" passengers. I worry that maybe the loadmaster won't understand how uncomfortable I feel as a DV.

The loadmaster and another sergeant are playing stewardess, handing out trays of food, with a "Coffee, tea, or me" in a fag voice. And everybody's asking them questions, but mostly it's the DVs. "When do we get to Pago Pago?" "That's pronounced Pango Pango, sir." "Can we get duty-free booze there?" "Right, sir, that's the only logistical reason for making the stop, no refueling, that's what they have to say on the flight plan." "How many hours we been in the air?" "What's the matter, sir, you ain't never had a wedgie?" "What's a wedgie?" "Well, sir, that's when they grab you right there by the ass of your trousers and give 'er a good tug." "What's the temperature at Travis?" Shrug. "Hey, pot roast?" "That ain't pot roast, sir, that's Canadian bacon, cain't you see them eggs lying there?"

Hours in the air. We talk and smoke and fidget in our seats, and think of the long miles and lose sight of the true value of time. We cannot enjoy it. Whoever said it flies? It stays, and to get away from it I go to the head up forward, and wait behind two sailors who are asleep on their feet but who wake up when the door opens and it's their turn. Inside there's a sign on the wall, IF WARNING HORN BLOWS, DON OXYGEN MASK. Someone has crossed out the last three words, and written JUMP over them in Magic Marker. I sit down, drink some brandy, and fidget some more. I get up again, and walk into the cargo area, hanging onto all sorts of levers and handles on the way. Inside, I lean against the lashed-down cargo and stare wearily out the porthole at the light, when a loadmaster yells at me, "Hey, sir, they ain't no O-Two in there, and if we get into trouble you'll die, yessir." I stumble out and back into my seat, and refuse a bourbon from the scientist next to me, who hasn't been talking much until now. He says he works in upper atmosphere physics, when he's sober.

He starts giving me a press briefing on his work, figuring it's time to kick and deal, as the sportscasters say, taking literally the advice in the NSF personnel manual that tells scientists, "Whenever possible, your attitude toward media that contact you should be one of complete cooperation. Remember, your research is funded by taxpayers who have a right to know about your work. Cooperation with the media will pay off. A poor attitude can do a lot of harm." The continent is vital to his work, he says. The magnetic field covers the earth like a huge umbrella, and it wards off many of the energetic nuclear particles that constantly bombard the planet. Except, of course, he goes on, at the magnetic poles, where the field dips to the ground. Charged particles reach the earth's atmosphere through these holes in the shield. He can measure their effects. Furthermore, stick an observatory at the geographic South Pole, on the earth's spin axis, and you have the advantage of being stationary relative to other points on the rotating globe. How do I like that jazz, huh? It thus affords a continuous look at the same point on the celestial sphere. He's been to the ice six times, two winters over and there is no doubt he loves his work. It's a nice place to work, he says, because it's good not to have to worry about time, what with six months of daylight and six months of darkness. You're not a slave to time when you're there, because you lose the sense that there is such a thing. If he feels like working, he says, he just does, even if it's sixteen hours straight, if he feels like frying up a steak at three A.M., then he does that, no day-to-day routine and all that. Get up when he likes, sleep when he likes, total freedom of movement, move when you want.

He also admits he's always liked ice and snow, coming from Minnesota and all, and the cross-country skiing is real nice outside Scott Base, not to mention downhill. He tells me he'll have to show me a diary he kept on one cruise he made to the ice, if I'm looking for some color. Suddenly it's mealtime. "What is it?" "Pot roast, sir, that'll be a buck-twenty, only we're callin' it beef bourguignon this time around." It is hard to eat, crammed in together as we are. I think that maybe I'm losing my taste, along with my hearing, because of a cold, but then the upper atmosphere physicist cracks open another bottle of bourbon, and I can smell it, so I realize the food is just plain lousy.

I tire of reading my press kit and staring at maps of Antarctica. The *Playboys* and *Penthouses* that keep getting passed around are starting to look like gynecology journals. The thought of all the hours ahead before we get to the ice won't let go, like nagging pain. Fantastic discipline for an impatient person. I think of Captain Bligh, who told his men during their open-boat voyage off the *Bounty* not to concern themselves with how far they had to go, but how far they'd been. We've just passed over Colorado or something. When we left, the total to cover was 10,853 nautical miles. We've gone about 2,000, and it's suppertime. Rotini and meat sauce, like it came out of a can, soggy green beans, grapefruit juice, two packs of Oreo cookies, one pack of cheese Nabs. I read labels like a child in a car reading passing signs.

8:10 P.M. and someone says over the intercom that we will all now practice patience. It's the captain speaking; he picked that up watching *Airport,* he says, but we can call him by his nickname, Colonel. Arrival at Travis is delayed. Another two hours. I go to the head again, and talk to a dark-skinned young sailor standing outside, a Filipino with a moon face and a smile full of teeth. He is a cook, and he's never been to the ice before, and he didn't volunteer either but he's going till February. He's not too cracked up over it, though, he says, it'll give him something to wow 'em back home with in the Cordillera. The temperature where he lives is always around 80 degrees and it's rainy as a bastard. When he goes back on leave those Ilokanos are going to stop and stare, he's going to be a big man, he's been to the ice, José Aguinaldo. He doesn't think he'll get to the Pole, though, that's just for guys like Barry Goldwater and the other DVs. He'll be at McMurdo. But he's going to climb that mountain there, with the cross on top that you can see for miles; he's got to do that even though they say that when you get up there it means you'll return to Antarctica someday. You know what else he figures he'll do, too, is maybe write a cookbook. *Antarctic Cookery*, he'll call it, exotic recipes, maybe seal meat and penguins and using penguin eggs, why not? He's been reading up on the livestock that's on the ice, and there's plenty of fish. If Amundsen could make cutlets out of his dogs why shouldn't he be able to fool around with penguins and seals? The early explorers did it, he says, but they weren't really cooks. Yessir. *Antarctic Cookery* could be a best-seller. Maybe the guys won't eat it, and maybe the CO won't let him serve it even, but he sure as hell is going to experiment in the kitchen when he's duty free and that's what makes a good cook, you got to experiment.

He says he won't stop there, either, just with the cookbook. You got to realize that things like penguin and seal and shag aren't exactly big items outside of Antarctica, so he figures that maybe he can work it so he sets himself up as an importer when he gets out in three years, get into the frozen food business, you know, have his buddies down on the ice supply him with the meat, just ship it back and he'll sit there in this big-ass office downtown in Manila with this big-ass secretary and become Antarctica Foods, Ltd. Then, who knows, maybe he'll open up a little gourmet restaurant and call it The Ice Box and serve Antarctican food like roulades of seal or stuffed cormorant or braised penguin breast Valdostino. Staff it with a couple of Eskimos, he laughs, because when most Americans think of snow they think of Eskimos.

We are on the runway at Travis, finally, dragging across the field to the terminal, off-loaded is the way the loadmaster puts it. It is after ten our time, after seven California. The captain has told us to stick close to the gate, it'll only be an hour or so.

34

That stretches into an interminable six; the problem was maintenance, the captain tells us with a laugh, when we are finally back aboard. Not in our front seats anymore, but in the sixth row. For some reason, the DV boarding pattern has gone awry, and it was a free-for-all for seats. There are now six Navy chiefs, a yard of hash marks on each of their arms, settling in for a long sleep in the front row, stretching their legs out luxuriously. There is no one with guts enough among us to tell them to move their asses. I am not thinking of personal triumph any more, or fun in the snow. I'm cramped and tired and have no legroom, and I begin to dread the flight back home when it's all over. We would have been in Honolulu now if we had gone nonstop. "Asleep," at three A.M., a blanket over my head to shut out the painful over- head light. It is like a movie theatre after the late show breaks, harshly lit. Jolted awake by the pilot's voice telling us that meals will be served, emphasizing the *will*, in twenty minutes, ready or not, gang. Unhungry, we eat mechanically, four or five in the morning; I've lost track. It's dry steak and limp lettuce with a load of vinegar, and coffee just as we start the descent to Hickam Field. The loadmaster hands out HELPFUL HINTS HICKAM AIR FORCE BASE, listing "useful information on military and civilian activities," like phone numbers for the Hale Makai barbershop, the Kalakaua 18- hole course, the Top-3 Club, SAC X-Ray SSB Radio and The Command 6486th Air Base Wing, who tells us in the letter with an Aloha! salutation that the base has been famous for its warm Aloha! spirit since 1935 and when we bid it a fare- well Aloha! he wants to add our names to his list of satisfied visitors. He signs his name under the closing, Mahalo. Some- one says let's phone the bastard and wake up his ass, Aloha!

We herd into gray buses in silence and drive slowly, dulled, into the warm mists seeping out of the Waianae mountain range to billeting in the BOQ. We pass the Schofield Barracks, ruined by Japanese planes streaking in low over Oahu from the west that December morning in 1941, and I am thrilled out of my lethargy at last. I am eleven again, as I was on that morning in that year, building balsa wood and doped paper models of those warplanes and prevented from lusting after Antarctica.

4

We sit by the pool at the Russley Hotel in Christchurch two days later, across the international date line. It is a warm November spring day of bright sun, two thousand miles from Pago Pago, where we made a liquor stop and paid a hefty airport landing fee, everyone refuses to say how much, after bidding farewell Aloha! to The Commander 6486th Air Base Wing at Hickam.

Our press group, now gathered at the hotel a mile and a half from Christchurch International Airport, consists of a photographer from the *Christian Science Monitor,* a writer for the San Francisco *Chronicle,* a freelance film producer who is shooting Antarctica for NSF, a writer on special assignment for *Rotor and Wing Magazine,* doing a story on the Navy's flying squadron on the ice, a member of the NSF Office of Government and Public Programs and a representative from the NSF press office who is really flacking hard, making sure we stick to the Revised Antarctica Press Visit Schedule. He seems a bit nervous, particularly when we ask questions about projects not listed on the schedule, saying we won't have all that much time, and there is so much to cover. This means he is going to push certain self-serving stories at us like cut-rate booze.

The NSF people seem to be worried about people like Senator Proxmire who go after frivolous-sounding government-funded projects, like love studies, or a study of the effects of tequila and gin on fighting sunfish, and wonder aloud whether the public is being screwed. We talk about that, and the feeling of the NSF people is that there are guys on the ice and elsewhere living off public monies, and there always will be, but NSF tries like hell not to fund light-minded research. Too often, one says, getting defensive, some of these congressional staff members come in with a jaundiced eye, distort a piece of research beyond belief, and go running to the media crying that it's absurd, a waste of the taxpayers' money. The titles of research work, however, often do not adequately describe the scientific goal of a project. Some of the work is so esoteric it cannot be understood by even a trained science writer, let alone an administrative assistant up on the Hill. Basic scientific research falls into that category. But because it sounds murky doesn't mean it's flippant. It is basic research, we are told, and the pitch is feverish now, that increases man's knowledge of his universe and you can't do any problem-solving, economic, social, or biological, without the nut, the nugget of knowledge provided by basic lab work.

But while the lecture is idealistic, the schedule is pure pragmatism. They are obviously sensitive to Senator Proxmire et al., and we go over what we will see and write about while on the ice starting tomorrow. Biomedical aspects of human adaptation to South Polar stresses, which may help others deal with the mounting pressures of daily life. Modeling of Antarctic freshwater and terrestrial ecosystems, which may sound awfully frivolous but if we're looking for a practical angle, why, what they're doing may help us in our quest for life on Mars and other planets. We'll understand how when we visit the Dry Valleys. Physiology and biochemistry of freezing resistance in Antarctic fishes. Don't laugh, what we're learning may one day be applied to the preservation of blood and sperm. Status and population dynamics of Antarctic seals. More than just movement and migratory patterns of the beasts. These things swim deep, you know, and for now until we get briefed on the ice, we are to let our imaginations find the obvious application to man.

The NSF representatives swing into an overall view of the research effort. Some $7.5 million in 132 grants for science projects on the ice, on research vessels and icebreakers and in laboratories back in the states. Another $16 million for logistic support by the Navy and civilian contractors; that includes transportation of investigators and other personnel, resupply of stations, construction and maintenance of facilities, and establishment of temporary camps. The principal export, of course, is scientific data, laboriously extracted from deep inside the snow-crusted continent, the skies above it and the icy waters surrounding it, a process that demands not only researchers skilled in their disciplines, but researchers with enough imagination to adapt their tried laboratory techniques to such a hostile environment. Remote and difficult to mine though it is, the Antarctic is a trove, a valuable laboratory. An understanding of the dynamics of the ocean and the atmosphere is necessary to learn how and why global climate varies, and to get this understanding scientists must look at the whole system, including Antarctica. Meteorology studies focus on the belief that the earth's poles are heat sinks by which the atmosphere gets rid of heat collected in the tropics, and on how the Antarctic weather pattern influences the weather over the entire earth.

One of the most intriguing questions under study is the possible existence in the distant past of a supercontinent called Gondwanaland, and whether Antarctica was one piece that broke off and drifted away, carrying with it a fossil record of giant ferns and the trunks of trees. In 1967, two young geologists working 325 miles from the South Pole discovered a bone embedded in rock. It turned out to be part of the jawbone of a labyrinthodont, a large lizardlike amphibian that flourished some 200 million years ago. One of the most significant fossil finds of this century, it was the first proof that a vertebrate land animal had lived in the Antarctic. Furthermore, since the animal could not tolerate salt water, it provided another piece of evidence that the southern continents were connected to each other in the Paleozoic era between 220 million and 600 million years ago.

Just as the air from Antarctica plays an important part in making the world's weather, the cold water flowing northward affects ocean currents as far away as the Northern Hemisphere. Oceanographers study these currents and the tides, and they analyze the mineral content of the waters. Samples from the ocean floor reveal much about the sea life of the past, and the rocks and stones are of interest because many have been dropped by icebergs which originally picked them up by scraping over the land as part of the great ice sheet.

But it is Antarctic life — in the seas and the scattered lakes, on the ice and land — that is capturing the attention of a growing number of scientists interested in how the seals, penguins, fish, and bacteria and other microorganisms that abound in the area adapt to the cold. The continent is an excellent place to study adaptation, a basic process of evolution, because the environment, though rugged and forbidding, is also rather simple. Since there are fewer factors to be studied, the whole process becomes easier to understand. Biologists are also aided by another simplifying factor in their study of the interrelation of the species of plants and animals with one another and with their environment. On the continent, there are frequently many individuals of a particular species — emperor penguins, for example — but the number of species, whether of plants or animals, is small. The number of interactions is, therefore, less than in other areas. Also, since the Antarctic has been less affected by man's activities than the rest of the world, nature may be observed more nearly in its original state.

The NSF people, however, do not say much about man, except for the small amount of work being done on various aspects of human adaptation. Human beings, they are asked, may not be indigenous to Antarctica, but does that mean they should be ignored amid the cosmic ray variations, the conjugate-point rheometer studies and the photometric observations of subvisual aurora? No one seems to give much thought to the motivations of the Antarctic traveler and the other softer issues such as human aspiration and self-realization. There's been a hard-science overkill, and the cultural anthropologist has yet to be invited to the Antarctic. The NSF people are sympathetic, but there are certain priorities. But there is an Antarctic culture, I insist, albeit newly transplanted and not transmitted by biological heredity. The way in which life is lived there, the social traditions, the capabilities and habits, crude as well as refined, all of these must have molded a unique ethnic group, the Antarctican. Yes, yes, they reply, they are well aware there is need for a better understanding of human behavior, emotion, and interpersonal attraction, and they are certain that future projects will deal with those things. But in the meantime, priorities must be ordered. Someone grows impatient and says, for Christsake, did we realize that when we step out of that Starlifter tomorrow we'll be back hundreds of centuries into a glacial age, the Pleistocene?

5

We are droning high over the earth in the Starlifter, headed for the ice, with only five hundred miles left of this journey to south of everywhere and anywhere, past the point of no return, the pilot informs us, so let's not be telling him that we forgot our parkas. We have those piled up in the cargo area, ready to pull on before we land. We are already wearing our long johns, baggy field trousers of black tightly woven cotton, without the heavy liners that we keep for the Pole trip, red plaid woolen shirts and shearling-lined shoes. Stowed in each of the orange survival bags issued us at the NSF warehouse in Christchurch, the contents of which we signed promises to return upon completion of this tour, are a woolen balaclava helmet, black watch cap, trouser liner, white rubber thermal boots, canvas mukluks, extra woolen socks, felt insoles, heavy gauntlets like bearclaws, woolen glove inserts, leather shell gloves, goggles, belts, earmuffs and a sewing kit. Thirty-four pounds of clothing in all, and if we think that's a problem, the New Zealander who fitted us out back in Christchurch told us, how would we have liked to be going in the good old days before modern fabric, and have to wear stuff like scratchy camel's hair drawers, woolen breeches, Eskimo overcoats of reindeer skin, six pairs of woolen socks, at the same time, two pairs of hair socks, and huge boots made of fur, soles and all, and stuffed inside with dried Norwegian hay, an idea they got from the Lapps. "Yes, gentlemen," he said, "it is bloody cold on the ice, cold enough to freeze the body's moisture and you'll look like you're encased in proper armor, if you're not careful." He said it happened several times to Scott's party, and they had to thaw themselves out before they could get some sleep. "Some of the blokes couldn't even turn their heads, so fast were they frozen."

Below us is the wildest water in the world, a zone of converging storm tracks. The only things that can get through are barrel-hulled Coast Guard icebreakers, carving channels in the annual ice of the Ross Sea, which runs eight to ten feet thick, and the giant T-5 tankers that bring in the aviation, diesel, and automotive fuel. Tom Kirkpatrick, a Coast Guard commander who has pulled duty in these waters, has told me they're the roughest he's ever sailed, and anyone who can avoid a tug and barge tow job down there does so. "Except for that little constriction between South America and the Antarctic Peninsula," according to Kirkpatrick, "there's nothing to stop the wind as it goes around the world. No continents at all, quite different in the Northern Hemisphere. Those roaring forties, those freezing and furious fifties, and screaming sixties have an infinite length of fetch. The sea just builds up, and anywhere you're going you'll have it right on your beam, it's that rough." I think of Dr. David Lewis, an incredible man I had read about somewhere, who is below us now in his 32-foot steel sloop, *Ice Bird*, obsessed by Antarctica and aiming to be the first person to make a single-handed voyage to the continent, and the first to circumnavigate it alone. In a few days, *Ice Bird* will be dismasted, her motor useless, her steering gear shattered, radios waterlogged, taking water in the seas of the sixtieth southern parallel after rolling completely over in a howling storm of snow, wind, and ice. Bailed out and jury-rigged, she will make it to Palmer Station on the peninsula, after a second capsize, two months after I am back home. Why is he doing this? Later, he will say little about that in the piece he writes for the *National Geographic,* except that there was an overmastering urge, Antarctica waiting, challenging. To try for it, relying entirely on his own resources, accepting the ultimate challenge of the sea.

Someone breaks in on my thoughts of him down there, yelling, "We couldn't last a minute, I'll tell you, if we have to ditch out here, freeze your ass right off, man." Alert now, and with a vacant feeling of fear in the pit of my stomach, I find this leg of the trip doesn't seem as tiresome as the past nine thousand, five hundred miles. I am anxious to land, and I think again of the long trip back, now made more unappealing by the stretch of bad water beneath, which we must cross again.

· Before human beings ever set foot on the glistening ice-age glacier that is wrapped around the underside of this earth, it had hold of their minds. Unaware that Antarctica was a frozen wasteland, the planet's most hostile place, early Greek geographers were convinced that a huge landmass lay to the south to balance the land areas of the northern hemisphere. The New Zealand Maoris, too, believed in a great southern land beyond the distant horizon — and their legends, handed down from ancestors whose big canoes may well have pushed far southward until stopped by rearing walls of ice, tell of an immense white island. Later, fifteenth-century cartographers, who had never seen it, drew startlingly good likenesses of the mysterious Southern region they called *Terra Australis Incognita.*

Armed with these rough maps and fueled by myths of a treasurehouse southern continent, a number of voyages were launched, the earlier of which resulted in the discovery of Australia and several South Pacific islands. Conceivably, some of these ships were blown off course by the violent storms

44

around Cape Horn and may have caught sight of an Antarctic isle or two, but it was not until New Year's Day, 1739, that the first documented discovery of land within the Antarctic Convergence was made. A French expedition commanded by Bouvet de Lozier sighted a snow-covered, fog-veiled island in the South Atlantic which now bears the name Bouvet. The young Frenchman guessed correctly that the huge tabular bergs he saw had been calved from a massive land south of him.

But it was Captain James Cook, the celebrated English navigator — who ranged over the Pacific in a brilliant succession of voyages to fire the imagination of eighteenth-century Europe — who became the first man to cross the Antarctic Circle, penetrating farther south than any other before him. Reaching latitude 71°10′ S., he was blocked by impenetrable masses of ice about 150 miles off what is today known as the Walgreen Coast of Marie Byrd Land. "I will not say that it was impossible anywhere to get farther to the south," Cook wrote in his journal, "but the attempting it would have been a rash and dangerous enterprise and what, I believe, no man in my situation would have thought of. It was, indeed, my opinion, as well as the opinion of most on board, that this ice extended quite to the Pole, perhaps joined some land, but if there is, it can afford no better retreat for birds, or any other animals, than the ice itself. I, who had Ambition not only to go Farther than any one had done before, but as far as it was possible for man to go, was not sorry at meeting with this interruption as it in some measure relieved us, at least shortened the dangers and hardships inseparable with the navigation of the Southern Polar Regions; Sence [Sic], therefore, we could proceed not one Inch farther to the South, no other reason need be assigned for my Tacking and Standing back to the North."

Cook, who drove his ships *Adventure* and *Resolution* on a

passage of some 70,000 miles between 1772 and 1775, sailed completely around Antarctica without sighting it. But he did skirt the South Sandwich Islands and South Georgia, spotting fur seals on the beaches of the latter, a find that would later draw hundreds of fur-hunters to the area. Braving ice fields, bergs, snowstorms, dense fog, and intense cold under sail, the sealers were probably the first people actually to see Antarctica. Though the issue is disputed, the young American sealer Nathaniel Palmer of Stonington, Connecticut, is generally believed by the Americans to have been first to sight the continent during his cruises in 1820 along the west coast of the Antarctic Peninsula, that spit of ice, rock, and islands that reaches toward Tierra del Fuego. (The British also claim discovery of Antarctica, maintaining that Captain Edward Bransfield charted Trinity Land on the opposite coast the same year. So, too, do the Russians.)

The first known landing on the continent was made by Captain John Davis, a sealer from New Haven, who, in February of 1821, sent a boatload of men ashore in Hughes Bay near where Bransfield explored, to look for pelts. "I think this Southern Land to be a Continent," he wrote in his log.

There were others who rode the winds south, and their names are well known to devotees of Antarctic lore. Faddei von Bellingshausen, the Russian naval officer who circumnavigated Antarctica between 1819 and 1821, discovering Alexander I Land on the peninsula. Lieutenant Charles Wilkes of the U.S. Navy, who sailed 1,500 miles along the coast in 1840 and furnished the first proof that Antarctica was a continent. James Weddell, British navigator, who reached a new "farthest South" in 1823, 74°15′.

And Sir James Clark Ross, the great British ice navigator, who discovered the north magnetic pole in 1831 and who, in January, 1841, rammed his well-fortified square-riggers, *Erebus* and *Terror*, into the ice pack that drifts north in the summer. Four days later, in a feat never before accomplished, his ships burst from the pack and, amid stinging snow showers and thick fog, glided into an ice-free, open sea which now bears his name. As they cruised, the fog began to disperse and, on January 11, Ross and his crews were stunned by the sight of the lofty, snow-covered peaks of what he named Victoria Land, rising in the west.

Thwarted in his attempt to discover the south magnetic pole (not attainable by sea since it is located in Victoria Land), Ross nevertheless continued to push southward to higher latitudes than that reached by Weddell, making landfalls on Possession and Franklin islands and sighting Mount Erebus. He also had the good fortune to witness the largest eruption of Erebus ever recorded — enormous columns of flame and smoke rising 2,000 feet above the mouth of the crater.

Ross was finally stopped in his drive south by the sheer white walls of the great barrier that bears his name, the floating Ross Ice Shelf, 180 to 200 feet high and covering an area about the size of California. One of Antarctica's most distinctive features, the massive shelf, attached to the land at the southern terminus of what is now McMurdo Sound, between Ross Island and Victoria Land, is afloat at the outside edges. Great chunks often break off and float away as flat-topped, or tabular, bergs, so astonishing early explorers like Ross that they called them ice islands. At one critical point in his voyage, Ross's ships were caught in a heavy swell that was driving them down upon an ice pack in which were counted, from the mastheads, some eighty-four large bergs. "Sublime and magnificent as such a scene must have appeared under different circumstances," wrote Ross, "to us it was awful, if not appalling. For eight hours we had been gradually drifting towards what to human eyes appeared inevitable destruction; the high waves and deep rolling of our ships rendered towing with the boats impossible, and our situation the more painful and embarrassing from our inability to make any effort to avoid the dreadful calamity that seemed to await us. We were now within a half mile of the range of bergs. The roar of surf, which extended each way as far as we could see, and the crashing of the ice, fell upon the ear with fearful distinctness, whilst the frequently averted eye as immediately returned to contemplate the awful destruction that threatened in one short hour to close the world, and all its hopes, and joys, and sorrows upon us forever. In this deep distress, we called upon the Lord, and He heard our voices out of his temple, and our cry came before Him. A gentle air of wind filled our sails; hope again revived, and the greatest activity prevailed to make the best use of the feeble breeze. As it gradually freshened, our heavy ships began to feel its influence, slowly at first but more rapidly afterwards, and before dark we found ourselves far removed from every danger."

The following year, Ross once more crossed the Antarctic Circle to examine the icy barrier which had blocked his progress and attempt again to pass around or through it. In February of 1842, he spied it, and approached within a mile and a half, in latitude 78°11′, the highest ever attained in the southern hemisphere. He could go no farther, however, and since the season was growing dangerously late, he gave up. But in the region in which he had traveled, he had sailed as far south as it is possible to go by ship. He had found the best way to reach the heart of the continent, and the closest navigable approach to the geographic South Pole, for in the Ross Sea, ships were within seven hundred miles of the spot at the precise bottom of the world, the attainment of which — more a symbolic than a practical goal — was to consume the adventurers of what has come to be known as the heroic era of Antarctic exploration. Just as the idea of a moon landing captivated us in the 1960s, so at the turn of the century the

48

public was taken by the probing of the vast untrodden snow desert far south.

I stare at our red nylon parkas heaped in the cargo area, with their blue and white Antarctica breast patches with the red letters USARP across a white silhouette of the continent, and suddenly I feel a strange urge to put mine on. The rare opportunity to set some footprints on one of the last truly mysterious regions of earth is moments away, and I am stirred up as hell. It is a chance to live a superlative, and my being singled out to do that puts an end to the occasional unsettling realization that I am farther away from the security of home and all of its comforts than I have ever been in my life, farther away than the majority of persons on this earth have ever been or ever will be.

There is murmuring now, and rustling and zipping of parkas. Camera shutters are adjusted, shoelaces tightened, watch caps slipped on. The wolverine fur of my parka is luxurious and warm as I snuggle in up to my ears and lean back ready for the landing.

6

We are down at last, not on the thick Ross Ice Shelf, where
the buildings and skiways of Williams Field are set, but on
what has to be the most remarkable airstrip in the world, the
annual sea ice of McMurdo Sound. Frozen ocean ten feet
thick for part of the year, broken up and unusable for aircraft
in the warmer months. We are impatient and out in a herd,
struck suddenly in the face by a volley of windy cold that
takes the breath away, now under the high silver wings of the
Starlifter, stamping on the rock-hard ice, fumbling with cameras, breathing in the sharp, clean air and straining to see
more clearly the glaring scene of sunlit white and blue that is
hinted at through the milling pack of parka-clad field crews
and scientists, and through the other parked aircraft and
ground equipment. Goddam, I think, here we are at the end
of the world, almost, beyond the sunset, and it is like sitting
behind a bouffant hairdo at the theatre.

We manage to move out of the crowd, but still all I can
see, except for the snow and ice underfoot and the blue sky
overhead, are trucks and more trucks, wheeled and tracked. I
do get a glimpse of Erebus in the distance, belching a column
of white steam that is bent almost horizontal against the blue
by a stiff wind, but only a glimpse, for we are rounded up
and sorted out and loaded aboard one truck or another, still
taking pictures of what little there is that's photogenic. We
aim our cameras through fogged windows, cursing as our

parka fur or thick gloved fingers get in the shutter's way. "Save it," says our driver, laughing, "you're just masturbating out here, the real stuff is out there, she's frigid but she'll pose."

McMurdo Station is about six miles away, on Ross Island, and we drive toward it cautiously, across the sea ice, bumping hard over the tidal crack that separates the ice from the southern tip of the island. In a while, we are onto the dirty gray ash and lava on which McMurdo Station is built. It is a bustling village of burlap and board buildings, classic Antarctic architecture, and sheet-metal huts, all strung together by miles of power lines, water pipes, and slushy roadways.

We drive past rows of trucks, motorized sleds, tractors, plows, and bulldozers. Past Trackmasters and Candywagons, past the Ross Hilton, and dirty burlap and board club, past the Penguin Power and Light Company, the Mickey Mouse Helo Hangar, the CPO Club, the mess hall, the Balloon Inflation Building, Rheometer Laboratory, Satellite Tracking Station, the Eklund Biological Center, the theatre, dispensary, and Chapel of the Snows. The buildings are green or red or gray, and every so often a door swings open as someone dashes out, revealing wild and brightly painted designs on its inner side, or a *Playboy* centerfold.

Someone puts on a pair of sunglasses, not the kind issued to us, and the driver warns him that he'd better not, the metal will stick to his ears. Also, we'd better drink a lot of water, especially if we have kidney problems, because we'll dehydrate fast out here, it's so dry. Outside of McMurdo it'll be worse so we shouldn't let all that snow fool us, it's really dry stuff and it's a desert. He says coffee and liquor will dry us out fast, too, so we should watch that. He grins because beer is okay, you've got to drink plenty of it, real fast so it doesn't dry out. "No problem," he says, "there's gallons of it, haul it

51

in special and, man, you want to see a pissed-off bunch if it doesn't get in on time. It's a total food, if you take it regularly like I do, with a One-A-Day vitamin."

The driver is a young man, Chuck Diatelli is his name, and he works for Holmes & Narver as a general field assistant, doing everything from preparing equipment for trail parties to pulling vehicles out of crevasses and broken sea ice. "There's a lot of cracks out there on the bay, and they put boards down so's you can get across, but every so often a scientist-type will overestimate the strength of the ice and cross it without laying his boards, and gulpo, he's in. This one time, this guy tries to cross a crack without his boards and he went in just after he got over; not the whole truck, it just dangled there, ass-end hanging into the crack, all four doors flying open and four people out of that can real fast. Had to pull it out with a track and a hook to the axle. Got it out real fast, but it cost the driver a case of beer for going through the ice. Anytime you fuck up out here, man, you pay." Once every four or five days, Chuck gets to clean all the buildings out, it's no glorious job but what the hell, he says, it's the environment he likes. "What's that ad say, you go around once in life so you got to grab all the gusto you can get?" He says he's been here two months and will be here for a whole year, and the only thing he's going to miss is the girls. Admiral Byrd put it another way, Chuck remembers from a book. "Said only one thing you'll miss is temptation. It'll probably get to me after a month or two more, I do get horny, I'm only twenty-three, you know. But I'll make up for it when I get off the ice and into Chee Chee next September, don't you worry about that. So I'll just have to learn to live without it for a while; they do it in the slammer all the time. Got no choice since there won't be any women wintering over this trip. Just a few here for a few months and you can't t near them that often." He shakes his head, he doesn't understand it. "Girl could make a fortune out here, God."

He figures he'll learn something about himself, maybe iron out some of the creases. "Like I've always had a tough time bending when someone gets on my ass. But out here you got to bend, and you don't go anywhere unless you do. I've already noticed that in the short time I've been here. One day you're out hassling with somebody, the next day he's buying you a beer, or you're buying him one."

Chuck stops talking and halts the truck. He points through the window on his side and we stare up at the principal landmark in the McMurdo area, a massive volcanic cinder cone about a thousand feet high, with a barely visible cross on top and a cluster of green buildings halfway up its side. The buildings are the nuclear power plant known as PM-3A, and they call the whole hump Nookie Poo Mountain. But its real name is Observation Hill and we can climb it, Chuck says, if we're in good shape. The huge cross, made of jarrah wood, was hauled up to the summit by members of Scott's last expedition in memory of the explorer and those who died with him. Just west of here, you know, he says, Captain Scott wintered his ship, *Discovery*, in Winter Quarters Bay, and we'll get to see the hut he built there. The view from Nookie Poo, he says, is super. Maybe we can do the hero thing, he adds, grinning, and climb her in jeans and parka, no long johns, no wind pants, no liners, "When you get up there, take off your hoods and just lean there against that wooden cross — it's a big mother, took Scott's men two days to get it up — and you just let that wind get a clear shot at you. It's something else, and they'll buy you a beer at the Ross Hilton. You got to do a hero thing while here, a real one, like climbing Nookie Poo in your skivvies, I don't know if anyone's done that yet, or standing bare-ass at the South Pole, or, like that helo pilot who parked his bird on the top of Erebus and took a piss into the crater so he could be the first one ever to do it. Man, that took balls. They almost stood that dude's ass up to mast when he got back, though. The brass were more worried that he might have wrecked the helo than fried his pecker off."

We stop at last, jolted by what one of the passengers exclaims is as out of place as balls on a whale. It is a genuine Swiss chalet, a beautifully built wooden structure sitting amid the ash and the unlovely military-style clutter of McMurdo. It is something like coming across the witch's cottage in the woods. It is the NSF administrative headquarters on the ice. Near the building is a patch of ground decorated by the flags of the countries represented in Antarctica, and a bronze bust on a black marble pedestal, Admiral Byrd. The inscription reads, "I am hopeful that Antarctica in its symbolic robe of white will shine forth as a continent of peace as nations working together there in the cause of science set an example of international cooperation."

Inside to hear, before dinner and assignment to our rooms, a Command Presentation for McMurdo VIP Tours by a Navy captain who tells us he's convinced his job is the best one in the military establishment, a mission that draws on military logistic capability but yet, here it comes again, someone says, is dedicated to peaceful constructive cooperation with several other nations. He talks about the world's most fascinating geography that is just outside that door, a streamlined Task Force 43, and about the flights of the Royal New Zealand Air Force. The lights go off, mercifully, and we doze as he tells us that during our tour we will see much evidence of logistic operations, 120,000 different line items of supplies, and that one of the ships involved in this year's operations is the USNS *Maumee* T-AO 149, and he gives us the draft loaded, the tons displaced, and the gallons of bulk fuel delivered at dockside.

He's sure we'll meet Commander Somebody-or-other and

his aircrews, and they'll be happy to answer our questions about the Antarctic capability of the LC-130. He's showing slides and we get the distribution of personnel at the major construction sites. We're finally out in the brisk air and the fierce sunshine, walking to our quarters in the huge barracks building nearby.

I suddenly realize it's ten o'clock at night, and I try to get some sleep, but coming indoors from bright sunshine at this hour makes that difficult, even though the room is darkened by black shades.

Also, I am thinking of the captain's efforts to mire us in tedium and make us remember, rather than forget, what we left behind.

7

It begins after breakfast of orange juice, rolled oats, minced beef, bacon omelet, buttered toast, cottage fried potatoes, and an ocean of coffee, all of which we consume with officers and USARP personnel in their special section of the mess hall. It is typical Navy caste in here, officers, chief petty officers, and the other enlisted men eating apart.

Even out here in the wild it is not that different, and we could be eating in the mess hall back at Quonset Point for all we can tell from the gray walls, the six-place metal trays, the heavy white mugs, the stainless steelware, the gleaming steam tables. Maybe this is not the place to be jolted out of conformity after all, to be unpacked from a bundle of habits. The only thing that separates us from the community organization of a base back home in the States is the row of parkas, red USARP and green Navy, hanging on hooks out in the hall, and the copies of the McMurdo *Sometimes,* "The World's Southernmost Newspaper," that we pick up eagerly at the door as the days draw on, since it is the principal source of news of the outside world.

The NSF press aide rounds us up and checks to be sure we are wearing enough cold-weather gear, and we climb into a red Trackmaster, tractor-treaded, a sort of armored truck with a hatch on the roof so we can get out fast if the thing goes through the ice. We sit facing each other on soft bench seats, enjoying the warmth of a noisy gasoline heater. With us is Dr. Donald Siniff, a biologist at the University of Minnesota who is collecting population data on seals, and we're going out onto the ice to see how he does it. We've also got Dacey Higgins, a chief journalist–photographer who's there to service us with photos for any stories we write. He sits huddled in a corner of the cab, blowing out vapor and muttering. Dacey's not as enthusiastic as the rest of us; he's been down fourteen times and the cold gives him headaches, and he gets a bloody nose at the Pole. He's never wintered over, no way, that's a bad scene out there, he says.

Siniff checks a note at the bottom of the Station Plan of the Day about restricted areas. "Seasonal ice shelf. Many of the areas of apparently secure and permanent ice will be carried out to sea in the mid to late Antarctic summer. All ice between McMurdo Station and Williams Field to the north of Cape Armitage, and particularly seaward of Hut Point, must be used with caution during the summer season because of tidal cracks, ice erosion from sea currents and frequent seal holes. Persons crossing this will be organized scientific parties and military personnel with specific duties in the area. All others must travel by marked trails only. Do not venture on the ice from Hut Point or the Quay area. This area is off limits."

We leave the volcanic ash roadway and lumber out onto the sea ice, struggling to hear Siniff over the noise of the heater, headed for Hutton Cliffs twelve to fifteen miles into the distant mist. We follow bright orange flags on our left, green ones on our right. The sides will be reversed on the way back, often the only way to tell direction, amid all the white and in the absence of prominent surface features. We pass vivid blue ice heaped against the shoreline, frozen waves of incredible beauty. We scrape across giant cracks marked by black flags, the gaps now frost-welded on this very cold day.

Siniff is telling us about seals. There are a number of different types. The Weddell, mottled gray coat, 10,000,000 of them in the Antarctic, haunting the coastlines. They weigh hundreds of pounds and are 9 to 10 feet long. Their stomachs are enormous and their bodies heavily parasitized. They use their teeth to keep air holes in the ice open. The crabeater seal is smaller and lives in the pack ice. It's a handsome creature, silver-gray, 30,000,000 of them in the Antarctic, 10,000,-000 in the Weddell area, small head, eats crustaceans. The Ross seal is in the ice pack, big and bloated with a greenish belly. It eats squid and jellyfish. Douglas Mawson said it reminded him of a pouter pigeon.

Starting in mid-December, Siniff says, the seal pup is born into its harsh environment. It has a furry, fluffy coat and is truly a land mammal at this stage. Birth weight is about 60 to 70 pounds, and in three weeks it's up to 150. In four months it's 200. There is only one in a litter, though there are reports of two pups being born to a female. But some adopt pups so it's hard to tell. Nine months' gestation. The Weddell is not particularly aggressive except that they bite you if they get a chance. There are tales of a leopard seal, a large carnivore down here that goes after penguins mostly, jumping out of a hole in the ice at some explorer, but that's usually if there's a penguin around at the same time. He laughs, and Dacey says he'll shoot 'em from the cab because the last time, he stumbled over one lying out there and it had this weird look in his eye. "There was one time," someone says, "that this penguin jumps into a boatload of scientists, it had been bloodied from something or other, and damned if this seal doesn't start following them under the water, and right under that boat. It's really flashing around under there, rearing up every so often trying to get that bird. They got back to dockside and there's that seal moving back and forth, leaping out of the water mad as a hornet, and the seal is shaking its fist, yelling, you fuckin' USARPS."

"Most of the males that compete for territory or females,"

Siniff tells us, "are six to seven years old and all teeth. They go for the chest and the penis with a bite, and they're just fierce, they don't mess around, kerboom." He makes a pincer-like chop with his gloved hand. Dacey grabs for his crotch and winces. "They fight in the water, though, and not on the ice, and that's to our advantage when we get near them. Underwater we'd be absolutely no match for one. On the ice they're sluggish."

Siniff says he's trying to get population data on the seals, looking to the future for possible use of the resource. "The pressure is great to harvest them, they're a marvelous source of protein, but we're not doing it yet. The Russians are, and so are the Japanese and the Norwegians. But U.S. ecologists have been pushing for a no-sealing position."

Siniff slows the Trackmaster. "There they are," he says, pointing through the frosted windshield at scores of black lumps scattered all over the ice about a hundred yards away, just at the foot of a high barrier of ice and rock. Dacey sighs as we start fumbling with our cameras. A few minutes later, Siniff pulls up and we emerge cautiously. I feel like I'm in a drive-through zoo, getting out of the car just where the sign says not to. The seals look as if they are floating in air, so white is the ice under them and the mist about them. But as we get closer we can see the urine stains on the snow, and occasional red streaks of blood. Mothers are protecting wide-eyed pups, all of them bleating loudly, the noise like someone vomiting strenuously in a bathroom.

"They won't bother us so long as we don't try to grab 'em," says Siniff. "Stay away from those teeth." We pick our way gingerly through the pack, snapping pictures, down on our knees, lying on our bellies for a close-up of a wary mother's face. At one point, I back up and fall over Dacey, who's on one knee, and he shrieks in fright, "Jesus Christ, you scared the shit out of me; I thought you were one of them."

Siniff is in the midst of the pack with two or three grad students who have been working in a nearby hut, and he puts on a demonstration of his work for us. "We do a little rassling," he says, motioning to one of the students, who is carrying a long canvas bag with ropes through eyelets in the mouth end. He says he's a coward so he has to blindfold them first. One of the students tosses a roped bag expertly over a seal's head, then leaps astride its back as it bellows and bucks. Siniff moves in from the rear, takes off his gloves and, working barehanded in the freezing cold with a screwdriver, fixes a small transmitter, a sonic tag, to the heaving beast's flippers. Inside the shack, which is jammed with biotelemetry equipment and underwater television monitors, the scientists wait for the seals to return to the water so they can measure the size of their underwater territory and changes in dominance characteristics. Each male, the scientists have discovered, protects a territory about thirty yards wide and hangs onto it for about a month. The sonic tag emits a signal that is just above the seals' range of hearing. The scientists record the signals and track the seals' positions. They're also using the tags to find out how often the Weddells have sex. Specially designed tags are fixed on male and female seals, and when the beasts begin copulating the male's transmitter goes off.

Also, since seals dive deep and for long periods of time in search of food — the Weddell can go to the crushing depth of 1,400 feet and stay there for more than an hour — Antarctic scientists are also interested in learning something about the influence of high oxygen concentration on breath-holding and oxygen consumption. It's known that seals can turn off the circulation in their extremities, thus concentrating the blood in vital organs. This conserves their oxygen supply, which they can store in amounts five times greater than a human's capacity. All of these pressure-effect studies have obvious application to man, be he a deep-diving oceanographer, an astronaut, or a patient in a pulmonary care unit of a hospital. The studies, it is hoped, will help physicians learn more about depth limitations, air embolism and decompression sickness, and lung collapse.

We are back at McMurdo in time for lunch, pepper steak and baked red snapper, and the grinning moon face of José Aguinaldo peeking out of the kitchen as I dump my silverware into a water-filled tray at the end of the line. I mention we've been out bagging seals, and he says, excitedly, "Oh man, just came across a goldmine of recipes for Antarctic cookery." He's culled them out of a stack of old books and records he found in the library. One of the things he's read up on is seal meat; it's supposed to be tasty if you can get rid of the strong smell. The explorers all ate it, but they'd blanch it first and strip all the blubber off. But the secret is to baste it with beef suet. The poor suckers will think they're eating pot roast when he lays it on them, says José proudly.

The rest of the day we tour the Eklund Biological Center. More seal stories. Anatomical, histological, and neuroanatomical studies, by Dr. Robert E. Coalson of the University of Oklahoma Health Sciences Center. The Weddell has the most enormous set of salivary glands he's ever seen on a mammal, and that's strange because the beast isn't supposed to chew. Comparative physiology of the echinoderm body wall with special reference to asteroids and echinoids, by Bruce Belman of Stanford. He collects his specimens off the bottom of McMurdo Sound by scuba diving through a hole in the ice in a fish hut. The dives are not supposed to be longer than thirty minutes but, off the record, he's been down for ninety. "It's orgasmic down there under the ice, just fantastic, great visibility," he says. Hydroids, sea spiders, urchins, comatulid crinoids.

The Southern Hemisphere is fifty-seven percent ocean, and the low temperature of the waters around Antarctica enable them to hold more dissolved nutrients and salts. Scientists are seeking data on the occurrence, distribution, and numbers of spore-producing marine fungi, both in water masses and in bottom sediments. Such information is useful for understanding the role of fungi as decomposers of plant plankton, the minute underwater organism, in the cycle of disintegration of organic materials. I listen and take perfunctory notes about the Stanford work, but about all I can get out of it is that the body wall of the Antarctic sea star *Perknaster fuscus antarcticus* has more protein than the temperate species. I quit when Belman starts talking about the oxygen consumption rate for both temperate and Antarctic sea stars as a measure of the body wall's metabolic activity, but come alive again when he tells us that down there, on the bottom of McMurdo Sound, along with all the echinoderms, are beer cans, thousands of them, and a ton of other inorganic litter — clothing, empty oil drums, tractors, bits of aircraft, fuel lines, and plastic. Most of this debris will last for years, some of it, like the plastic, probably forever, and will kill everything lying beneath it. Bacterial decomposition is slow in the Sound because of the cold. Sponges are particularly sensitive to litter, and die quickly beneath the weight.

While the continent still rates high marks for cleanliness, compared to the notoriously spoiled areas of earth, a slow filthifying is underway. It is unavoidable, given the pace of activity and colonization. It is more than beer cans and abandoned equipment, however. DDT, not used on the continent because there are no insect pests, has moved in on airborne dust, in migrating microorganisms, and in surface slicks, and its traces are found in the fatty tissue of penguins, seals, skua gulls, and fish. It has been found on the Polar Plateau. Radioactive fallout has left its imprint on the glaciers; heated seawater flushes into the Sound from the nuclear-powered distilling plant. Organic food waste and garbage are dumped on sea ice that is later smashed to bits and scattered by ice-breakers cutting channels.

The continent's ecosystem is fragile. Damage to the nutrient-rich water that flows northward could have an adverse effect on the organic life it sustains in other oceans, and if offshore drilling becomes a reality here, as many believe it will, oil spills will pose a special hazard to krill, a protein-rich crustacean whose numbers in the Antarctic waters are believed to equal the total fish protein in all of the earth's seas combined. This larger shellfish version of plankton makes up the chief food of the baleen whales, crabeater seals, penguins, petrels, and terns. It has been estimated that the whales alone, swimming through swarms of krill, gorge themselves on 200,000,000 tons of it a year.

"And on top of it all," someone remarks, "you still hear some fool suggesting every once in a while that Antarctica would be a good place to dump radioactive waste, all that unused space, you know. Just dump it onto the ice and let it melt its way down to bedrock. None of these idiots seem to understand that glaciers move."

Someone else is intrigued by the idea that everything dumped out on the ice usually winds up being preserved for generations, and notes that he's heard viable bacteria has been obtained from feces left by the Scott and Shackleton expeditions.

"Fantastic," says Dacey Higgins, "fantastic. Only place in the world where you can shit and it becomes a national shrine."

8

There are three old wooden huts near McMurdo, remarkably preserved and with that white-brown weather-scoured appearance so typical of Cape Cod homes. All three are protected as historic sites, probably the most famous on the continent, under the Antarctic Treaty. It is a special privilege to enter them.

One is Sir Ernest Shackleton's at Cape Royds, built for his abortive 1909 expedition to the Pole, the other two, at Cape Evans and Hut Point, built by his rival, Robert Falcon Scott.

We are heading out to visit them now, on a slow flight from McMurdo aboard two rattling, orange-red Navy helicopters, our heads and ears encased in flight helmets that muffle the loud noise of the rotors. The view from aloft is fantastic. We can see the eruptions of steam from Erebus trailing white against a shining, robin's egg blue sky, and the sun circled in rainbow, a phenomenon caused by a sprinkling of ice crystals high in the air. Seaward are giant, tabular bergs, hundreds of feet tall and caught in a frozen ocean that looks like marble, awaiting the summer temperature shift that will free them and send them, drifting and cumbersome, out into the shipping lanes, where they will give ice navigators fits until shoved out of the way by straining icebreakers, three to a cyclopean hunk. Every so often, the pilot banks and allows one of us to slide open a side window, and we lean out, held back by our safety straps, to take a quick picture before someone yells, shivering, "Show a little mercy, man, that ain't Waikiki down there."

Trying not to miss anything, and painfully aware that I probably will never see any of it again, I try to ignore Lieutenant Garcia, the pilot, who is bored and flying with his mind on Automatic, prattling about all that guano, that's bird-shit, sir, out there on them sea rocks. He gets out of the service, he says, he's going to get him a decommissioned helo and pick up all that shit and load it. I'ts got lots of phosphate in it because the gulls eat lots of fish, and it's super fertilizer. He's going to sell it back in the States and make a bundle, *beaucoup* gold. Call his transport system the Shit Ships, man can make a big mother of a living.

We are fluttering low over Cape Royds and Shackleton's hut. It looks so natural sitting there, crude and dark against a sky that has deepened its blue, that I expect to see smoke puffing from the pipestack chimney. There is a helter-skelter of footprints in the snow drifted around its base, and it seems to be leaning into the chill wind that has increased.

Robert Falcon Scott's National Antarctic Expedition of 1901–1904, sponsored by the Royal Geographic Society, carried explorers for the first time since Ross into McMurdo Sound. A crew of fifty and Shackleton accompanied the moody, sensitive Royal Navy officer turned explorer aboard the *Discovery*, a 700-ton ice-strengthened ship. The expedition proved to be one of the most important to enter the Antarctic. Scott's sledging traverses opened a new era of inland exploration, ranging for 380 miles south over the Ross Ice Shelf, climbing the Victoria Land Mountains, and reaching the Polar Plateau for the first time. The expedition discovered and named Mount Discovery, the Royal Society Range, and Edward VII Land, and did a good deal of pioneering work in meteorology, zoology, and geology. On December 30, 1902, Scott, Shackleton, and the physician-naturalist-artist Edward Wilson — who was to perish later with Scott on the ill-starred Polar trek — sledged to a new farthest south of 82°17′.

On the return trip, Shackleton was struck snow-blind, contracted scurvy, and began coughing blood. He was invalided home soon afterward, with a hint of reproach, by Scott, who apparently felt that he had failed to meet the challenge.

In 1907, Shackleton mounted his own expedition to the Antarctic, sailing from England aboard the *Nimrod,* a small but sturdy sealing vessel. His objective was to reach both the South Pole and the south magnetic pole and to explore King Edward VII Land. "Men go out into the void spaces of the world for various reasons," he explained, "some actuated simply by love of adventure, some have the keen thirst for scientific knowledge, and others again are drawn away from the trodden paths by the 'lure of little voices,' the mysterious fascination of the unknown. I think that in my own case it was a combination of these factors that determined me to try my fortune once again in the frozen south . . . the stark Polar lands grip the hearts of the men who have lived on them in a manner that can hardly be understood by the people who have never got outside the pale of civilization."

An incident that casts some light on the ego and possessiveness of Scott occurred just prior to Shackleton's departure. This involved the hut at Scott's old Discovery base in McMurdo Sound. Shackleton had asked his former leader if he could use it and Scott, whether out of dislike for Shackleton or petulance over his plan to get to the Pole, refused, saying he hoped to camp there himself on a future trip. Wilson was called in as mediator and an agreement was reached whereby Shackleton promised not to move into the hut unless forced to. As it turned out, Shackleton was compelled to use the hut, an act that angered Scott, who wrote, after revisiting it in 1911, "Shackleton reported that the door had been forced by the wind, but that he had made an entrance by the window and found shelter inside — other members of his party used it for shelter. They actually went away and left the window open; as a result, nearly the whole of the interior of the hut is filled with hard icy snow, and it is impossible to find shelter inside. . . . I went to bed thoroughly depressed. It seems a fundamental expression of civilized sentiment that men who come to such places as this should leave what comfort they can to welcome those who follow and finding that such a simple duty had been neglected by our immediate predecessors oppressed me horribly."

Shackleton set out with Manchurian ponies and a specially designed motor car, the first ever brought to the Antarctic, but it proved incapable of negotiating the ice. Plodding slowly across the Ross Ice Shelf, the young naval officer and his men headed south, killing ponies and caching the meat for the return trip, huddling in tents and sleeping bags, hunting for a break in the mountain chain that would serve as their gateway to the Pole. On November 25, 1908, he wrote: "A day to remember, for we have passed the 'farthest south' previously reached by man . . . and this latitude we have been able to reach in much less time than on the long march with Captain Scott. We celebrated with a four-ounce bottle of Curaçao."

Later, he noted, "It falls to the lot of few men to view land not previously seen by human eyes, and it was with feelings of keen curiosity, not unmingled with awe, that we watched the new mountains rise from the great unknown that lay ahead of us.

"November 29. The worst feature of today's march was the

terribly soft snow in the hollows of the great undulations we were passing. During the afternoon one place was so bad that the ponies sank right in up to their bellies and we had to pull with might and main to get the sledges along at all. . . . We did fourteen miles and are tired. . . ."

A few days later, Shackleton made one of his most important discoveries. "There burst upon our view," he wrote, "an open road to the south, for there stretched before us a great glacier running almost south and north between two huge mountain ranges. As far as we could see, except towards the south, the glacier appeared to be smooth, yet this was not a certainty, for the distance was too great. . . . There was no question as to the way we should go now." Shackleton named it the Beardmore, after Sir William Beardmore (later Lord Invernairn), a financial backer of the expedition. The largest valley glacier in the world, the Beardmore was the long-sought icy highway to the Pole.

On December 7, they lost Socks, their last pony, in a crevasse, and the next day they themselves were dodging and crashing through the thin snow bridges, some a thousand feet deep, saved only by their sledging harnesses. They moved slowly up the glacier into a cold north wind, collecting rock samples on the way, talking mainly of food now as their supplies dwindled. At the higher altitude, 5,600 feet above sea level, the heavy pulling became more trying, the going more slippery as the surface, now half ice, half snow, began to resemble "the glass roof of a station." On December 22, Shackleton wrote, "Please God, ahead of us there is a clear road to the Pole."

New Year's Day found the party still pulling uphill, 172 miles from the Pole, minus-14-degree temperatures. They suffered nosebleeds and headaches, and Shackleton wrote, "The Pole is hard to get."

Considerably weaker now, the party weighed whether to

push on or put an end to it and return. "I must look at the matter sensibly," wrote Shackleton, "and consider the lives of those who are with me. I feel that if we go on too far it will be impossible to get back over this surface, and then all the results will be lost to the world. We can now definitely locate the South Pole on the highest plateau in the world, and our geological work and meteorology will be of the greatest use to science. But all this is not the Pole. Man can only do his best, and we have arrayed against us the strongest forces of nature."

On January 7, a blinding, shrieking blizzard with 90-mile-an-hour winds struck the party and pinned them down all day. The temperature dropped to minus-70 degrees, and the snow drifted high up over their tent. Two days later, Shackleton put an end to the trek: "We have shot our bolt, and the tale is latitude 88°23′ South, longitude 162° East. . . . We hoisted Her Majesty's flag and the other Union Jack afterwards, and took possession of the plateau in the name of His Majesty. While the Union Jack blew out stiffly in the icy gale that cut us to the bone, we looked south with our powerful glasses but could see nothing but the dead white snow plain. There was no break in the plateau as it extended towards the Pole, and we feel sure that the goal we have failed to reach lies on this plain."

Shackleton had gotten to within 97 miles of the Pole, farther south than any other explorer, and by the time he reached his home base again, he and his party had covered 1,600 miles in 117 days.

"Oh shit," exclaims our press aide as we hover over the Cape Royds hut, "we haven't got the goddam key." "Sonofabitch," mutters Garcia. The press aide tells us we also don't have the key to the Cape Evans hut. "Sonofabitch," says Garcia again. He wants to know what he's supposed to do now. The press aide says we'll go to Evans anyway; at least we can look around outside. He has the key to the Discovery Hut, though. "Yessir," says Garcia disgustedly, yanking a lever and sending us veering off sideways and up, "it's only gas."

A short time later, we're down on the rocky western coast of Ross Island, facing McMurdo Strait, and walking toward the neat wooden hut built by Scott's Terra Nova expedition in 1911, his second and last. It was from here that Scott undertook his most notable journey, the fateful trip to the Pole, and prowling about the site now there is a sense of abandonment about the place, of men having left in haste. Cans and broken bottles are strewn about, just as they were left by Scott and his party, nails and bits of board, pieces of white, porous bone that might have come from the seal carcasses the explorers used for fresh steaks, or from their dogs. When members of Admiral Byrd's 1947 task force landed here, in fact, they found the frozen carcass of a dog standing on its four legs as though alive. I pick up an unopened can of sardines, the label still legible, and start to put it in a pocket. The press aid sees me and shouts, "Uh uh, that's a no-no, leave it right there where you found it, exactly." I can see his point, for over the years people have ripped the place off. I recall an article in *Holiday* magazine in which the writer boasted of distributing, on his return from Antarctica, a dozen boxes of matches left by Scott and still striking perfectly. Today, removal of any article or material from any of the huts, either for souvenir or scientific purposes, is strictly forbidden.

We walk away from the hut, climbing up over heaps of volcanic ash and rock, looking for wind-polished stones to take home — those are free — stuffing them along with bits of bone into our pockets. There is a large cross here, too, on Wind Vane Hill, erected by a later Shackleton expedition in memory of three of its members who died nearby. Strolling along back to the helicopters, I overhear a shivering crewchief complaining to Garcia that there must be something wrong with these guys, there's nothing here but a bunch of old cans and a shack. Garcia shakes his head and says nothing. It is all in the point of view, I suppose, Central Park from the sixteenth floor of the Plaza Hotel doesn't look the same as it does to the person walking through it at night, alone. The crewchief is a moth at a concert. He got in free but he didn't hear a thing.

"Up, up and away," says Garcia wearily, and we're heading back to McMurdo and Hut Point Peninsula. Our press aide reassures us that he's got the key to this one.

We land again, leap out and into a waiting van, which takes us to the old hut overlooking the ice of Winter Quarters Bay, 200 yards away, where cargo ships unload in the austral summer, and where the *Discovery* was moored. Scott never intended to use the hut for living quarters; the ship, iced in during the winter, served that purpose. But he did use it as a workshop, for drying furs and skinning birds, and as a playroom. Nearby is Observation Hill, with its huge cross dominating the landscape, and toward the annual ice of the bay stands another cross, a mute memorial to the first man to die in McMurdo Sound, a sailor from the *Discovery*, George Vince, who lost his footing on the ice and went into the sea.

The hut has a pyramidal roof and overhanging eaves and was brought here aboard the *Discovery* from Australia. It is in perfect condition, having been cleared of its ice and compacted snow and restored by the New Zealand Antarctic Society and the U.S. Navy. There are skeletons of Scott's ponies about, and entering an attached lean-to, we step on the huge body of a frozen seal, ropes still lashed about it, left there by the *Discovery* men. We open a padlocked door and enter the hut.

In museums as we know them, the specimens and memorabilia are locked safely behind glass, untouchable, and that is sometimes frustrating, for we often yearn for some tactile sense of the past. To touch a relic of the True Cross, to hold a cup from which Alexander drank, to smell a sample of Cleopatra's perfume, rolling the vial about in our fingers. Here, inside this darkened museum that was lived in, with its iron-braced overhead beams to guard against roof collapse from heavy snow and its brown stained walls, we can touch and smell, if not keep, the things of years gone by. I sneak a bite of a biscuit that is still edible, though rock-hard and pasty-tasting, fondle cans of oatmeal, bottles of fruit and pickles, and the fur in a boot, cold but still soft. Pieces of seal meat still lie in a skillet atop the old cookstove, and fried eggs. I savor the odor of a smokehouse that arises from the dried penguin and seal meat hanging in an alcove. Stacks of wooden packing crates marked British Antarctic Expedition, and pony fodder, newspapers, rough furniture, and hanging sleds, all as though left only moments before our arrival. But no dust to cover the past, for this hut that meant survival for the men of the *Discovery* stands where there is none of the powdered grime of mortality.

9

We drink beer at midnight in the nearly pitch-black Ross Hilton, also known as the Polar Big Eye Club after the insomnious condition that afflicts everyone who spends a spring and summer here. Outside, a bright sun, now due south, marches slowly around in the cold, gray sky to its own cosmic rhythm, refusing to set, on its way to due north at noon. It is unable to pierce our privacy this time, though, because there are no windows in here, only dingy black burlap walls stretched tight over a wooden frame.

It's good to get away for a while from this sun that has overstayed its leave, as when it pours in and floods the white-tiled head that I must stagger into, bleary-eyed and bladder full, at three A.M., down the darkened corridor from my sleeping quarters.

The club is full of men only and noisy tonight with honest vulgarity, and everyone is talking to someone, whether they're listening or not. Every so often, someone comes in out of the cold, stamping his boots on the floor to knock off the snow. Nobody is lost in a martini, like in a real Hilton bar.

There are mostly Seabees in here at this hour, drinking Budweiser at the huge bar beneath a gigantic blowup of a spotlit supine nude with mountainous breasts. These Seabees are fiercely proud of their gun- and tool-toting bumblebee emblem designed by Walt Disney, and of their heritage from World War II, although only a few of these men were in it then when the Seabees were organized into fighting construction battalions and gained their reputation for efficiency and bravery under enemy fire. Petty officers and chiefs, utilities men and electronics mates, builders, equipment operators and machinery men, specialists all, they are on leave from or en route to the high plateau they call Dry Gulch City, the South Pole, 840 miles across Titan-reared mountains, luminous blue ice and deep crevasses.

Out there, over the ranges, a new U.S. research station is rising slowly out of the white to replace the existing under-ice facility built in 1956, now settling and slowly being crushed under the weight of drifting snow. These men, technically men of the sea, do not know or care about the difference between a fo'c'sle and a quarterdeck, and in that they are unlike their predecessors on this continent. They boast, however, and grouse, and in that they are no different from those who hoisted sail and holystoned decks. But the things they talk about every so often in here, between the obscenities and the jokes, are peculiar to their Navy, tube drills with castellar cutting sides, snowmillers, tricone bits, candy wagons, Jamesways, coring augers, and Rodriguez wells. And, The Job at Pole, without precedent on earth, that makes the Alaska pipeline project, with all its PR and TV ads and newspaper articles, look strictly Tinker Toy. The Seabees aren't shy about saying that. Someone wants to know loudly, "Why is it that every time you mention the South Pole to anyone, the assholes always say, 'Oh yeah, I read about those guys working up in Alaska, saw it in the Geographic,' or they tell you, 'Oh yeah, the South Pole, I was stationed in Greenland during the war,' and 'Oh yeah, I been to Kodiak or Newfoundland with the Coasties,' those fuckin' shallow-water sailors, Hooligan's Navy?"

"Right," says another, "bush leaguers all of 'em, the Coast Guard and the pipeliners and them pussy-stripers up in Newf."

I am thinking of the background stuff in my press kit, on the Pole project, that I read last night and I cannot begrudge these men their feelings about The Job, the superlative they are working on atop the wind-raked Polar Plateau. A geodesic dome, a low-profile igloo 52 feet high and 165 feet in diameter, with an aluminum skin over a framework of extruded aluminum struts. The dome is to protect from wind-blown snow, the three buildings that will go up inside to house laboratories and living quarters. Any heated building in Antarctica, no matter how well insulated, loses enough heat to melt the snow blown against it. The resulting moisture causes the building to deteriorate. The dome will not be heated, and the average temperature inside will be around zero. There will be a hole at the top, like Hadrian's Pantheon in Rome, to bleed off accumulated heat.

The Job means flying thousands of tons of heavy equipment and supplies and hundreds of thousands of gallons of fuel oil on hundreds of daily, turn-around missions aboard the Navy's ski-equipped Hercules planes, the Southern Trail's Most Experienced Airline, Antarctic Development Squadron Six, VXE-6 on your ticket.

The men who deliver the cargo — off the ice runways of McMurdo and hauled high over mountains with royal names like Queen Maud and Queen Alexandra — and who work on The Job, must fight the constant subzero cold and cutting winds, and they must race the oncoming darkness, which means sharper cold and no more flights, and no work except that done by the scientists who will stay the winter in harsh isolation in the old station beneath the ice.

"It's a real ball-crusher," says a First Class Utilitiesman they call Haulaway Joe, who was there in 1971 when they started the construction with surveying and laying the foundation. "Fuckin' tools get brittle and break, you know, and you don't use poured concrete for the foundation like

75

you're buildin' one of your suburban bungalows. Use milled snow; that's dense stuff, man. First you tear it all up with a rotary plow, you dig this here eight-foot-deep trench in a circle in the ice, and then you walk in there with this Swiss-made Peter snowmiller to cut up the snow and pulverize it. Pour the stuff in the trench and it packs hard as a mammy-jammin' cement load. Buildin' the whole fuckin' station on milled snow, can you believe it? I mean pourin' snow back onto snow; Congressman sees that, he'd like to have the shiverin' fits, he's so used to haulin' it away so's he can park his limo outside the embassy. But it works, goddamit."

Haulaway says they wear all the standard issue cold-weather gear, special sunglasses to cut the glare and heavy fur bearclaws. "Tryin' to grab a pair of pliers in them babies is worse than tryin' to take a piss in hockey mitts," he says laughing so hard he shakes. "They're going to make it easy for us, though, when we put up the aluminum panels on the dome. They'll have these blind rivets in them in holes and we'll be able to do the joining with a simple rivet driver, so they tell us."

On a good day, says Haulaway, the Bees can work outside for a half-hour before going back into the shacks to warm up for a half-hour. On a bad day, that's when the temperature falls down below minus-sixty degrees, when the planes are grounded, they have to cut the work to fifteen minutes outside, forty-five in. " Eat and drink like a loving pig," he says, patting the bulge under his parka. "Got to keep the furnace stoked four, five times a day, and I was layin' in five thousand, six thousand calories a day, not counting the booze."

He asks me if I'm going to get to Pole on this tour, and I tell him I hope so, but it all depends on weather and space. He shakes his head. "Ain't nothin' there, you know," he says. "Nothin' but what we're puttin' up and the old station. Ain't nothin' like what's up in Alaska where they're stringin' that pipe, and that's what pisses me off *beaucoup*. I mean those civvies up there are at least gettin' good dough from the oil companies that want you to think it's real tough out there so that when they jack up the price of gasoline again in a few years they'll have an excuse; it was tough gettin' it out, you know, they'll say. We're gettin' shit, Navy wages, and the government's gettin' it all built by U.S. coolies. At least up on the pipeline they got Valdez and Anchorage, Fairbanks, and you got lots of people. It's no Vegas, that's for sure, but man, they got casinos and clubs and places to go, and they got ass, lots of ass, for the guys on the line. At Dry Gulch, all you got is memories."

The only thing worth seeing at Pole, Haulaway Joe says, is what the Bees are building. "But," he acknowledges, "what the fuck, you come this far south and don't get to Pole, it ain't like comin' down at all, even though there's nothin' there, of course." He says he figures the Bees have done God a favor, putting something out on the ice for Him to show off to the press, and when it's done, man, it's going to look like a Turkish whorehouse, without the quiff, of course, unless Uncle Sugar comes to his senses and realizes that man doesn't live on bread alone. There'll be a gym, wood and vinyl paneling, red wall-to-wall carpeting, beams in the ceiling to hide the pipes, fluorescent lighting, coach lamps on the bulkheads, an observation deck and lounge with large tinted plate glass windows and skylights so the scientists can watch auroras, brownish-yellow glass in the windows of the living quarters to make you think of a Renaissance castle.

"Scott," says Haulaway Joe, dropping his voice and going serious out of respect for the man's memory, "would shit, wouldn't he?"

The conversation has suddenly turned dirty around us, maybe the natural evolution of too much talk about coring augers that are more efficient in working deeper holes. A young sailor at the bar, his parka fur just the right feminine touch to frame a face that is unnervingly like a girl's, says, dead straight in his beer, boy, it must be rough on those winter-overs, no chicks and all. And someone near him laughs mockingly, "Hey, belay the last word, Pogie Bait, if you ever see a cunt you'd take an ax handle and try to beat it to death." "Ah, fuck you, Big Bee," says the kid defensively; he knows what's coming, it always happens to him. "Be the best piece of ass you ever had, mate" is the reply that is lost in a roar of whistling and laughter that puts an immediate end to a tentative conversation nearby about the 150-pound sack of mail that the Royal New Zealand Air Force dropped through the ice at Scott Base and not on it.

The sailor called Big Bee, a bearded hulk, tears open a can of Bud and sucks at the foam that bursts from the popped top while someone shouts at him to do the Shakespeare. "Oh Jesus," says a voice next to me pulling on a black watch cap in flagrant violation of the house rule against wearing head covering in the bar at the penalty of buying a round for all hands, "let me the fuck out, I'm going to the flicks and see John Fucking Wayne." Ignoring the bartender's frantic ringing of the bell that signals a scofflaw, he goes out the door, deliberately leaving it open to let in the light and the wind and the cold. "Prick," says someone, attacking the door, as Big Bee, taking the pressure off Pogie, acquiesces to his fans' demands and stands up, holding his beer aloft. With a huge grin, he starts up and I half expect it will be a pithy line or two by that mass of mirth he resembles, fat John Falstaff. But he does Jaques from *As You Like It* and not too bad, I suspect, if I could hear him well enough in the din.

They are shouting and bellowing laughter, and Big Bee pauses, tears open another can, and goes on. When he gets to the part about the soldier, full of strange oaths and bearded like the pard, they are hysterical, and someone wants to know, choking, "What's a fuckin' pard?" Someone tells him, "You know, a pard, like a padre, a monk," and Big Bee stops abruptly and just stares at the man with the answer. "You ignorant shit," he says, annoyed, "a pard is a leopard." And he shakes his head, saying, "No class, no class."

Before we turn in, I ask Big Bee where he picked up the Shakespeare and he tells me he only knows a few lines, and he can do Friends, Romans, Countrymen, and Is this a dagger that I see. "Naw," he says, "never really read that shit, but I check the book reviews in the Sunday *New York Times,* impresses the Christ out of the quail in Chee Chee."

10

Cocktails in the NSF library before supper, gallons of the best British gin, American bourbon and vodka, the real stuff from one of the Russian stations east over the vast ice plateau. Military men in full dress, even ties, us in red plaid shirts and jeans, parkas hanging on the ubiquitous hall pegs. A huge picture window frames an impressive panorama of blue shadows on a treeless, snow-white expanse that stretches glittering out to the far peaks of the Royal Society Range.

In the tranquilizing grip of a strong martini, I stare at the scene, trying to convince myself that it is not one of those giant-sized nature murals that can look so real in a bar under the right lighting and libation. Dacey leaves us after taking a few pictures of the base commander chatting with our group, which includes a full-bearded Russian geophysicist, Khabanikhov, and two NSF scientists. Dacey whispers that there's a closed-circuit showing of *Deep Throat* at 1900 hours, and they're trying to get a couple of the broads over. He doesn't like being around so much brass for too long, he says, not because he's uncomfortable with them, he's been in this end of the game too long for that, but it's just that they know he's closer to us than they are, and they worry that he's being irreverent, or truthful. And they start giving him looks. Just before he pulls on his parka, Khabanikhov asks him what he plans to do when he gets out of the Navy. *"Playboy* photographer," says Dacey. "Can you imagine, sir, coming home at night and saying, man, what a hard day I had at the office today?" The Russian laughs generously and remarks that he's heard Dacey has a collection of pictures in his lab that he shows to special guests. "Yes," Dacey tells him, "got some *Playboy* rejects, didn't make the centerfold, and I'd be ashamed to show them, they're such dogs, almost guys. You know, only out to here instead of out to here." But, if Dr. Khabanikhov still wants to see them, well, he'd be happy to oblige. The Russian nods and says he'll be over later, anything would be good, he's just come back from a winter at Vostok.

I ask Khabanikhov about his work, and he tells me he's been handling the reception for the Doppler-shift network, something to do with monitoring traveling ionospheric disturbances. I get him off, at last, of neutron monitors and cosmic rays, and onto talking about life at the remotest of all Antarctic stations, the coldest place on earth, cold so intense, it is said, that it freezes the carbon dioxide right out of the atmosphere, air drier than all of the world's deserts. The world record for cold was set at Vostok — 126.9 below zero. Heart rate doubles there, he says, downing a vodka and pouring another from a chilled gallon jug, and it hurts in your chest when you breathe in the cold. Because of drastic differences in the boiling point of water at the outpost, it is difficult to sterilize medical instruments, and even minor procedures become major operations. Wounds take longer to heal there, and foods take longer to cook, three hours for boiled potatoes, fifteen hours to cook beans and peas. "They did the first abdominal operation at Vostok a few years ago," he says, beaming under his beard. "Acute appendicitis, performed an appendectomy in the mess hall under local anesthesia, took one and a half hours, and a day later the patient resumed his work as an aerologist."

A dozen or so men winter at Vostok, and they have to melt snow blocks regularly for drinking water, just as the Americans do at the South Pole. Work seven days a week, plenty of hearty food, movies, a broadcast from Radio Moscow, dominoes and chess. Not much different from life at the remote U.S. stations. U.S. exchange scientists visit and work there regularly, just as the Russians visit McMurdo. He says he much enjoys the friendly relationship that exists between the U.S. and the Soviet Union on the ice, and that it is good not only for science but for better understanding of each other. He says he tried to give Russian language lessons to Americans, but that's where the understanding fell apart.

Khabanikhov says he's fascinated by unusual phenomena in the Antarctic, and he is collecting reports of them for publication. One involves the voice in the snow, acoustic illusion. In the middle of one polar night at a Russian station, a radio operator decided to go outdoors for a brief walk. He returned excitedly to the mess hall and announced that he had just heard a call for help. The men counted heads and determined that this was impossible, since all eleven members of the wintering party were accounted for. There was not another human being for hundreds of kilometers, and the men looked at him as though he were gone mad. Later, one of the other men went outside onto the snow-covered roof of a station building to shovel snow into a melting tank. He, too, heard a voice in the distance. He stopped, and listened, but the cry was not repeated. He resumed shoveling, and heard the voice again, calling for help. He stopped, and stood perfectly still, but the voice had stopped again. He looked carefully about, and suddenly he understood the source of the cry — it came from beneath his feet. The snow was creaking. He verified it by placing a foot in the snow and turning it slightly. He heard a faint sound, as if from a great distance. Apparently, the structure, thickness, and low temperature of the snow cover had produced sound of an unusual quality very similar to a distant human voice.

Another time, the driver of a Caterpillar tractor was moving slowy along over a snowfield under a sky covered with a continuous layer of dense clouds. The tracks, because of the whitened condition, were completely invisible to the driver who relied on them to orient himself. He had the illusion of floating in air. Every once in a while, he would open his door to inspect the surface in an effort to find his way, and at one point he saw another tractor coming at him.

It turned out it was a vehicle that had been following him earlier. In his search for his tracks, the driver had made a 180-degree turn without noticing, and was driving in the opposite direction. Then, says the Russian, there are the mirages, very bright. ones, such as those observed on one occasion on a traverse from Vostok to Molodezhnaya Station. The silhouette of a tractor that first extended upward in the form of a column and then split into five individual silhouettes, half of them inverted, was observed through the telescope of a theodolite.

We are interrupted by a middle-aged American scientist whose tongue has been loosened by too much V.O. After a few tentative jabs he admits loudly that he doesn't care much for the press, they always misquote him, and they put those awful misleading headlines on all the stories about his work. He says he's had just about enough of having to cooperate with the news media just because NSF and the public is paying the freight. The FBI, after all, doesn't always tell the public what it's doing, and neither does the military. Anyway, he runs on, a lot of his work is too esoteric to be reported on by reporters who don't have Ph.D.s. It has something to do with sounding the ice cap. He says he has a rather limited amount of time in which to do his research, and he really is tired of being disturbed, or forced into releasing preliminary findings that may change after more detailed analysis.

Furthermore, he says, his temper rising, he's fed up with all the questions about how he feels about all the ice and snow out there, and what it's like working in this environment. He says he's never ever thought about what it means to be out here, he's only interested in his work. "You mean you've never heard the voice in the snow?" someone asks. The scientist shoots him a look of donnish scorn. "That," he says, "is just the sort of thing you people are best at reporting." "Well," says his questioner, "try this. Is it true that all glaciologists and geologists in Antarctica are really prospectors in drag, and you've made a real big mineral strike, maybe gold or uranium, out there in the Pensacola Range? Maybe that's what it means to be out here?" The scientist lifts his glass in a mock toast and says, lip curled, "No, what we're really doing is trying to determine the rate of melt of the ice cap so we can let you know just how long it's going to take before all your asses are drowned." "Now that," says the questioner, "is a helluva story," and he pulls out a notebook and feigns a scribble. "But, doctor," he adds, "which came first, the problem of glacial deterioration, or your grant?"

After the scientist leaves in a huff, we vow to misspell his name in a no-comment story about reported mineral strikes out in the boonies of Antarctica. Khabanikhov laughs and says he's convinced there is plenty of fuel and minerals under the ice, and offshore, that it's more than pure speculation, and we can quote him on that. He says our own government has estimated something on the order of fifty billion barrels of oil on the western continental shelf, and a hundred trillion cubic feet of natural gas. Shackleton discovered coal seams, and Byrd reported a vein in the Queen Maud Mountains full of enough coal to supply the entire world. The Soviet geologist Ravich believed that East Antarctica, where the Russians currently operate, contains diamonds, gold, mica and iron as well as coal. There have to be such deposits, Khabanikhov says,

84

because of the very strong possibility that Antarctica was joined at one point in time to Africa, South America, Australia, and India, and each of these continents possesses rich deposits. Take the Transantarctic Mountains, for example, an extension of the Andes. There are mother lodes of copper in both ranges. Of course, the problem of getting all of this out from under the ice is a formidable one, one that the Americans, the Russian says with a smile, must have anticipated since most of their stations are concentrated in areas that facilitate mineral exploitation. But the Soviets have generally worked the intensely cold eastern interior, with ice almost three miles thick covering whatever is underneath. Maybe, he says, that's why the Soviets have concentrated on what they consider to be the best exploitable resource in Antarctica, the wildlife, notably seals, whales, and krill.

Conservation experts do not share Khabanikhov's enthusiasm, however, particularly with regard to krill. Not too long ago, officials of the World Wildlife Fund charged the Russians with indiscriminate fishing for the microorganisms, sucking up both plankton and krill in huge factory ships and converting it all into fishmeal and poultry food, and threatening the very bottom of the food chain on which the entire fauna of Antarctica depends.

Khabanikhov shrugs off the criticism, saying that he is a geophysicist interested only in science, but that he can understand the feelings of those who want to see more tangible results than those derived from pure research. It is no secret, he says, that there are heavy demands today for food and fuel, and no secret also that America's research in the Antarctic, because of its expense, is moving closer to satisfying those who are demanding such things as an oil or mineral strike. He says he personally is distressed at such an attitude, there is so much yet to learn about the earth's geological history, for example, about the pollen and dust, and micrometeorites

85

that are all trapped in the ice, preserved in layers like the growth rings in a tree, a record of the earth's atmosphere for 100,000 years.

"But then," he says, smiling, looking through the picture window at the mountains beyond, "perhaps the scientists have been here too long, perhaps it should not be our own special preserve any longer. Perhaps there is more here to be satisfied than intellectual curiosity."

11

Some people set out to be Polar explorers. I never did. I have always enjoyed the tropics — balmy weather, swimming from warm, sandy beaches, the sight of graceful palm trees swaying in a gentle breeze. My first voyage to the Antarctic was the result of an impulse. After that, these things just happened to me.
— ADMIRAL GEORGE DUFEK

Rear Admiral George J. Dufek was a crusty, blue-water sailor, fifty-three years old and one of the U.S. Navy's best ice navigators when he took command, in 1955, of Operation Deep Freeze, the Navy's logistical support for America's effort to establish and maintain its Antarctic bases.

In December, his Task Force 43 supply ships, led by the ice-breaking *Glacier*, steamed into the Ross Sea, smashing a 400-mile path to the towering ice barrier. Dufek's Seabees swarmed ashore at McMurdo and set up two stations. Little America V was at Kainan Bay, 30 miles east of where Admiral Byrd, now sixty-eight, with the largely honorary title of Officer in Charge of U.S. Antarctic Programs, had set up four previous Little Americas. Another was built on Hut Peninsula.

Dufek was racing time and the weather. McMurdo had to be ready for air traffic and scientific instruments had to be in place when the International Geophysical Year began in 1957. Working double 12-hour shifts under floodlights and in temperatures that went as low as 70 below zero, the men who remained through the winter after their ships returned to Christchurch got their jobs done. In October of 1956, one day after the airstrip was completed, a Navy Skymaster with Dufek aboard hit the ice. "It was," said Lieutenant William

"Trigger" Hawkes, Dufek's pilot, "like landing in a bowling alley in somebody's basement."

The 1956–1957 season saw the greatest invasion of Antarctica in history. The U.S. sent 12 ships and more than 3,000 men. In addition, naval aircraft and eight Air Force Globemasters landed cargo on the ice and began dropping supplies and building materials at the South Pole, where a new station would be constructed.

But before that, Dufek took a crew aboard a modified DC-3 nicknamed the *Que Sera Sera* and headed for the Pole to try for a landing. Lieutenant Commander Conrad Shinn was the pilot, "Trigger" Hawkes the copilot, and Dufek the observer.

"I look up at the members of the crew," Dufek wrote in his book, *Operation Deep Freeze*. "There is no indication that this is an unusual flight. Pilots, navigator and radioman are at their tasks, occasionally yacking small talk over the intercom. Doug is slumped over in a corner on some soft luggage, sound asleep. Strider is at the hot plate brewing some coffee and making me a toasted cheese sandwich. I have no feeling of excitement either."

Their ski landing was without incident, and Dufek was the first out of the plane. It's the first landing ever made at the South Pole, October 31, 1956, the first humans at the spot, since Amundsen and Scott. It's more valuable symbolically than practically.

"Strider opened the door and I stepped out onto the South Polar Plateau. It was like stepping out into a new world. We stood in the center of a sea of snow and ice that extended beyond our vision."

Working quickly in 60-below cold and fierce wind, Dufek chopped an 18-inch hole in the ice with an alpine ax and stuck in a bamboo pole with an American flag lashed to it. He stuffed in a letter to verify he was there.

"Trigger came up to me and said, 'Boss, I can't move the

fingers of this hand. I think they're frozen. We've done everything here we can. I suggest we leave.'

" 'Good,' I said. 'Let's get the hell out of here.' "

They climbed back aboard, exactly 49 minutes after they landed, and slammed the door shut. They strapped themselves in, and Shinn revved his engines. But nothing happened. The plane had not moved. The skis were frozen into the ice.

With engines turning over full power, Shinn fired off four JATO (jet assist) bottles, a 30-second burn with the force of one engine. The plane shuddered but did not move. Shinn exploded four more, and the plane rocked and bucked forward. Four more, and still not free, then the last three blew and the *Que Sera Sera* wrenched loose of the ice, bounced heavily over the rough surface and staggered into the air.

Inside, Dufek leaned back and closed his eyes and thought about what he had done. They had been the first Americans to set foot at the South Pole, and one of his haunting concerns had been laid to rest. For weeks he had been worrying that the Russians, who had been the first to land at the North Pole, would get there first.

He is seventy-two and retired now, living in a lovely home overlooking the James River in Newport News, Virginia, not far from the Mariners' Museum where he has been director, retiring from that in 1973. He could pass easily for sixty, but not as easily for a civilian. Lean and gray, he is wearing a white Navy shirt, black trousers, black socks, and black shoes. He drinks several cups of coffee as we talk.

"Why did I go there in the first place? I was an aviator, flying off the Saratoga, and it was getting a little monotonous, you know, doing the same thing over and over again. All of a sudden this all-Navy dispatch comes out, looking for volunteers to go with Admiral Byrd to Antarctica. I was a kid, you know. 'They won't take me I'll volunteer' kind of stuff, and I came up to Boston, became navigator of the *Bear*. It was just an impulse.

"Well, the war was coming up and I was a regular Naval officer who shouldn't be off on some jaunt, so I went back and went through the war. And I was a Captain, and one day an old skipper friend came up to me and says, 'I got a task group going up to the Arctic to build a weather station and I want you to go with it,' and I said, 'Oh oh, that looks like it'll be long.' So he said, 'What are you doing?' and I told him I'm on a board that's rewriting the Naval regulations; you know, takes a thief to catch one. Well, I liked the guy so much I went with him. And after that we just turned around and went to the Antarctic. When the IGY came along, Byrd was too old and I got the command.

"So, first I went out of impulse, then loyalty, and then I got some experience and I was in the right place at the right time.

"But you know, we didn't consider ourselves explorers, and I never considered myself an explorer. We were just in the Navy doing our job. Some of the real explorers, like Finn Ronne, they'd never have thought of building a base like we did at the South Pole. Impossible. Seven hundred fifty tons, for eighteen men for a year. Ronne was still thinking dogs, small airplanes, small ships. But when the Navy got the job they thought of many people, many bases, lots of equipment. And we had the ships and the planes and the tractors, these great big Cats, and it was tough. But we didn't feel any sense of historic achievement, really, it was a job like any other, so go ahead and do it.

"The Pole landing. I don't think, looking back on it now, that I had any real feeling of history. Oh, it was the first time, but the only way to build that base there was by plane, not with dogs or tractor-train, you just couldn't carry seven hundred fifty tons up there over those crevasses and mountains.

"I don't think I even felt any identity with Scott when I landed there. We admired those people, of course, for their courage, the meager equipment they had, their limitations. And although we admired and respected them, we looked at it in a different way. This was not exploration we were doing this time; it was development. We were fortunate we had the equipment developed during World War II available for this job. But when I look at what they've got today, compared to what we had back twenty years ago, our stuff was pretty meager then. Look at that DC-3; that wasn't big enough to haul what we needed. It could pick up five tons at a time, but you're talking a hundred and fifty trips. So that's why we brought in the Air Force with the big Globemasters. They couldn't land at the Pole but they could drop a helluva load. Now you've got Hercs on skis that land there all the time. We had to go through agony.

"When I think of some of the things we had to do. Take that Pole trip. It wasn't any stunt, you know — we had been planning it for two years — but we were concerned about landing there because we didn't know whether it was too soft, whether we'd squash in, or it was too hard, maybe, and we'd snap the skis. So one day, Trigger came in and he said, 'Boss, don't worry anymore, we can land and take off safely at the South Pole, I just figured it out.' I said, 'What makes you so optimistic?' And he said, 'Well, I got this photo of Scott standing there and I enlarged it, figured out his weight, the size of his shoes and how much he had sunk into the snow. Then I figured out the pounds per square inch under the shoes, and pounds per square inch of the plane on skis, and, Boss, we got a safe margin.' And I said, 'Okay, we'll do it then.'

"Things are a little different now. Oh, the people are pretty much the same, I suppose, just as enthusiastic, just as proud of what they're doing. They may have it a little easier, I guess, but I wouldn't say the danger is any less. But, their equipment is more reliable, they have a better weather net, better communication. And that flight from New Zealand to the ice, twenty-five hundred miles, over the most dangerous air route in the world. You go down there, you're finished, forget it, you die in three minutes. When we did it, it was twelve hours, now it's four. Twelve hours, and over that water."

Dufek learned, from an unnerving experience, how cold are the waters surrounding the continent. In 1947, while he was being transferred by a highline between ships lying-to off Byrd Land, the hulls of the vessels began rolling in opposite directions. Dufek was in a chair suspended from a trolley that ran on the highline wire. With a sound like a pistol shot, the highline broke as the ships heaved and Dufek was thrown upward, hitting his head on the trolley, knocking him unconscious. He plunged 25 feet into the icy water and vanished.

A momentary mountain of water between the hulls sank into a gulf, and Dufek surfaced, still strapped in the chair, then sank again. The cold water brought him to and he freed himself, but his water-soaked polar clothing began to pull him down. He struggled and was able to pull the toggles that released compressed air into his life jacket. One ship heeled over into a sharp turn to pick him up and came to a halt 40 yards away. A moment later, a whaleboat was in the water, and he was pulled aboard.

When Dufek was back on his ship, the physician rushed him to a shower and turned the water on hot. Dufek's clothes were cut away and he began shivering like a patient with malaria fever. He pleaded for the water to be turned on hotter. Expedition medical doctrine called for immersing such exposure cases in a bath of 115 to 120 degrees Fahrenheit if the person was unconscious, otherwise no more than 110 degrees, since the higher temperature might be too painful to a conscious person. The treatment given Dufek was a radical departure from the old belief that a frozen body should be warmed slowly. He suffered no permanent harm, thanks to the therapy and the fact he was rescued in eight minutes. In a somewhat similar mishap, a month earlier, Dufek had another narrow escape when his helicopter crashed into the sea and sank. A nearby boat pulled him and the pilot to safety.

"Do I miss it? Yeah. It stands out in my mind more than anything else I've ever done in the Navy. I've commanded ships, the carrier *Antietam* in the Korean War, but this stands out. I made some good friends. It left me with a sense of accomplishment. And the environment. It's something I'll always remember. The isolation, the snow. It's engraved in my mind, and sometimes I can still see it.

"We had some laughs. This guy Beveridge, Lieutenant Beveridge, was an unusual fellow, spent two years at the South Pole. At the end of his first year, I said, 'Beveridge, why don't we take a plane, go up to New Zealand, raise some hell, get drunk, then come back?' He said no. He wants to be the man who spends two consecutive years at the South Pole. And he had this husky he was attached to, and he brought it back to McMurdo from the Pole. He had asked me if he could leave the dog up there, after his two-year hitch, because the animal was used to it. I told him no, they've got new people coming in up there and they have their own dog, they aren't going to leave theirs and take his. So, he brought it back to McMurdo, and he didn't know what to do with it. The dog was with him all the time. I told him to put it with the dog teams, and Beveridge said, oh no, that kind of dog he couldn't lower by putting him in with any team. He has to be by himself, that dog does. So, I said why not take the dog

93

home, you're going home, and Beveridge says no it's too big and he's got a small apartment. So I told him to leave it and I'd figure something out, I'd get rid of it or something.

"Well, Father Dan Linehan was there, and I said, 'What shall I do with that guy?' and Dan says, 'Get him out of here as fast as you can, two years up there, you know.' So I called my operations officer and I told him to get Beveridge out as fast as he could.

"So they got him on a plane and off it went, and I said, well there goes old Beveridge. Pretty soon, Beveridge walks in, and I said, 'What the hell's the matter with you? You're supposed to be on that airplane. And he says, 'Well, I just couldn't leave my dog.' And I said, 'Oh God.'

"Anyway, in a couple days, another plane is leaving and I got my aide and I said, 'Look, I got a quart of bourbon here, my last quart, and I want you to take that Beveridge and get him drunk, and get him on that goddam plane and get him the hell out of here.'

"So, the plane goes off and I said, that aide never misses, he's pretty good, a damn good aide. Beveridge's gone. Well, pretty soon, in walks my aide, and he's holding the bottle of bourbon and there's about that much left in it, about an inch off the bottom. And my aide says, 'Shir, Beveridge don't drink.'

"Well, I finally got him the hell out on the third plane, told the air ops officer that I didn't care if he had to hogtie him, I wanted him the hell out. . . .

"God, these guys were wonderful, though. Twenty years ago it was damn rough, and they'd work twelve hours a day seven days a week, week after week, to get their jobs done. Women would have been in the way. But, I have to explain my feelings about that. There was this movie called *Quick before the Ice Melts*, and it was a funny little thing, a bunch of kids and a woman slipped in, and the admiral was a sort of takeoff on me. Women, you know, we're not going to have any women down here on the ice, and anytime mentions women this admiral takes off and yells, 'No women.' So I got the reputation, no women. And this girl reporter comes down, got as far as New Zealand, and she said she had permission from the CNO and the Chief of Staff and the Air Force and everything else to come down. Well, I was on the ice and I got this message that this girl had this and this and this, so I sent a message back and I said, no dice, the CNO didn't tell me anything, the answer is no.

"So, she goes back to Los Angeles and she's interviewed or something and she calls me a misogynist, and I had to look it up to see what the hell it was. A woman-hater.

"Well, look, our living conditions were austere, really rugged. I had a little room about this big, that's all I had, and I was the admiral. The captains had similar rooms, except they had double bunks. Because living conditions were like that we just could not afford the luxury of separate dormitories, toilet facilities, and so on, for women. So I said no. It was money, that's all. The price of that operation was terrific. I'd figure it all out and go to the CNO, and he'd throw up his hands and go see Eisenhower, and the CNO'd come back and say, George, the President says this is all you get, do the best you can with it. It would have been a waste to duplicate facilities.

"As things eased up later, they built some facilities for women, and I see nothing wrong with them being there. If they can do their job, there's no reason why they shouldn't be.

"It's different now. Now we've got the Navy slowly being replaced by civilians down on the ice. And if you want to know why, it's because I think that President Nixon was sold a bill of goods by the NSF. They told him the civilians could do it cheaper than the Navy. Someone asked me, and I said

95

go and look at the DEW line and see how much that costs. What are you going to pay a cook at the South Pole? And why were they selling a bill of goods? Well, the Navy never really wanted to go into the Antarctic. It was an extra expense for them. The money that went into the Antarctic was taken out of the Navy's budget and they could probably have had a sub or a couple of cruisers, something like that. Instead of spending the money there. So, the Navy never liked it in the first place. I know that. When I started, I was bucked, it was slow getting people. But the Secretary of Defense told the CNO, you do it, and that's how the Navy got into it; they were ordered in by old Engine Charlie Wilson. Do it, so they did. The Navy wanted out as soon as they could. Well, the scientists are a little jealous of Navy running the show, and they wanted to do it. So they sold it to Nixon, we've got the money, we can get civilians to do it just as well and cheaper. The NSF wanted to take over, and that's what happened. Now the Navy's being replaced by civilian contractors, and hell no, they can't do it cheaper, and I know damn well they can't do it better. Take a weatherman, electrician, cook, a diesel engineman that's in the Navy, getting sailor's pay, compared to a civilian who goes down there, he gets overtime.

"Anyway, it is a psychological lift to know that the American flag is flying at the South Pole. And our international cooperation has also been fantastic on that continent, better than anywhere in the world. The reason, of course, is that all we're getting out is science. But discover something else, well, that goodwill to men is going up the pipe.

"From a military standpoint, I don't see any strategic value there today, except maybe weather, a global entity. If you look back at World War II, the allies were in a better position on weather than Germany, and this helped our air operations. It was so important that the Germans even put subs out as weather observers up around Greenland, when they needed those subs to be sinking our shipping. Now, it's a little far out, but I don't think too far out, to think that if we control the Antarctic . . . and had the weather reporting there . . . both the polar areas, you know, heavily influence circulation patterns over the whole globe . . . well, we would have the advantage over any opponent who didn't have it. . . .

"And you know something else, I could do things there that I can't do here. Like when Fuchs and Hillary showed up. Father Linehan was with me, and I said to him, 'Look, Father, the Americans were here first and we went through all this to build a base out here, I want the Americans to be the first to take a sounding and see what we're sitting on. Is it all ice down there, or ocean, or land, or what?' So he said, 'All right, I'll help you. You have to dig this hole down several feet, get all this equipment in, and you set your ears out and a pin goes down and so on, and you blast and measure the shock and so on.'

"While all this is going on, it's pretty hard work, and it gets to be noon, and I said, 'Father, I'll go up and get us a couple bottles of beer and some sandwiches.' So, I go and get the food and tucked a bottle of beer under each arm so it wouldn't freeze out there, sat down, and I give Father Linehan his beer and sandwich. Well, he's drinking the beer but he's not eating. I said, what's the matter? He says he's hungry, yeah, but it's Friday. 'Look,' I said, 'if you just take two steps over here, it'll be Thursday.' And he did. Two steps into Thursday; I can't give that kind of an order any more."

12

This work of Antarctic exploration is very different from the work I had planned for myself some years ago. And yet I do honestly believe that God's will is being worked out for us in what we are doing, and though it may seem to some rather more "worldly" and "scientific" than "spiritual," yet there *is* a spiritual work to be done here. And as for its main object, the acquisition of knowledge pure and simple, surely God means us to find out all we can of his works, and to work out our own salvation, realizing that all things that have to do with our spiritual development are understood and clearly seen in things created, and if it is right to search out his works in one corner of his Creation, it is right for some of us to go to the ends of the earth to search out others.

— EDWARD WILSON

The headline writers like "Earthquake Priest," not out of any awe at his sermons but because it's what they call a grabber. He practices seismology, too, emeritus now at the age of seventy-two, high on a green hill in Boston College's Weston Observatory. The Reverend Daniel M. Linehan, Society of Jesus and Harvard alumnus in geology, as comfortable with Aquinas as with the seismic refraction system he perfected, locater of the north magnetic pole (it was 100 miles north of where cartographers thought it was), prober of Vatican Hill for the tomb of Peter, three times to the Antarctic, one of a handful of Americans to have circumnavigated the continent close to the ice front, first person to determine the depth of the ice at the South Pole.

He was also, he says proudly, talking easily in his rock-cluttered office from behind a desk heaped with scientific journals, the first priest to say Mass on bare earth on Antarctica, right outside Scott's camp on Ross Island. Some other chaplain had said Mass there, but it was on floating ice, he is quick to point out. He was also the first to say Mass at the South Pole itself.

Celebrating those two Masses, he says quietly, was a high point in his life. They were also Antarctic firsts, rating a mention in a Catholic almanac, or a nice thing to drop at a Knights of Columbus dinner. When he was eleven, in 1914, his mother and father took him to a movie house to see films of Captain Scott's last expedition to the Pole.

"Some of those scenes, I can still remember," he says. "The bow of the *Terra Nova* cutting through pack ice, the platform built out over the gunwales from which the pictures were taken, skiers herringboning across snow-covered slopes, men crawling into sleeping bags and drying out senna grass for their boots. I forget the rest, but the picture must have made an impression. Ever since that, I wanted to visit the Antarctic."

The first time Father Linehan went to the ice was in 1954 aboard the icebreaker USS *Atka*, at the invitation of Admiral Byrd, to help scout for possible landing areas for IGY activities, and to determine the thickness and type of ice at various locations.

He went back in 1955–1956, "same sort of stuff, and to make tests for airstrips which would be permanent," and he helped establish Little America V at Kainan Bay. "They built it on shelf ice, eight hundred feet thick, floating on a thousand feet of water, and so I gave it a three-year safety factor. They built the camp and abandoned it three years later, and it broke up and went to sea, just like the old Little America site on the Bay of Whales." A touch of sadness creeps into his voice. "We found that earlier, and four hundred or five hundred square miles of ice had broken off the shelf and gone. You could see right up the face of the break-off, the line where the old airstrip was, oil and stuff on the snow, some GI tents and trash barrels. That was all there was left to it." He shakes his head, and I do not know exactly whether it is in remorse over the end of a monument, or nostalgia.

"Yeah, that Dufek was something else," says Father Linehan. "I remember a time we were flying into Little America from McMurdo, and we had one of these DC-3-type planes. We had an extra thousand gallons of gas tanked down the middle aisle, and we were sitting behind it, with the admiral up front. He used to get in flying time now and then, and he'd swap with the copilot. We'd just started to circle the field at McMurdo but we weren't landing and we didn't know why. The plane was wobbling an awful lot, and the copilot came back and said, the ski on the starboard side's dropped. The cable had broken and the ski was just hanging there, weighing close to half a ton, you know. And it was shaking in the wind and vibrating the plane, and the pilot said he didn't know yet what he was going to do. So, he says, we'll be circling for a while while they get things ready on the ice. Said we couldn't retract the ski, and anyway, we looked out and there were the firemen down there, with spray guns to let us have the foam.

"There were twenty-six of us aboard, and while we were circling I remember looking out and they had this big X marked on the runway where they wanted us to hit, and foam tanks on sleds, and they were putting out these litter baskets. Fifty of them I counted, and there were only twenty-six of us on board.

"So we made a couple of passes about a mile and a half from the strip, lashed everything down, took things like fountain pens out of our pockets, hid them, took our glasses off. There was this doctor sitting across from me, and he pulls out one of those ocarinas and starts to play, 'Happy Days Are Here Again.'

"Well, the copilot comes out and he says, 'Of course, Father, you'll be giving out absolution if it happens?' And he wants to know if it'll take care of them up in the cockpit, too. I told him it'd reach all the way to the Pole. Well, it started vibrating more and more, the ski, and finally one of the starboard engines cracked open. It blew, and there was fire all over the place, and I looked at it and it was really blazing. That was no fun. I kept watching it, and all of a sudden the pilot went for the ice. He landed it a mile away from the X, in soft snow, snapped the ski off, he did, one in a million chance, and we had a guy ready at the door who pulled something and loosed the whole plane frame. We got out as fast as we could, and we put the fire out ourselves.

"And the last thing I remember was Admiral Dufek standing at the door — he was the last one out after the pilots went out through their hatches, and he's standing there, yelling, 'Where's my photographer?' of all times, 'Where's my photographer?'

"Dufek, he brought me up to the South Pole with him, where I measured the thickness of the ice there, for the first time, by setting off explosions and timing them and so forth. Explosive wave goes down to the rock, comes back up and you time it. One of the difficulties there was that the camp generators were making so much noise, I had to sort of shoot between them. But I came up with a figure, a little less than nine thousand feet, the depth of the ice. Then the English party came along with Vivian Fuchs, and they made some seismic tests, but they came up with a lower figure, less ice. But they weren't right at the Pole. Around the Pole it's like a big bowl, and they were away off on one side of it. But I hit it right in the center. . . .

"I loved it there, I really did. The beauty, the geological phenomena, the penguins raising their chicks, and the sunsets we'd get there in the summertime just when the sun starts to go below the horizon. The colors, the same colors you can see up here, but here they're just up in the sky and down there they're reflected on the ice, and the whole world looks to be on fire. Under the right conditions, you get new suns in the heavens, parhelia surrounding the earth like jewels, and there's that intense whiteness, sheer blueness, awful brilliance, and the total silence that you can only experience in Antarctica.

"But those sunsets, you can't look at them too long without beginning to see what must have been the beauty of the Creator who designed them. Then you watch a big iceberg — and we saw one that was larger than the state of Connecticut, we measured it — and you see that thing plowing along from subsurface currents. There's about eight hundred feet of ice going on the bottom, picking up lower currents, and it's moving along like a big ship, right in the teeth of that wind as though under its own power. It'd come into a field of pack ice and smash right through it, didn't bother it a bit. Well, something like that, to see the ocean doing more work than all the icebreakers in the world, and you say, this couldn't be an accident. You begin to see some of the power of the God that created that berg and keeps it moving. And you see how the little skua chicks survive in that weather, how man's blood adapts, and it all points, for me, to the gentleness of the Creator, His gentle touch that lets these living things get along.

"And you realize that every crystal of ice, every speck, forms a six-sided crystal, following a very definite mathematical pattern, and here you've got like five-and-a-half million cubic miles of ice, each made up of individual, microscopic crystals, each with the same math working, and yet perhaps no two looking exactly alike. It teaches you something about what we mean by infinity. We speak of God as knowledge, as power, as time, so no matter where you look down there on the ice it backs up all your theology as well as your science. It makes an impression on everyone, I think.

"Many times, I'd be sitting there on the ship, say, looking over the rail at a sunset, or sailing by that ice, and someone, a sailor or a scientist, he'd come over and say it, 'This sure makes you feel pretty small, doesn't it, Padre?' It just humbles everyone, that immensity and beauty, perfect beauty. Even on stormy days, and it made all the guys you worked with wonderful people to live with, to play with, and sometimes to suffer with.

"One time, I went into this place in a small 'copter to make some measurements, see what the snow was like and so on, and these 'copters we were using then were small, just held two people, pilot and passenger. And one of those whiteouts occurred. In those days, the planes only had a gasoline gauge and a magnetic compass on the dash, and the compass was no good. And you don't know whether you're flying upside down or not unless you look out at the horizon. In a whiteout there's no horizon, and it's the milk bottle that they talk about. I just happened to look out and I saw a couple of specks and I thought they were penguins, so I nudged the pilot, said, 'Let's go down.' They weren't penguins but some of our men, and that's how high we were. We weren't supposed to be up there like that, and when we got down I said to the pilot, 'Look, when you get back to the ship tell them not to send any more flights out till this thing clears.'

"Well, this was his first time flying out here, and out over the water there was this dark sky, what we call water blink, while over the ice it was white sky, snow blink, during a whiteout. So I said to the kid, over there is your ship, and I could actually hear the generators running from where I was. I said, 'Get up as high as you can before you start to push.' Normally, the 'copters start taking off sideways, but I wanted him up high. I said, 'Keep your eyes on that black part and when you get over there you'll see the ship, but make sure you don't let anybody else come back here.' So he says, 'Okay, Father,' and he starts out. He went in the right direction, and I knelt over and put my skis on, got some gear together. And then I heard his engine, and I knew he was coming back. He must have taken his eyes off the ship. Well, he thought he was going level, but he wasn't, and he went straight down into the ice, and he hit a hundred yards from me. I was waving my arms at him trying to distract him, show him where he was, but he went into the ice, and the whole plastic shell was shattered and it was into his body and his clothes. I was over him and I reached for my knife to cut his straps and get him out, slashed myself in all that plastic embedded in him, but I got him out. The ship never did catch fire, but I thought it was going to. Another plane came over, and they had these big bags for landing gear in those days, pumped up with air, and I waved them off because it would have been all over if they hit any of that scattered plastic, they'd be out of luck, too.

"We got the pilot onto a sled, I baptized him and gave him Absolution and everything. Strapped him on the outside of a 'copter, onto the pontoon, and they got him back to the ship in twenty minutes. And he couldn't make it himself, only a few minutes before. And he died two hours later. It's a kind of hard thing. We let the skipper know we were okay, and not to come get us, and we stayed out there a couple days. There was an ensign there with us, and the skipper told him to tell me I was in charge, so the first thing I did was get the guys started digging a hole in the ice, climb down into it for protection. I really just wanted to keep them busy, take their minds off that dead man. No heat, we ate some chocolate, had to walk around a lot to keep warm. We couldn't tell in that whiteout where the crevasses were, so we set up a big flag to mark where we were, and it all worked out okay.

"We got back to the ship finally when the weather cleared, and the skipper asked me to talk to the men, said he was afraid of a mutiny. They got a dead man aboard and this doesn't have a calming effect on men on a ship. So he said, 'Father, you've got to talk to these guys.' I was sort of the informal chaplain, you know, and it was a marvelous way to study different men, not that I was trying to do that. But you can't help it under those circumstances.

"And these were great boys. I came away with a really positive feeling about them, not a negative one. You know, you read some camp books and diaries and you find out that when a new crowd comes in at the end of winter, nobody in the old crowd is talking to each other anymore, sick of each other after the winter. But I don't think that was true of the American camps as much as the foreign ones. I only heard of one that didn't make out too well; the officer-in-charge was to blame. Everyone that I know came out with that *noblesse oblige,* and we had the best camps in the Antarctic. I used to tell the guys, look, when you winter in bring along some language books, you can get up a language while you're there, and each language you learn makes you another man, a second person. . . .

"Sure, there were dangers out there, and I always considered those, and watched for them all the time. But, you know, I had a previous experience when we went looking for the north magnetic pole that sort of set me up. There was this fellow in New York, a maritime lawyer who also held a master's license so he could sail any ship from the *Queen Mary* on down, and he wanted to go on a vacation for himself. He knew navigation, and he and his son decided they'd like to go into the Canadian Arctic. Well, you have to do some scientific work to get permission from the Canadian government to go there, so he said, we're going to relocate the north magnetic pole. He was talking to some bank in

New York, ran into a vice president who had been a former student of mine who told him, well, why don't you contact Father Linehan, he's a geophysicist, does magnetic work and all that stuff. So, I get a call, he's fitting out a ship, would I like to go along, and I said, yeah, that'd be wonderful.

"Well, when I get up to South Portland, Maine, to get aboard I've got this load of seismic and magnetic gear. And I'm out on the dock looking for the ship, and I couldn't find it. The reason was it was low tide, and the ship was below the dock level, only sixty feet long, for God's sake, and some high school kids for crew. Well, we went to sea in it, put in at Halifax, up to Greenland, and then through the Northwest Passage.

"Now, this little ship . . . it's a little one, remember . . . well, we're going through the Davis Strait and it's pretty rough water, and I was on watch from three to eight, with the skipper and his partner, and I looked around the cabin and there was water leaking in through the overhead. The skipper tells me everyone's sick below and he's been up all night. So I said, 'I'll take over; go get some sleep.' He takes off and here I am, all alone, and we start passing some icebergs, and I start to worry. I'm steaming along eight or nine knots, downhill, and we had a gyro, but on a small boat they don't work well; all that rocking throws it out. But the magnetic compass was okay. Anyway, I was worried about those little growlers out there, could send us right to the bottom if we smacked into one, and there's water coming in over the bow, and I tell you I was frightened to death.

"So, I started my meditation, wondering what the boys were doing back home at Weston. They're getting up soon and so on, and I made my meditation on the Sea of Galilee, Lord, ye of little faith, you know, why do ye fear? What am I worried about? The guy I work for made these bergs. So I just sat back at the wheel and whistled, figured if He wants us to hit it'll happen, if he doesn't, that's it.

"And it worked. The sun came out, icebergs all around us, and I stuck it out at the wheel for ten, twelve hours. I don't worry too much after that. When I get on a plane I just figure we're gonna crash, we're gonna crash. That's it.

"So, yeah, I've always considered the dangers. But they don't really bother me, and anyway there's a pull about the place, things you just got to do. It's like when you're a kid and you see a field after a snowfall, where nobody has been before. The first thing you want to do is go out and make tracks on it. We do the same thing in the Antarctic. It's like breaking open a rock and finding a fossil fern, or a clam, inside, something that may have lived five hundred million years ago, and you break open that rock and sometimes you can even see the little bore hole of the bug that dug in and killed whatever lived inside, and you're the first human being to see that clam or fern inside the rock. The only other was God almighty. . . ."

13
Notebook

There are peculiar ironies here on the ice. We have refrigerators in the barracks to keep our food from freezing. Outdoors, there is intense cold that scorches. Barren land touched by frigid and inhospitable waters rich with animal and plant life. Flightless birds that walk like men; strange wingless flies the only insect life; millions of cubic miles of freshwater ice, yet a desert. Dry valleys of sand that are chilled and licked by a glacier's tongue, megatons of snow where it rarely snows. The dry, white bones of one of Scott's ponies nearly run over by a buzzing motor toboggan, the tin dog of the Antarctic. Nansen sledges, the mainstay of polar explorers, still in use, their beautifully grained wood rubbed and polished and lashed with rawhide for give, but with runners of plastic. A New Zealand dog team puts on its show for us tourists, yelping and dashing and panting alongside our rattling Trackmaster to shouts of their driver, not mush but more onomatopoeic, *tweet tweet, aurrrukkk,* and *ahhh ahhh.* Mean dogs that snarl and fight in their traces and on the trail, and yet they nuzzle and lap us as we kneel beside them, gingerly, amid the sculptured blue-green ice shapes flung up out of the sea near Scott Base, in the urine-yellow snow.

More often than not we do not have the time to absorb what we see and hear, and we find ourselves scribbling frantically with chilled fingers in bulky gloves, wondering how we're going to tell it all, never being alone with any of it long enough to store it up in large quantities to be drawn on later, when we are back home.

We take hasty pictures, and the camera sees more than we do. We move on, leaving it all behind, to come back, I hope, in a dream. I am reminded of a visit to Jerusalem and how I could not concentrate on the Via Dolorosa because a bothersome pack of Arab kids kept tailing me, pestering me for paper money, not the Kennedy half-dollars I tried to tempt them with, while they swore to me that they were Christians, too.

Often, I am not certain that what I record later is as I saw or heard, or whether I am entranced by being here, led on by the things that I have read or heard from others who have visited and who have stirred me to dreaming. How can one, for example, read a description by Wilson that blends science and color and not try to emulate? "In the North at noon there was a splendid sunrise with a heavy bank of cloud arranged for all the world like wavy hair, and wherever the sunlight caught those waves and curls it was broken into the most delicate opal mother-of-pearl tints; all colours of the rainbow, pale rose, pure lilac, emerald green, lemon yellow, and fiery red — blending but with no apparent arrangement, so that a wisp of cloud standing like a stray curl in the blue sky would be lit by pink and brilliant lilac, and then would begin to shine at one end with a light that can only be compared with the light you see in a vacuum tube with a current sparkling through it, or perhaps the colour is more exactly what you get with incandescent barium. It seems far-fetched to go into chemical details to describe a sky, but neither lilac nor amethyst describes the colour I have spoken of as lilac, but the light of incandescent potassium does exactly. One can describe the yellows more easily because all our ideas of light vary from white to yellow and orange; but for red I like to refer to strontium, though a rose-pink describes a certain light chiefly perhaps because one so often sees light shining through a petal of the commonest form of rose.

"If a dozen rainbows were broken up and scattered in wavy ribbons and flecks of curl and fleecy forms to float against a background of dull grey, it would be something like the beautiful appearance of this cloud colouring."

Scott, too, though he lacked the keen artistic perception of his friend Wilson, was caught on occasion in Antarctica's spell and moved to jot down a few "impressions" in his diaries, imprints that went a bit beyond his usual meticulous accounting of miles traversed, temperatures recorded, and supplies on hand. He wrote of the seductive folds of the sleeping bag, the small green tent, and the great white road. The whine of a dog and the neighing of steeds, and the driving clouds of powdered snow. The crunch of footsteps as they break the surface crust, the crisp ring of ponies' hooves and the swish of the following sledge over windblown furrows. Patter of dog pads and booming of full-force blizzard. Some of it I feel and hear and see, on a long and quiet walk onto ice fields back of Scott Base with a friend who, thankfully, does not talk. Out here, we all want to wax poetic, as they say, and are driven to do it in a diary. I stand in the lee of a fluttering canvas hut, and I write things that I am certain have been written by everyone who has been to this spot. A moan of cold wind, ice like lace, clothes billowing in heavy gusts like a sailboat running downwind as we skid over the ice. Ocean spray freezing as we watch, into columns of pale blue. A blurred sun, weakened by a dull sky, snow devils whirling in from the great white desert farther south.

Crevasses that we prod with pikes, nature's pitfalls covered lightly as by a hunter. How many ways can I say snow? I am tired of powder and flour and crushed chalk. Ice? There's sleet and hail and cold glaze. And cold. I am thinking of my newspaper and my days on rewrite, when cold was always bone-chilling and knife-edged. Try Mawson on blizzards: "A plunge into the writhing storm-whirl stamps upon the senses an indelible and awful impression seldom equalled in the whole gamut of natural experience. The world is a void, grisly, fierce and appalling. We stumble and struggle through the stygian gloom; the merciless blast, an incubus of vengeance, stabs, buffets and freezes; the stinging drifts blind and choke. In a ruthless grip, we realize that we are poor windlestraws on the great, sullen, roaring pool of Time."

Poetry reading in the mess hall after the so-called night meal that is served only to "authorized working personnel possessing a meal card who must leave table promptly after eating to provide room for others." It is near midnight and the menu is cold cuts — the Navy calls it horse-cock — on great slabs of warm bread, with pies and milk and coffee. Poems must deal with Antarctica, a severely limiting factor. Everyone's a Robert Service fan, particularly that ad for Yukon Jack liqueur, a tall man enveloped in a great bearskin coat, sipping from a glass against a backdrop of frozen northern wilderness, with Service's lines: "I have flouted the Wild. I have followed its lure,/fearless, familiar, alone;/Yet the Wild must win and a day will come/When I shall be overthrown." Service is ruled out of order, but not before someone else, unstrung on the bottle of brandy we have brought along, chants, "Let us probe the silent places,/let us seek what luck betide us;/Let us journey to a lonely land I know./There's a whisper on the night-wind,/there's a star agleam to guide us./And the wild is calling, calling. . . ./Let us go."

Someone recalls an old sledging song: "Give me your strongest, those who never fail./I am Blizzard, King of the Southern Trail."

A midwinter poem by Anonymous: " 'Twas the night before midwinter and all of the Bees/Were asleep in their beds catching some ZZZs./The Marsgrams were sent to BUPERS with care/In hopes that choice orders soon would be there./ The hippies were stoned, their eyes heavy as lead/While visions of grass danced in their heads./The captain in his nightgown, the XO in his cap/Had just settled in for a long lifer's nap./When down at the club, there arose such a clatter/The master chief ran to see what was the matter./And what to his mil't'ry eyes should appear/The Kiwis were drinking and shouting for beer."

On cold: "It melts into your mind/And stiffens the grease on the gears of thought. Cold/Suffusing in/Leaving no escape/Slowing the clock."

From one called "Midwinter Night" by someone calling himself "Nemo" with one of Shackleton's expeditions: "The revels of Eros and Bacchus/Are mingled in some of their dreams/For the songs they gustily gurgle/Are allied to bibulous themes./And subjects re barmaids and bottles/Whisky and barrels of beer/Are mixed with amorous pleadings/That sound decidedly queer."

"Aurora Australis," during the same expedition: "Darling, you really love me?/Stutters one dreaming swain./The watchman whispers, 'Never,'/and the dreamer writhes in pain."

One by Pat Lynch, wife of a member of Deep Freeze 66: "She called, this white-veiled beauty/From her realm across the sea./She beckons with an icy hand/And takes my love from me./She calls, and he must follow/Her winds echo in his ear./This mystic, snowy beauty/Sings a song I cannot hear./I know that he must answer/Her pleading, distant voice./For adventure deep within his soul/Leaves him with no choice./ She never calls the faint at heart/She only wants the strong./ Her sunless days and dark nights/Are cold and very long./She offers him no comfort/Within her icy walls./But still he cannot turn away/From her constant calls./Who is this icy beauty/Who takes him for a year?/She's known as The Antarctic/And she holds a new frontier."

We end on a note from something called "The Adelie Blizzard": "Eddy — wraiths o'er the splintered schist — /Torrent spume down the glacier hissed!/Throbbing surge of the ebbing seaward gust/Raping stillness vast in its madd'ning lust." No one understands it but we all cheer.

At the last minute, they cancel our trip to Pole this morning, even though it looks like ideal flying weather, a fierce sun, bright and blue and not a cloud. It is, however, too cold at Pole, our pilot tells us, growing impatient with our impatience. Minus sixty-five eff, he says, walking away from us, shaking off our pleadings. Bad enough to freeze up the hydraulics. Oil pours like Karo when it gets that low, your kerosene turns to Jell-O, rubber around the electrical systems breaks apart and you short out, your engine metal gets brittle and cracks up, and do we need any more reasons why he isn't about to risk his loving ass?

We spend the change in the schedule learning about ice, with a field trip and a lecture. The field trip is an invigorating hike in crisp, clean air across the blue and white sea ice of McMurdo Sound, led by an older man, a New Zealander from Scott Base, who strides ahead of us, jabbing his long pike into crevasses that we barely notice, leaping nimbly over each crack, telling us to step lively, laddies, or it's the blue grotto below that'll take us all. To prove his point, he does a running broad jump and lands with both feet piercing a long seam in the snow-covered ice, plunging in and saved by arms stretched out straight and stiff from his body. He looks like a man buried to his armpits in sand, as he mugs for our cameras. We haul him out, laughing, and follow him to some gigantic pressure ridges that rear up to our right, squeezed out of the water by the considerable force of the Ross Shelf against Ross Island. He leads the way up the side of one of the ridges, cutting crude steps as we ascend, and we pick our way, boots slipping, gloved hands trying to grab some protuberance. It is like trying to get a grip on a refrigerator.

We are up, at last, on a narrow, icy ledge, thirty or forty feet off the sea ice, five of us scared to death, not him, he's shouting into the mouth of a cave that he's kneeling at a few yards ahead of us. "Hah-loo, Bert, you there?" We weren't expecting this, but Bert, who's inside the cave, answers, "Aye, Chippy, coom darn, coom on." Bert's head, in a green tam with a pink pompon in the center, pops out of the hole, then his shoulders and finally a gloved paw waving a lighted lantern. "Coom on," he says with a wide grin, "the wee chap first wi' me." He means me, five-foot-five. It is one of those moments I wish someone would call off, but no one does and I live another blustering lie. It is like being sixteen, swaggering up to a bar for the first time, hoping I won't choke on the straight shot of rum. Bert backs into the hole and I follow him, a queasy feeling in the pit of my stomach, feet first and on my belly so that I won't see whatever it is that's coming.

It is an icy tunnel, round and so narrow that I feel like a piston in a cylinder. All the morbid dread of confined places that I've ever had is jammed in here, and I have an overwhelming urge to stand up and run. But that is impossible, filling this burrow as I do. I manage a strained head-turn and over my shoulder I see Bert's lantern light reflecting orange in the icy tube, and then all of a sudden it disappears and it's coal black, and cold damp.

Then I hear Bert's voice, and it sounds far away and below me somewhere. "Noo then," he shouts, "ye gaun tae jine wi' me, nae fear, nae fear, laddie." Before the echo has died away, I am sliding down helplessly as the tunnel takes a quick dip.

It is a deliciously sick bobsled run with arms outstretched, hands trying to catch hold of anything that will slow the ride, chin pulling against the ice. It is over abruptly as I shoot out of the tunnel and drop about three feet to the icy floor of an immense cave, lit reddish-yellow by Bert's lamp and another set atop a glistening white hummock. He sticks his head into the hole and yells. One by one, they slide down and pop out of the hole until we are all standing unsteadily on the slippery ice, all but Chippy, who is, Bert reassures us in this gleaming dungeon, waiting topside to help us out.

We are in something the likes of which none of us, save Bert, has ever seen. A frost-encrusted chamber, jeweled and sparkling in the reflection of Bert's lamp and the blue-green light filtering through the ice somewhere above. No mold, no moss, no crusting calcium carbonate, none of the earthy, moldy odor of the caves in the sides of dirty hills. It is a fairyland of glitter and clean-smelling cold, of stalagmites and stalactites of ice, some as big as I, and tiny icicles that now and then break and tinkle to the floor. There are shiny heaps of snow that have melted and frozen, melted and frozen again into a candle-drip effect.

It is the most eerily beautiful place I have ever seen or been in, and there is no need, indeed no inclination, to animate this Nature that is so pure here, that has its own special excuse for being. It would be presumptuous to mar it as we do laughing brooks and smiling suns and sermons in stone. I wonder, in here, whether we have any right at all to compare ourselves to Nature, to look to it for moral strength, to imitate its awesomeness, to pit ourselves against it.

I want to draw in as much of this immaculate splendor as I possibly can, to carry on a fleeting affair and then get out, hauled up through the slippery tunnel on the end of a rope that Chippy has let down. The rope has distracted me from the beauty, and the claustrophobic feeling seizes me once again. I am anxious with thoughts of dying in here, in a fitting icy tomb. I am as far away from home as I could possibly be, not only at the bottom of the world but beneath the ice that, with the rumble of a plane overhead could come crashing in on us all, destroying all the fairyland, like the carpeted and once music-filled lounge of a 707 jetliner scattered over a cornfield after a midair explosion.

I don't really know why, but I am thinking of when the news broke that Martin Luther King had been assassinated. I was saddened, but not so much for his death as over my own ambivalence to his cause. I wanted to be able to tell him that I had been meaning to help in some way, but had put it off. It was too late, and the sorrow and the helplessness were as strong as they would have been if I had had a bitter argument with my wife and she died before we had a chance to make up.

I am also wondering, while waiting for the rope, who it was who said that everything that we are hanged for or imprisoned for is going on in Nature, that it is quite indifferent to our values, to us. A mindless killer, it can do me in as it did Scott and his men only a few miles from this place into which we have burrowed to gaze at an unheralded wonder of the world that may not be here when the next press tour comes down.

Thoughts of death and near-death do come easily here, for it is a place where the heroic and the foolish and those marked for accident met their end, a place of lonely crosses in the snow. The Scripps graduate student killed when his tracked vehicle broke through thin ice on McMurdo Sound and sank in two thousand feet of water. The manager of the biology lab, a Holmes & Narver employee, dead in a truck plunge down an icy slope a mile from here. The ice runway at Williams Field, named after CD3 Richard Williams, who died when his tractor went through the ice of the Sound.

The earth sciences lab at McMurdo, dedicated to the memory of Dr. Edward Thiel, a polar geophysicist killed here in 1961. And before all of those, the Douglas Mawson expedition working west of here in 1912, Lieutenant Ninnis crashing through a snow bridge and falling to his death with a load of food and the best dogs, and a little while later, Dr. Xavier Mertz dying on the trail. And Mawson himself, struggling to return to his home base alone, the thickened skin of the soles of his feet separated in a complete layer, flapping loose, the new skin underneath abraded and raw. Mawson crashed through the lid of a crevasse on the trek back, and dangled in his harness at the end of a rope hitched to a sledge jammed luckily on the edge of the pit. His thoughts of death before he managed to haul himself up. "Exhausted, weak and chilled, for my hands were bare and pounds of snow had got inside my clothing, I hung with the firm conviction that all was over except the passing. Below was a black chasm. It would be but the work of a moment to slip from the harness, then all the pain and toil would be over. It was a rare situation, a rare temptation — a chance to quit small things for great, to pass from the petty exploration of a planet to the contemplation of vaster worlds beyond."

We are up and out, hauled from the ice-coated cavity by Chippy's rope, but not before we sign a guest book that someone has left in a niche cut into a wall. We laugh at the sign over a tincan, DROP ALL CASH HERE.

Standing unsteadily on the ledge, dazzled by the sun's glare on the snow and ice below, it is sighing relief to be outside, but with a twinge of disappointment, now that the potential danger is past, over the absence of anything untoward or dramatic occurring, no crumbling walls of ice, no narrow escape to make Page One, no snatch from the jaws of death to talk about tonight in the mess hall. I have been reading too much Mawson and Cherry-Garrard.

Later, three scientists try to teach us that there's more to ice than the solid state of water, and I get only shreds of what they are saying. I am still piqued that I wasn't pulled from that icy cave as though from a coal-mine disaster, and I feel I have given Antarctic lore a bad name. The glaciologists are covering things like the bubble pressures in ice cores, and Wilson's theory of Ice Ages that has something to do with surges in the Antarctic sheet and, yes, the purity of polar ice is just as high as the purest laboratory water and, yes, ice does have the ability to emit microwaves. Then there's the loud ping you hear when a floe snaps apart into a hairline crack that opens into a 400-meter lead, and of course there is the strong possibility that ice in West Antarctica is crumbling and deteriorating for some mysterious reason. They're all sure that anyday now a bunch of old ladies will be calling radio talkmasters complaining about all these weird changes in the weather caused, undoubtedly, by scientists messing around at the South Pole.

The best ice story, however, belongs to Commander Kirkpatrick of Coast Guard ship operations, who has designed what is called the Ice Pier, a giant ice cube 650 feet long, 200 feet wide, and 30 feet thick, floating in Winter Quarters Bay and used to dock and off-load ships. The construction effort, in the dark and the cold, will probably never make a seminar at the Harvard School of Design, and it probably will not make the newspapers until the pier starts to crack and break apart, which it shows signs of doing. Kirkpatrick's Kube, or Wally's Wharf, after Seabee Jim Wallace, who supervised the job, will undoubtedly be forgotten, the inventiveness behind it melted away with its bulk.

But for the time being, Commander Kirkpatrick, who probably doesn't find many people besides Antarcticans willing to listen, talks about it this way:

"Well, we came up with the idea of building up a bank of

cold, an ice wharf. Back in the early Deep Freeze years, if we could have found a twenty-five-foot-thick ice floe up against the shore we would have made for it very quickly as an obvious place to off-load. We don't need to be very ultrasophisticated, you know, to off-load a ship or two a year at the end of the earth. But ice floes don't grow twenty-five feet thick, so we had to make one, to order.

"And we first needed some cheap and easy way to contain the water we were going to pump in and let freeze. But when you're talking about something as big as we were, there isn't that much available timber down there. And I had dreams all along of using bales of straw soaked in water and stacked up as you'd stack up building blocks, let 'em freeze. Then, I reckoned that as we built up a four-foot wall of straw bales we would lay a heavy layer of plastic film on the outside of the wall, and to hold it up we would put chain link fencing alongside it. Hold that in place with fence wire passed right through the bales before you wet it and froze it. This still fascinates me, but when you work out how many bales of straw you need, you see half a ship capacity being used to get it down here. I also thought about getting a big shredder to shred up most of what goes into the garbage dump at Mc-Murdo, and if not using it for the outer perimeter walls, at least for surface covering.

"Well, that would take hours and money and the people who control those things didn't share my enthusiasm. . . . So, I discussed the problem with the winter-over crew and I told them to use their imaginations and come up with something better.

They formed the idea of building plywood forms, foot apart, four feet high, and they filled these with a mixture of snow and water and allowed them to freeze, for forty-five minutes, it turns out, then move the forms along and repeat the process. Slip forms, they're called. This was a hard, cold, miserable job, but they did it, and that's how they built the walls that formed the vertical outer face. They pushed up snow, four foot high on the shore side and the sides, and you can imagine how that was. They had all hands down here shoveling up snow, carrying buckets of water, in the dark and in bitter cold and wind, and it was hell.

"The water to fill the form came from three pump houses out on the natural ice, on which the wharf was started. The crew figured that the best way to go was to keep one pump running, run it till it drops because once you get it up to temperature that's half the battle. Well, they worked more than diligently, and they built up twenty-five feet of ice.

"I didn't want the wharf to touch bottom because as the tide rose and fell it would have cracked. So, to keep it from floating out and away we put in five steel bollards, two wires to each, and held it to shore. That's essentially the state of the wharf today. The cracks that developed in her have refrozen, but it's losing thickness along the bottom because the water down there is slightly above freezing. But it's been used successfully and we'll use it again. Dirt is poured over the top for insulation and, to get a working surface, volcanic dirt. But the weight of the dirt pushes the wharf down into the water at least three feet.

"It's not much to be proud of, really; it's just a freak application. I am happy, though, if I have diverted attention away from the standard civil engineering construction techniques that were being used here. It's not very complicated, you know. It's no big thing. But, you know, what I would like to do is refine it; we've got good deep water here and we can bring a ship right up into the head of the bay, and this is a nice cargo-handling area here, and the bay is almost sheltered. I see coming out almost half the width of the bay with a wharf that looks like this. Maybe I'll redraw this a little bit, and I think we might be able to flood it with a single pumping station right here in the center of the damned thing, with a movable nozzle that will push the water across the surface in either direction, and . . ."

I hope it stays around here a long time, this dirty, amorphous monstrosity that lies cabled to the shore near the memorial that is Scott's hut, trucks driving on and off it over a pontoon bridge. Some of the men who worked the cold night of winter to build it were on hand when it was put to its most demanding weight-bearing test. The cargo ship *John R. Towle* had been nudged through broken and brash ice by the icebreaker *Staten Island* and tied up at the wharf. The first piece of cargo to be unloaded was the largest and heaviest, a ninety-thousand-pound mobile crane plucked from the ship's deck by a massive lift boom and swung out to maximum reach onto the ice. As the crane set down lightly on the wharf, the vessel which had disgorged it rose suddenly in the water, but the wharf did not sink nor even shudder. The collective wincing that accompanied the lowering of the crane and its lighting on the wharf gave way to a spontaneous cheer when the ice cube bore the load without a tremble. As the crane lumbered across the wharf and over the bridge onto shore, a sailor turned to a companion, chuckled and said, "Ain't nothin' like hand-made goods."

The machine age has descended on Antarctica, and though we can rightfully lament its coming and mourn the passing of yet another last frontier, the ice wharf, in its ugly simplicity, stands as a crude reminder that all is not lost to the past here, that response to challenge need not be a frivolous leak into Erebus nor computer-directed. Antarctica needs this pier, doubtful throne of ice that it is on summer seas.

14

"Noo then, you twa," cried the Emperor Penguin, "what the deevil are ye daein' here? Ye ken vara weel this is private property. Let me see what ye hae got in your pockets."
"We are from the British Antarctic Expedition of 1907."
"Mphm! Are ye though? Ye're queer folk, man! I often wonder what brings ye here."

— From *Aurora Australis*, first book
ever printed, written, illustrated, and bound
in the Antarctic

"All right," enthuses our NSF press aide, "let's get packing; we're going bird-watching." We are into the warm helicopters again, bellies full of breakfast steak and eggs, cans of beer jammed into the side pockets of our parkas, two cans to a pocket, ready to be stuck in a snowbank when we get to where we are going. Lieutenant Garcia is excited because we'll be scouting for penguins on this trip; he loves the little buggers. Also, he's promised José Aguinaldo he'll cop one for him if he can get away with it. Molesting the birds is prohibited by the Treaty, and that means you can't fly a helo over them or drive near their rookeries. "You've got to treat them gentle," Garcia says, "and not go barrel-assing through their colonies because that makes them desert their nests, and the scientists really take a spastic if you start trying to screw Mother Nature." Garcia is a fact sheet on penguins, he's been out here so many times; he calls them flightless wonders and junior birdmen. Seabirds, they do not fly, but they swim like Spitz. Their food is fish and shrimp, and that's why they don't move too far away from the water's edge.

There are seventeen varieties, seven living in the Antarctic, and around McMurdo we'll find emperors and Adélies.

Adélies are small, maybe about a foot and a half tall, about fourteen pounds. They don't live out on the ice, but build nests of pebbles where snow has melted. Since the chicks don't take long to grow, the parents come ashore in the spring, lay their eggs, and raise the young during the Antarctic summer season. When fall comes, the chicks are old enough to care for themselves, and they head out to sea with the adults. In the winter, they stay near the edge of the pack ice where the food is. "They're lively little porkers," says Lieutenant Garcia. The emperor is much bigger, three feet tall and going about sixty pounds. They live out on the sea ice, and in the fall they lay their eggs, one egg to a mother. The chicks are born and raised during the Antarctic winter, under the most extreme conditions any bird knows, in the cold and dark. Garcia says the best part of the whole story is the male emperor juggling the egg on his feet for two months in the middle of force-ten wind and minus-seventy cold so it won't freeze up. "That's real macho, man, that's what this ice is all about." Or, he adds sourly, it's what the ice is supposed to be. "Place is turning into a regular powder room nowadays."

Dacey Higgins, sitting half asleep in the center seat behind Garcia and the copilot, pockets bulging with camera equipment that had grudging priority over the beer he had to leave in the barracks, mumbles, "Oh yeah? What's the poop, Garcia? You queer for penguins?" Dacey doesn't seem to worry about Garcia's officer status and winds up, before falling fast asleep, telling him that he doesn't object to women on the ice; they keep his morale rising. He pats his crotch. Garcia grins and says, "What can you expect from a peon?"

About an hour out of what Dacey calls McMadhole, we are chattering down for a feather-light landing on a stark white snowscape that blends into the distant sea. Off a few miles to our right is the steep, irregular terrain of a hostile heap of volcanic rock, cliffs, and snow, Cape Crozier, at the eastern end of Ross Island, where it joins the great ice Barrier. Vicious winds lash the cape regularly, and we are slapped with them as we emerge from the helos. The cold grips us, and it is hard and dull like the daylight this morning. It makes us ache and angry. No jonquils in the garden here, no dandelions on the lawn, no bare-limbed trees silhouetted darkly against the sky. Only the monotony of white, marred by the dirt of Crozier far off, and a sky drained of its bright blue. We trudge toward the water over surface that is like pulverized chalk, rippled by the strong wind, and for the first time I begin to imagine what it must have been in those cold old days before the machine age clattered in.

I move as quickly as I can in all of my cumbersome gear, not to escape the cold, for that is impossible and that is what makes us irritable, but to get away from the group. Baggy trousers make that rubbing noise they used to make when I was a boy in corduroys. I am walking alone now so no one can detect my daydreaming, playing make-believe with head down against the wind that is piping shrilly, eyes fixed on the hard powder and my heavy white boots. I had read about this place last night in the library, and it was spellbinding, Cherry-Garrard's account of what he called the worst journey in the world.

On June 27, 1911, as a member of Scott's *Terra Nova* expedition, Cherry-Garrard joined Edward Wilson and Lieutenant Henry R. "Birdie" Bowers on what Wilson called the "weirdest bird-nesting expedition that has ever been made." Setting out from Cape Evans in the winter darkness, they manhauled two sleds, roped one behind the other, 757 pounds to draw, headed for the big emperor penguin rookeries at the foot of Cape Crozier's rocky cliffs 67 miles away. "It is going to be a regular snorter," Wilson wrote to his wife, "I can see that. But I have got the two best sledgers of the whole expedition to come with me. Scott has allowed me to have them, and they are desperately keen to come. . . . I don't think anyone has tried traveling in midwinter before, and yet as there is no way in the world to do this particular piece of work, I think it is up to me to try it."

Wilson's interest was in the penguin's ancestry, and he hoped to shed some light on the primitive bird's past by collecting emperor eggs at a particular stage of incubation. Men of the earlier *Discovery* expedition had found their breeding grounds, but this was during the spring, and the only eggs that were procured were deserted ones, with no early embryos. "The possibility that we have in the Emperor penguin the nearest approach to a primitive form not only of a penguin but of a bird," Wilson said in a monograph published by the British Museum, "makes the future working out of its embryology a matter of the greatest possible importance."

The journey was, true to Wilson's prediction, a "regular snorter," but it was also more horrible than he could have imagined. It stands, in fact, as the worst trek of its kind, if only because the three could have quit and returned without disgrace before they reached the penguin rookeries and their goal. For it was on the outward march that they took all the weakening punishment that Antarctica could deal. It was slow and frightfully hard pulling in moonlit fog over poor snow surfaces, crevasses, and jagged pressure ridges that creaked and groaned and split like glass, maybe making two or three miles in eight hours, a constant battle against fierce winds, temperatures that dropped as low as 77 degrees below zero, frostbite, and exhaustion. Their sweat froze, breath turned to ice on faces, and at night they had to crawl into a tent of thin canvas and into hardened sleeping bags that had grown increasingly difficult to thaw.

"Our bags were awful," wrote Cherry-Garrard. "It took

me, even early in the journey, an hour of pushing and thumping and cramp every night to thaw out enough of mine to get into it at all. Even that was not so bad as lying in them once we got there."

Wilson, compassionate and considerate always, began to feel responsible for his two companions, repeating over and over that he was sorry, that he had never dreamed it would be as bad as it was turning out. One man's scientific curiosity was taking them all through the worst possible conditions on earth. But Cherry-Garrard saw it in another light. "When leaders have this kind of feeling about their men they get much better results, if the men are good; if men are bad or even moderate they will try and take advantage of what they consider to be softness. Always patient, self-possessed, unruffled, he was the only man on earth, as I believe, who could have led this journey."

Now they were pulling upward, and at 800 feet over the sea, nineteen days out, they built a hut of hard snow and stone, roofed with a rag of green canvas. Later, they picked their way along cliffs black in shadow, and over convoluted ridges, and crept through channels hollowed in the ice, and at last were stopped by an icy wall thrown up against a face of rock. A hole pierced it and wriggling through they saw their emperors under the Barrier cliff, disturbed now and trumpeting in metallic voices, no nests in sight, and trying to shuffle off with their eggs on their feet. "After indescribable hardship," said Cherry-Garrard, "we were witnessing a marvel of the natural world, and we were the first and only men who had ever done so."

They quickly gathered five eggs, hoping to carry them safely in fur mittens tied about their necks, to be pickled later in alcohol. They killed and skinned three penguins to get blubber for their stove, and, roping themselves together, headed back to the hut. But the going was torturous over cracked sea ice, through thick gloom and up icy ridges, and the two eggs that Cherry-Garrard carried broke in his mitts.

A blizzard struck a few days later, and the heavy blocks of snow and stone placed on the roof to secure the canvas blew away. The canvas billowed and tore, and finally was carried off. A smother of soft snow was in on them and they huddled in their sleeping bags, warmed somewhat by the heavy wet blanket. "I expect the temperature was pretty high during this great blizzard," wrote Cherry-Garrard, "and anything near zero was very high to us. . . . And so we lay, hour after hour, while the wind roared around us, blowing storm force continually and rising in gusts to something indescribable. . . . I think it was blowing a full hurricane. Sometimes awake, sometimes dozing, we had a very uncomfortable time. . . ."

The following day, the storm over, they shook themselves out of their snow-covered bags and had their first meal in forty-eight hours, picking hairs, penguin feathers, and dirt from their pemmican and tea. They found their tent, which had also blown away, weighing close to a hundred pounds with its coating of ice.

Suddenly, the sky to the south turned sinister again, and blacker now without moonlight. Hours later, another blizzard was on them, holding them down in the shabby tent, fuel oil dangerously low, for two days more. Miserable, they waited it out, shivering in sleeping bags too stiff now to be rolled, and frozen so hard that any attempt to bend them split the skins. Their socks and mittens were crusted with ice, and the temperature rarely went higher than minus sixty. Finally, they started down from the cliffs and, leaving one sledge behind, made for Cape Evans, slithering over snow slopes, crawling along drift ridges, snow-blistered and ice-burned, in harness roped to the squeaking toggles of their sled, past glaciers burnished silver, under steel-pointed stars and a cold, black sky, and out over the gray, limitless Barrier, which seemed "to cast a spell of cold immensity, vague, ponderous, a breeding place of wind and drift and darkness. God! What a place."

In pitch darkness, they felt gingerly with their feet for the treacherous crevasses, or listened as best they could in the whistling wind for the ominous crack of ice beneath that warned of their presence. Periodically there was a muffled explosion as the ice in the bay beyond constricted in the harsh cold.

Suddenly, Bowers was down in a crevasse, out of sight and out of reach from the surface, dangling in his harness, his weight straining at the rope and the sled above him. Hanging there, with a bottomless pit below and ice-crusted walls around him, Bowers called for an alpine rope with a bowline for his foot. Cherry-Garrard lay across the crevasse, which was a narrow one, and lowered the bowline, which Bowers put on his foot. "Then he raised his foot, giving me some slack," said Cherry-Garrard. "I held the rope while he raised himself on his foot, thus giving Bill some slack on the harness. Bill then held the harness, allowing Birdie to raise his foot and give me some slack again. We got him up inch by inch, our fingers getting bitten, for the temperature was minus forty-six degrees."

Slowly, they plodded toward Cape Evans. "The horrors of that return journey are blurred to my memory and I know they were blurred to my body at the time," said Cherry-Garrard. "I think this applies to all of us, for we were much weakened and callous. I know that we slept on the march, for I woke up when I bumped against Birdie and Birdie woke up when he bumped against me. I think Bill steering out in front managed to keep awake. . . . I know that our sleeping bags were so full of ice that we did not worry if we spilt water or hoosh over them as they lay on the floorcloth, when we cooked on them with our maimed cooker. . . . The day's march was bliss compared to the night's rest, and both were awful. We were about as bad as men could be and do good travelling, but I never heard a word of complaint, nor, do I believe, an oath, and I saw self-sacrifice standing every test. . . . Always, we were getting nearer home, and we were doing good marches. We were going to pull it through, it was only a matter of sticking this out for a few more days, six, five, four . . . three perhaps now, if we are not blizzed. . . . 'You've got it in the neck, stick it, you've got it in the neck' — it was always running in my head."

The party reached Cape Evans on August 1, and the thirty-five-day ordeal was over. Standing unsteadily at the door of the moonlit hut, encased in snow and ice and trying with frozen fingers to extricate themselves from their stiffened sledging harnesses, they were a sight that Scott took note of in his diary: "They looked more weather-worn than anyone I have seen yet. Their faces were scarred and wrinkled, their eyes dull, their hands whitened and creased with the constant exposure to damp and cold. . . . That men should wander forth in the depth of a Polar night to face the most dismal cold and the fiercest gales in darkness in this effort in spite of every adversity for five full weeks is heroic. It makes a tale for our generation which I hope may not be lost in the telling."

Some time later, Cherry-Garrard carried the three eggs, for which he and his two companions had risked their lives and taxed themselves to the limit of human endurance, to the Museum of Natural History in Kensington to be cut open and their contents examined. The study indicated that the development of a penguin embryo is comparable to that of a duck or chick embryo, and that a flying bird was the ancestor of the penguin. The worst journey in the world, all but forgotten now by Britons, never heard of by most Americans, was not in vain.

Cherry-Garrard put it thus:

"There are many reasons which send men to the Poles, and the Intellectual Force uses them all. But the desire for knowledge for its own sake is the one which really counts and there is no field for the collection of knowledge which at the present time can be compared to the Antarctic.

"Exploration is the physical expression of the Intellectual Passion.

"And I tell you, if you have the desire for knowledge and the power to give it physical expression, go out and explore. If you are a brave man you will do nothing: if you are fearful you may do much, for none but cowards have need to prove their bravery. Some will tell you that you are mad, and nearly all will say, 'What is the use?' For we are a nation of shopkeepers, and no shopkeeper will look at research which does not promise him a financial return within a year. And so you will sledge nearly alone, but those with whom you sledge will not be shopkeepers: that is worth a good deal. If you march your Winter Journeys you will have your reward, so long as all you want is a penguin's egg."

Before I realize it, I have walked into a whole community of strutting, trumpeting emperors, purple heads and golden-orange necklaces. They are surprisingly tall, larger than I thought they would be. Some are only about a foot and a half or so shorter than I. Comic caricatures of men in tuxedos, they waddle, tipping from side to side, occasionally flopping on their shirt-fronts to propel themselves over the ice with feet and scaly flippers churning.

They are inquisitive birds, having encountered few, if any, humans. They have lived in the Southern Hemisphere, from the Galapagos to Antarctica, for thousands of years. Men have come only recently, and the emperors have not yet learned to fear us. They are generally placid, except when tormented by scientist, sailor, or journalist. Garcia says he's heard they have a twenty percent divorce rate. "Momma sometimes doesn't come back when she goes over the hill, but old Dad takes care of things; he's a *macho*."

I notice that when I stop to look at them, or get down on my stomach on the ice to take their picture they'll approach and surround us. But the moment we get up and walk toward them, they turn, en masse, and toddle off, making their queer squawking sounds. Everyone wants to be photographed shaking one of them by a flipper. "How are ya, babe, nice to meet you" or sitting next to one, an arm around what should be its shoulder. Nobody is successful, and one of our group even gets a flipper whack across the thigh by one particularly agitated bird, who then goes after him, pecking with its long curved beak, and beating with a single flipper. The penguin reminds me of a nun throwing punches with one arm tied behind her. "Go lightly," says a New Zealand journalist who is with us, "the bugger weighs about seven stone and he can bloody well cold-cock you, break your arm anyway, with that flipper." He mentions that Sir James Ross's seamen had a high time of it when they landed on Possession Island and were attacked by thousands of the birds, who pecked at them and finally drove them out with beaks and the stench of their guano.

Ross managed to catch several and bring them aboard his ship alive, killing them with a tablespoon or two of hydrocyanic acid. "That was more blessed than doing them with a bludgeon on the ice; they make such fearful cries, you know," says the New Zealander. "He brought the first specimens to England, preserved whole in casks of strong pickle, and when they cut them open they found up to ten pounds of pebbles in their stomachs, swallowed, no doubt, to promote digestion."

Zoologists have long been intrigued by the great distances penguins are able to walk, some fifty miles from the sea to their ice rookeries at mating time, and by their astonishing ability to fast for up to four months. Back at McMurdo, scientists from Duke University have been trying to determine just how the emperors' metabolic systems function in seventy-below-zero temperatures during breeding time, how they expend and conserve energy and control heat release. They study them by fitting penguins with face masks that monitor their intake of oxygen and outflow of carbon dioxide, and start them walking on a treadmill.

We buck the knife-edged wind back to the helos, covering about 200 yards, and as we climb in, glad to get away from the biting, unrelenting cold, Garcia nudges me and asks with a grin if I've ever eaten penguin. I look at him with my mouth open as he pats a bulge under the armpit of his flight jacket, and I tell him he didn't dare, he couldn't have. "No, no," he says quickly, "nothing like that; they'd have my ass two-block to the masthead if I ever snapped one." No, he says, he just found this little carcass lying out there, near the edge, all stiff like it came out of the frozen food chest at your local Super-M, and he figured, W-T-F. "W-T-F?" "Yeah," says Lieutenant Garcia, head cocked toward the window, watching the crew chief who is standing outside in the freezing wind steadying the rotor prior to takeoff, "what-the-fuck."

Dietland Muller-Schwarze knows a lot about penguins, more than Lieutenant Garcia, because they are his business. He's been to the ice several trips to study their behavior, and sixty years after Wilson's expedition, in 1971, he and his wife, Christine, from the Department of Wildlife Resources of Utah State University, walked from Cape Crozier to the stone hut the three explorers had built. From a distance, it could be mistaken for a pile of rocks. A closer look, however, turned up parts of the green canvas roof, personal items, shirt and socks, all perfectly preserved. At the entrance lay part of an emperor penguin. There was also a wooden box, still unopened, containing the pickling solution that Wilson and his men had brought along for their work.

One of the things that interests Dietland Muller-Schwarze is why people consider penguins so cute, why the birds are such public favorites. First, he says, they have to have an upright postion, then they have to be a certain size. Chipmunks stand up on occasion, but they're too small to attract large crowds. Dietland Muller-Schwarze says other animals, like bears, are too large. The best bet to receive affection is an animal of child-to-adult human size, and penguins are the only group, among birds, that put together the right body size, upright posture, manlike gait, and social traits, which together make them acceptable to man as little brothers. This is in spite of the fact that they lack a large field of binocular vision, one of the attributes that gives owls and monkeys a human look. They have adapted well, of course, to their environments, but occasionally a catastrophe occurs. In the early 1900s, an estimated ninety-five percent of the chicks perished in the Emperor colony at Cape Crozier because of a breakup of sea ice. In 1968, some 1,000 chicks were killed at Cape Crozier by fierce storms. They communicate by sound, naturally, and make a short "kok" noise when hailing a marching group, and a soft "arrp arrp" after going ashore. It's "rrak" when they're lined up onshore but are reluctant about leaping into the water.

Dr. Muller-Schwarze is also interested in man's impact on Antarctic birds, and one of the peculiar problems found on the ice is psychological, the hatred of predators. Just as farmers in many countries have declared total war on many species of birds of prey or mammalian carnivores, he says, so he has observed that those on the ice he calls the ecologically less enlightened stone the gull-like skuas that abound here, shoot them or torture them, for instance, by feeding them hot dogs that have a long nail inside. A considerable effort, he says, will be necessary to overcome this prejudice. Sledge dogs are also a menace to Antarctic birds. There's really no need for the dogs now, what with all the mechanization. The New Zealanders at Scott Base keep them around to show the tourists, and we should seriously consider banning all dogs from areas where birds breed or seals haul out. There is, in fact, a real danger of dogs establishing themselves as free-roaming predators. In 1957, Dr. Muller-Schwarze says, a Japanese expedition evacuated in a hurry and left fifteen huskies behind. A year later, when they returned, two dogs greeted the new party. They had survived the Antarctic winter, not by eating the other dogs, but by living on the droppings of the Weddell seals.

15

Everything that lives in the Antarctic — seals, penguins and skuas, the scant mosses, lichens, and algae of the peninsula, even the many-celled organisms that are found in the occasional patches of soil and sometimes in the ice — is equipped by Nature to survive. Here, it is all adaptation, accommodation, and adjustment. For the animals, it is inherent. For the humans who come it is forced, a truce with the environment. They must carry government-issue orange survival bags and overheat their huts, and go booted and furred and complaining. They must pass a psychological test if they are to winter over with the animals.

We are in a green Sno-Cat with Arthur L. DeVries and his wife, Yuan, both young Ph.D. biologists from the University of California at San Diego. They are interested in biological adaption, specifically why Antarctic fish don't freeze to death in the chilly waters, even when they are resting on or hiding among the large aggregates of ice crystals known as anchor ice, which form during the winter on the bottom of McMurdo Sound. Grinding out over the annual ice toward where the DeVrieses do their science, Arthur explains that if one were to take a black perch from the ocean off the coast of California and place it in the waters of McMurdo, it would immediately freeze, because its freezing point is about a degree higher than the temperature of Antarctic seawater (the water temperature here is minus 1.9 degrees centigrade, the freezing point of seawater). The reason that Antarctic fishes do not frost up, DeVries says, is that the temperature at which their blood and muscle tissue freezes is minus 2.1 degrees centigrade, just below the freezing point of the water in which they live.

Stopping the Sno-Cat at a red plywood hut out on the ice, he invites us inside so he and his wife can show us what they do out here every two or three days during the spring. In the center of the apparatus-crammed hut there is a hole, about four feet in diameter, cut into the eight-foot-thick ice. The water is blue and clear and deep, and the icy walls of the hole narrow considerably as they funnel down from the warmth of the hut to the colder temperatures below. Standing on the slippery edge of the hole, I think of Poe again, this time it's the pit and the pendulum, because hanging just over the hole are a number of large hooks and a basket attached to a thin steel cable. The cable passes around a pulley in the ceiling and is connected to a gasoline-driven winch. DeVries has already baited the hooks with fishes about a foot long, and it's obvious he's going after something bigger.

He throws a switch and the winch hums and swiftly lowers the cable and hooks down through the hole until a depth of 1,600 feet is reached. He turns it off and we wait. "He'll bite soon," says DeVries, "*Dissostichus mawsoni* in his name." It's a cod of sorts. DeVries has been fishing it since he was a graduate student at Stanford in 1965.

After about ten minutes, the cable yanks taut and DeVries throws the switch back on. Slowly, the winch hauls the hooks toward the surface, and we gasp as a *Dissostichus* breaks into view through the thin film of ice that has begun to form over the hole. It has to weigh two hundred or more pounds. It is writhing and flopping about with fins and tail. It is mottled and black and ugly and its face reminds me of pictures of the coelacanth, that primitive fossil fish that still shows up alive from time to time. Looked at head-on, the eyes are round and staring and set wide apart, the lips, torn by the large hook, stretch from one side of the grotesque face to the other and seem almost to wrap around the sides of the head.

DeVries and his wife wrestle the fish out of the hole, and we grab fins and tail and help lay it in a long water-filled wooden box, where it finally lies placidly. They insert a hypodermic needle into its body and withdraw a quantity of blood, which is squirted into a test tube and sealed. "It's all in here," says DeVries, holding the tube up to the light. "Antarctic fish," he explains, "carry slightly greater quantities of the usual protective compounds—salt, urea, amino acids, potassium, and calcium—in their blood, but these account for only half of what lowers their blood freezing point." The rest is a kind of protein, an antifreeze, that DeVries has managed to isolate. "The mechanism by which the fish antifreeze supercools or lowers the freezing temperature of water is not fully understood," says DeVries. One explanation may be that the proteins bind to the surface of ice crystals and stop their growth by preventing water molecules from settling onto the crystal surface.

The significance of the antifreeze to humankind may be greater than first expected. Not only does its discovery provide an explanation of why Antarctic fish do not ice up and die, but it also poses the question of how a simple protein can interact with water or ice to prevent freezing. "It is possible," says DeVries, "that these proteins may become useful probes for investigating the structure of water and ice, which, in part, still remain a mystery to scientists." Studies of the mechanism by which the antifreeze protects Antarctic fish may also yield information that eventually may be applied to the problems of preserving biological tissues, human and livestock sperm, and red blood cells in a frozen state. The antifreeze molecule's ability to slow the growth of ice and prevent a buildup of high salt concentrations during freezing are pluses for cryopreservation, he says. It is possible, too, that the antifreeze may influence the types of ice crystals formed so that less damage occurs to cell walls when cells are subjected to freezing, or they may prevent ice crystals from entering the cells. Furthermore, the importance of understanding what chemical compounds impart resistance to freezing in organisms is obvious to people like plant breeders. Cold snaps in Florida and California do millions of dollars' damage to citrus crops. Such damage, says DeVries, would not occur if frost-resistant strains were available. The example of the proteins as an antifreeze in Antarctic fish may provide clues to plant biochemists as to what sorts of compounds are responsible for frost hardiness in plants, and once the compounds are identified, plant breeders could select for strains of plants which produce large amounts of chemical compounds with antifreeze properties.

Before we go, DeVries reaches into the basket at the end of the cable and fishes out two bits of rock, with a white encrustation I cannot identify. "Here," he says, tossing me the fragments dredged up from 1,600 feet below, "there aren't many people who can have these." I put them in my pocket and zipper it shut. Common rock, but from an uncommon place, scoured off the ocean floor by eroding and strong circumpolar currents, and I am only the second person on earth to touch them. I wish DeVries had let me pluck them from the basket myself.

DeVries and his wife drag a wooden lid onto the crate containing the fish and we lift it, like pallbearers, and carry it to the Sno-Cat. Back at McMurdo, he dumps the fish into a tank, where it floats lethargically. There are several others there, in different tanks kept at different temperatures, and DeVries is hoping to learn what happens to the concentration of antifreeze as the fish grow accustomed to warmth.

That evening we feast on marinated, deep-fried *Dis-*

sostichus in the NSF library, and drink cocktails and beer. Yuan has prepared it with a teriyaki sauce and it is incredibly delicious, boneless pure white flesh that tastes remarkably like a combination of lobster and crabmeat with the texture of sole. "God," sighs someone, "put that on a menu in a fancy restaurant and you'd have them paying Lobster Savannah prices without batting an eye." "Guess who's considering fishing it commercially?" asks an NSF official, looking over his shoulder at Khabanikhov, who's digging in for seconds.

16

Notebook

Puzzled by the following blurb in my press kit: "Just about the strangest clock and calendar conflict on earth may be demonstrated at Siple Station, 1,552 miles from McMurdo. On the same meridian as Chicago, Siple operates on Central Daylight Time. However, it uses the same day of the week as McMurdo, and since McMurdo is on the other side of the International Date Line, Siple's clock time is the same as Chicago's, but the day of the week is a day later." Maybe my brain is glaciating out here, but I'm thinking about the little man who wasn't there, he wasn't there again today, oh how I wish he'd go away.

Another conundrum before breakfast: "The Earth has three pairs of poles. One member of each pair is in the Antarctic. The *Geographic Poles*, which are often referred to as simply the South Pole and the North Pole, are determined by the daily rotation of our planet and are the two points where the axis of rotation passes through the surface of the Earth. The *Geomagnetic Poles* are used to describe the Earth's basic magnetic field, most of the characteristics of which could be created if a powerful bar magnet were buried in the center of the Earth with its axis tilted at 11.5° to the axis of rotation. These Poles are the two points where a continuation of the axis of this theoretical magnet would cut the

Earth's surface, approximately 78° 30′ N., 69° W. and 78° 30′ S, 111° E.

Because these points are part of an explanatory theory, they are imaginary and do not move. The *Magnetic Poles* (sometimes called the *Magnetic Dip Poles*) are real. If the Earth's actual magnetic field were exactly the same as that which the hypothetical magnet would produce, your compass needle would be horizontal at the Geomagnetic Equator and would lead you to the North and South Geomagnetic Poles, where it would be vertical. This is not so. Other, local magnetic fields in the Earth make the real magnetic field near the surface different from the theoretical field. So, your compass leads you to the magnetic dip poles at . . ."

José Aguinaldo has given up on *Antarctic Cookery* after roasting penguin breast and serving it at the late meal, when one of the diners was Big Bee. Spitting and cursing after finding it wasn't the chicken that Aguinaldo insisted it was, Big Bee grabbed the cook, dragged him yelping outside, yanked down his pants and shorts and performed the Antarctic ritual known as "packing ass"—burying a victim up to his waist in a snow-hole, minus lower garments. Afterward, Aguinaldo gave me the recipe: "If you can get by the smell, you've got it licked. The worst part is removing the breast, which is the best-tasting. Wash it first, soak it in water with wine vinegar. Then boil it and skim off the scum. Rub it with salt and pepper and lay some lard on top. Roast at 350° for one hour, basting with pan gravy made with sherry, garlic powder and tarragon added. This kills the strong taste, somewhat. But if it's an old bird, forget it; it will taste like shit."

Listener survey, taken by Station AFAN, is in. Here's what they like, in order of preference: rock, 16 percent; Top

Forty, 14 percent; classical, 12.8; country & western, 12; oldies, 11; folk, 11; easy listening, 10; soul, 7.8; beautiful music, 6.3. "World's coolest music," says E. J. the D.J.

When you near the location of the South Magnetic Pole, the ordinary compass with its horizontal pointer is useless, since the magnetic field is vertical and one end of the needle dips straight down. You can use a shadow compass, which is the reverse of a sundial in that time is known and you work out directions with the position of the shadow.

"Did you hear about the guy at Pole," someone asks, "broke his dental plate? No dentist there, so he lost forty pounds 'cause he couldn't get any chow in. Finally fixed it, with airplane glue."

Scientists from the University of California are studying egg whites and yolk proteins of penguin eggs. I ask José Aguinaldo if he's tried cooking with them.

"Yeah," he says, "a couple times. But you can only scramble with them or mix them up in meatloaf. Best thing to do is heave out the yolks; they taste like shit. Stir powdered egg, good old Navy issue, into the whites with a little sherry, salt, and red pepper."

A further note on native and explorer-staple Antarctic cuisine: Expeditions here typically dined on fried seal liver, tinned meats and vegetables, loads of butter and biscuits and cheese, tea and cocoa, lime juice, bouillon, pemmican and pea flour, malted milk tablets, oatmeal, raisins, and powdered milk. Onion and curry powder were popular spices. Beef quarters and hog and lamb carcasses were hung in ships' rigging or in shacks on the ice. The principal foodstuff, for both humans and dogs, was seal meat, and Amundsen's expedition stocked up on 120,000 pounds of it during his 1911 winter-over. Seal meat, particularly the flesh of the crab-eater, according to those who have eaten it, resembles steak. Comparing raw seal meat to beef, one nutritionist figured that it's richer in protein and iron, poorer in fat, and produces fewer calories. Seal brains, according to old explorers, are a delicacy, blanched first, freed from blood clots, washed in cold water, and cooked au gratin, in fritters, or in omelets. Cormorants and penguins, with rich, dark and gamy-tasting meat, were also regarded as good food by some members of Scott's and Byrd's expeditions, but Aguinaldo bets those guys would put catsup on french fries.

17

The Dry Valleys of Antarctica, well-known to Scott and
Shackleton, lie in Victoria Land, some sixty miles due west of
McMurdo Station, in the Royal Society Mountain Range.
They are the ice-sheathed continent's contradiction, bare and
rock-strewn and nestled between 10,000-foot-high, chocolate
brown spires. The Valleys take up about 4,000 square miles
of snow-free terrain, and are among the few places in Antarctica swept of white.

Eerie and silent, windy and wintry-raw, the Valleys are
scenes of glacial retreat, where mummified seals, seen also by
Scott, lie scattered mysteriously, far from the sea that normally harbors them, some here for five thousand years. Here,
too, the valley floor often heats up sufficiently to permit
working in shirtsleeves, and there are lakes of delicate and
unique biochemical properties, as baffling as the seals and the
absence of even a patch of snow. There is Lake Vanda, with a
bottom temperature of eighty degrees Fahrenheit, and a foot-
thick cover of ice. Don Juan Pond, six inches deep and with
water so salty it does not freeze, even when the temperature
drops to seven below. So simple is its ecosystem that but a
single species of bacteria lives in the brackish water. And
Lake Bonney, five miles long and a hundred feet deep, holding an azure sky fast in its icy grip, fed by glacial meltwater,
where algae and fungi and bacteria thrive.

We are on the ground in one of the Valleys, in a debris of
rock, gazing up at the crests of cliffs rising high on either

side of our helicopter. Fingers of ice spread down the sides of some of the rock, prying it apart in places but stopping abruptly just off the valley floor. At each end of the wide corridor in which we stand, the receding edges of the glacier are plainly visible. Something has chased them away, leaving an environment so simplified that a careless person urinating outdoors or in one of the lakes would upset the ecological balance for ages to come. Trash and garbage and human wastes are packaged and flown out, burning is prohibited, and even cigarette ashes are flicked into tin cans carried in parka pockets.

We had flown low over the glacier, the sediment-streaked Ferrar, thirty-five miles long and three to six miles wide. Named after the geologist of the *Discovery* expedition, the Ferrar spills its glistening bulk through the mountains, grinding over the land underneath all the way to the Mc-Murdo Sound coast of South Victoria Land. We flew high over the Kukri Hills, the Asgard Range, and Cathedral Rocks, all familiar to Scott and Shackleton, and again I felt a closeness to the men who walked years ago through this silent place.

"Just think," said Garcia, who had been flying extremely carefully and saying little, eyes fixed on his compass and his gauges, "just think, those guys weren't able to go back to McMurdo for a martini the same night."

Antarctic flying, even in the spring with continual daylight and generally crystal-clear weather, is no simple matter. There is the problem of compass orientation. On the continent, the horizontal direction force of the earth's magnetic field is feeble, and magnetic variation — the difference between magnetic north and true north — is often a drastic one. Travelers on and over the continent must know the variation figure for a certain area of operations, and take this into account when using a compass. "If it isn't known," Garcia says, "it can be determined by checking the angle between true north from the sun at noon and north from the compass reading." The sun's bearing is also important for determining approximate directions. At about six in the morning, it bears due east and at about six in the evening it is due west. It moves around the horizon, a 360-degree arc, at fifteen degrees an hour. It's due south at midnight, due north at noon. Except at the South Pole, where it bears due north all the time.

"You really have to fly with your ass," says Garcia. "There's hardly any landmarks that you can follow with any certainty. A rock looks like a distant mountain if you look at it long enough, and a mountain might fool you into thinking it's a distant rock, and that, man, is fear when the dawn breaks." Stratified temperature inversions create images, mirages, and you get upright mirror images of objects not ordinarily visible around the earth's curve. "The whiteout is a bitch," he says. "Light bouncing from snow to clouds, back and forth, everything gets white and hazy and if you're on the ice you start walking around in circles, no horizon, no reference points. Tougher in the air. On the ice you can at least stay where you are and wait for it to lift. Sometimes it's limited to only a few kilometers. But in the air, man, it's one hairy scene, *beaucoup* trouble. Man can get wasted easy in the milk bottle. Good thing no one flies in the winter, that's worse. Only time aircraft ever land at McMurdo in the dark is in extreme emergency." Garcia says he's heard of it being done only two times, in cases of medical emergency when the lives of a couple of guys were at stake. "The Kiwis," he says he's heard, "are going to try a mail drop, round trip from Christchurch to McMurdo, in midwinter. It'll be a first, five thousand miles in twelve hours, the crazy fuckers." He shakes his head, but it's in envy, not disgust. "WTF," he says, "everybody's got to do his hero thing."

"But aside from the risk," Garcia adds, "there's all that shit you got to know in the winter about the Southern Cross, the only constellation you can use in an emergency. There's this imaginary line through the long axis of the cross, the True Cross, and it points toward the South Pole. You can't confuse that with the False Cross, that's not as bright and the stars are spaced farther apart. The falsie has also got five stars, the True Cross but four. Over the Pole, there are no stars. It's so dark there in winter compared to the rest of the sky they call it the coal sack. You just got to see Pole, even in spring. That is some place."

From the single seat behind Garcia and his copilot, the view through the windshield is startling, more so than the scene spread out through the side windows. Guiding the helo expertly, Garcia would set a course straight for a giant snow-topped peak and hold it, dead ahead, until we were so close it filled the windshield, its crest lost somewhere above. Then, he would pull up ever so slowly, just, it seemed, in the nick of time to avoid a head-on crash into the bare rock walls. He repeated the maneuver over and over, and each time we would gasp I could see the corners of his mouth turn up. "Compliments of the Southern Trail Tourist Bureau, no tipping please," he said the last time he did it and just before he set us down in the valley.

We walk toward a hut set near Lake Bonney, clambering over wind-carved and angular rocks that give this place the look of a moonscape, and are greeted by two young women, undergraduates from Virginia Polytechnic Institute. They are in shirts and jeans, gloveless and hatless in the zero weather. We are booted and in parkas and windpants, and I quickly uncover my head and remove a glove out of embarrassment. My hand nearly freezes, I think, and I figure they're putting me on or doing their own hero thing. We head for indoors, past a sign sticking out of the ground, DONT

DO IT IN THE LAKE. Someone's crossed out the DO IT and marked PISS over it. Inside, they make us coffee and grudgingly share a six-pack of beer. It is warm and cozy. The women live out here with the leader of the scientific team and three other men. On the door, next to a dish-filled sink and across the room from an array of laboratory glassware and apparatus, are chalked two notices. One reads, "Let no one say it to your shame, that all was beauty 'fore you came." The other, "Love is life and life is love, drink is life and life is drink, so get bombed."

We sit and talk about what the scientists and their assistants are doing out here, while Garcia and his copilot stand against a wall and stare at the girls as though they'd never seen one before. I find myself doing the same thing. It is like a time I recall not being able to take my eyes off a girl modeling a bikini in a department store. On the beach, I would hardly have noticed her.

The VPI group is modeling, too, but it's freshwater and terrestrial ecosystems. Geological surveys are underway gathering data for comparative analysis with photographs to be returned from the Viking Mars mission in 1976. The scientists believe the ice-free Valleys may provide one of the best terrestrial analogues of the surface conditions thought to exist on Mars. The Valleys are distinguished by a low magnetic field, high ultraviolet radiation, desiccating winds, low humidity, intense cold, eolian dunes, patterned ground with cracks like dried pottery, and cavernous weathering—all thought to be present on Mars.

The soil studies may also help in the quest to discover life on the red planet. A VPI team, trying to determine how life can exist under the harshest conditions, such as on Mars and in these valleys, took several soil samples in which there were no visible microorganisms. Later, a single population of bacteria was found in the same area, showing that with the passage of time and improvement in the environment, there was an ecologic sequence of microorganisms.

Even more exciting was the recent find of two scientists from the Darwin Research Institute of Dana Point, California, and California Institute of Technology's Jet Propulsion Laboratory. Working with a multinational team investigating the continent's evolution, Dr. E. Roy Cameron and Frank A. Morelli, both of whom had also been doing research in the Antarctic under NASA's space program for extraterrestrial life detection on Mars, went to work on several sediment cores drilled out of the permanently frozen ground at sites on Ross Island and in the Valleys. They first passed a butane torch flame over the tubes containing the samples to wipe out any contamination, then, using a sterilized hand drill, bored into the centers of the cores and extracted chips with sterile cotton swabs. The samples were taken to germ-free labs at the Eklund Biological Center in McMurdo and put into a nutrient broth to see what might grow. It turned out that there were microorganisms in the cores, that they had been there for anywhere between 10,000 and a million years, and, more startling, not only were they revived when taken to the lab, but they grew and reproduced.

Only one type refused to grow, although it lived. "We could all see them wiggling when we observed them under the microscope," said Dr. Cameron, "but conditions were apparently not right for them to grow." One type formed unusual doughnut-shaped colonies that grew or flowed in toward the center as the colony expanded, then, according to Dr. Cameron, took on the shape of an inactive volcano. None of the bacteria has yet been identified although all were motile — that is, equipped with fine, hairlike appendages that propel them. The results of the core experiments, Dr. Cam-

149

eron feels, could have tremendous relevance to understanding the ability of microorganisms to remain frozen in a state of suspended animation for hundreds of thousands of years. Further, he believes, scientists attempting to detect life on Mars might well speculate, on the basis of the Dry Valley borings, that if no life forms are found on the surface of the planet, the subsurface permafrost may hold the key to ancient and living organisms buried deep within it which thrived at some distant time when the Martian atmosphere was more hospitable to life than it is believed to be now.

One of the other scientists who is working here is Dr. Wolf Vishniak, an internationally known microbiologist from the University of Rochester. Also well-known for his lunar and planetary work for NASA, he has been testing for microbial life in the valleys, an area which he believes contains less bacteria per gram than the Mojave Desert or Death Valley. "The Dry Valleys are a tropical paradise compared to Mars," he says. One of his major objectives is to determine where the microorganisms living in the sterile soil get organic matter which they must consume to multiply. He is looking for a missing part of an ecological cycle. "Although there is periodic replacement of water, the water content of the soil is extremely low in Antarctica. Water activity is especially low in the Valleys. The bacteria may have the ability to take water from the soil, even though it is dry."

Vishniak was the deputy team leader of a seven-man group which devised the instruments that will pick up and study the soil samples for signs of life on Mars during the 1976 Viking landing. He is also planning to establish a "Little Antarctica" in his Rochester laboratory to examine the structure of the bacteria and learn how they solve the problem of water accumulation.

But Wolf Vishniak will not finish his work, for a year after my trip to Antarctica, while in the seven-thousand-foot Asgard Range, he will leave a marked trail and fall five hundred feet down a slope to his death.

We are off again, to the New Zealand station at Vanda, and Garcia's spirits are lighter. "Those Kiwis are a blast to visit. They like parties." He's carrying them their mail, copies of the *Sometimes,* and a variety of packages and bottles. They love to see him coming, says Lieutenant Garcia; he's their flying rummy-runner. He wishes there was some way, he says, he could run them in some poontang, a little space-heater now and again to take the chill off. Garcia's Survival Kit, he'd call the service. Specializing in the finest lays in the Antarctic Command. "A man could make a big buck with a flying fuck," says Garcia.

We land on the floor of the valley and are into a sea of exuberant New Zealanders. They are shouting, waving their arms, clapping us on the backs, and hustling us off to their shack. It seems strangely warmer here, the few moments I am allowed to remain outdoors, possibly from some underground thermal system not fully understood. Garcia says people often lie around in their shorts, suntanning. It's not exactly that warm, but I do take off my glove when I start shaking the Kiwis' hands, and it is not that uncomfortable. Back home, I'd have them on in this temperature; it's still around five or ten degrees. Maybe it's the absence of wind on this day, or the speed with which the New Zealanders drag us inside. Or maybe I'm learning, at last, to adjust to my surroundings. Maybe now I'll be able to take my gloves off in the wintertime back home. Or else everything is going to be the same, very soon.

I get a quick glimpse of a decrepit farm tractor, its treads hanging off in steel shreds, parked outside the hut, and they tell us, inside, as they start breaking open bottles and bags, that it was used in the British Commonwealth Expedition of 1957–1958.

The main party of that expedition, under the leadership of Sir Vivian Fuchs, was to land on the shore of the Weddell Sea and travel overland through the South Pole and on to Mc-Murdo. It was one of the last great challenges facing Antarctic explorers — crossing the continent from sea to sea by way of the Pole — and in accomplishing it, the British expedition had made a dream of Sir Ernest Shackleton come true.

A supporting party from McMurdo was to lay depots of food and fuel on the Ross Ice Shelf and the polar plateau for use by Fuchs and his party during the final stage of the crossing. The depot-laying was mainly a New Zealand operation under the leadership of Sir Edmund Hillary, who a few years before had been the first man to climb Mount Everest. Starting out in October, the New Zealanders, using slightly modified farm tractors, pushed across the Ross Ice Shelf and up the Skelton Glacier to the polar plateau. They laid depots of supplies and marked a trail for Fuchs to follow. Originally, they had intended to go about seven hundred miles from their base at McMurdo and then return. Hillary found, however, that he had enough fuel to push on to the Pole. He arrived there on January 4, 1958, the first man to travel overland to the spot since Scott and Amundsen.

Fuchs started out on November 24, 1957, from Shackleton Base on the Weddell Sea, riding in two kinds of American-built tracked vehicles, a Weasel and a Sno-Cat. A dog team pulled a sled ahead of the vehicles to find the best route over untraveled terrain. But even with the dogs the trek was dangerous and difficult, and several times the Sno-Cats, big enough for men to live in, fell partway into crevasses. On January 19, 1958, Fuchs reached the South Pole. They rested for a few days and moved on, and because Hillary had marked the route the dogs were no longer required. They were flown to McMurdo. A few days out on the trail, the Weasel began to break down and was proving itself to be slower than the Cats. Fuchs abandoned it, and managed to finish his trip before another winter broke on them, arriving at New Zealand's Scott Base on March 2, 1958.

"That tractor out there," says a Kiwi, raising a glass of gin, "is a bloody monument." We all drink to that. "To Scott's ghost," says another, and we drink to that, too. Someone remarks that he hopes Scott didn't do any pissing in Vanda, that delicate ecological balance and all, and that's a drink.

There is some light and easy talk about matters scientific, such as the ten-thousand-year-old, five-square-mile salt bed discovered out here in one of the Valleys a few years ago, and the evidence that the Valleys and Antarctica were tropical a long time back. Cores taken from the bottom of Lake Vanda contain marine fossils, suggesting that this part of the continent was a fjord with a mild climate. Maybe that explains those long-dead seals outside that are as hard as boards.

We talk a bit more about their drilling projects and how the cores they've dredged up out of the valley are a record of the region's entire history, but it is not the science that I will always think of when I think of Vanda Station. That is not meant to disparage their science, for it is as good as any done on the continent. It is the camaraderie, the cheer in large measure that I will long remember, the oilcloth on the table heavy with plates of oversized scones, freshly baked for our coming by men not boastful over what they do out here, nor given to intellectualizing about the experience. The pounds of yellow butter squatting on thick blue china dishes, hot apple crumb cake served in soup bowls, black currant jam and orange marmalade, song and laughter, and much pouring from bottles of English gin, and pots of high tea, even Nescafé prepared special for us. It is a place to pause near a quiet lake, a chance to get off this tour, off the Southern Express that often travels so fast the sights we see are as blurred as reflections in a swift-moving river.

We throw darts at a *Playboy* nude tacked on the wall, and drink some more, Garcia too, I think, and it doesn't seem to bother any of us that he's got to take us home. I laugh with a young geologist who tells me that I am now an IAE, Intrepid Antarctic Explorer, because that's what you are when you come down for the first time. When I leave, it'll be OAE, Old Antarctic Explorer. If I ever come back I'm OAE and QM, Quite Mad.

We climb into our helo and someone is still singing indoors, about some queer wee chap named Jamie Shaw, him an' his wife and his mither-in-law, who went an' jint the volunteers, a pair o' Tartan breeks he weers, mairchin' off tee fame and gloree.

Fluttering off into the sky and heading toward the steam-plume of Erebus, I wave out the window at plaid-shirted men growing smaller and smaller and soon out of sight in the snow-free valley. I hate to leave the fun.

18

Notebook

A visit to PM-3A today, the nuclear power plant 300 feet up on the side of Observation Hill. Built on solid volcanic rock foundation by Seabees, it went critical in 1962, then 24 months of operational testing and it was turned over to the Atomic Energy Commission for operation by the Navy.

PM-3A was built to help reduce the enormous fuel requirements at McMurdo Station lying below. They gulp it right up down there, says the lieutenant commander who is showing us through. Diesel generator fuel, fuel for oil-fired heating units, fuel to melt snow for water, fuel for internal-combustion engines, for the aircraft, you name it. This is the first nuclear-powered electrical generation and water distillation plant in the Antarctic, he says proudly, and it's manned by two officers and twenty-five or so enlisted men who have received their training at Fort Belvoir, Virginia, along with on-the-job operation and maintenance qualification training in an operational, pressurized water, nuclear power plant.

We are inside one of the green buildings. There is little activity, none of the humming and whining of machinery I had expected. We pass a sign on the wall, GOD BLESS ANTARCTICA, LOVE IT OR LEAVE IT, pass the POWDER ROOM, pass another sign, THE BEGINNING IS THE MOST IMPORTANT PART OF

THE WORK. The ubiquitous *Playboy* calendar and another voluptuous nude are pasted to the back of a door, the doorknob protruding precisely where the right breast should be. Against another wall, is a life-sized, paint-by-numbers nude, a sign tacked under it, SHORT-TIMER. Someone has added, LONG-TIMER NO SEE. "Thank God," says Dacey Higgins, unlimbering a camera and getting off a quick shot of the artwork, "a safe house. Means there's no faggots in here. Lab without a nude, scientist is a faggot." He grins.

The commander gives it all to us rapid-fire, cutting us off when we try to ask him why no one seems to be doing anything. We haven't seen but one or two crew. Steam is produced by heat created by the splitting of atoms in a pressure vessel, the reactor, and the steam drives a turbine-generator that produces electrical power and light to distill fresh water from the sea. PM-3A, he runs on, is a contained pressurized water reactor with a low enriched pin-type core and magnetic jack-actuated control. 1800 KW electrical, gross, 264 elements per fuel bundle, 6 bundles per core. Fuel type is UO-2, 9.6 percent enriched in U-235 isotope. It costs about a million bucks a core; estimated core life is five years at 9.51 megawatt thermal. Radioactive waste? "Easy," he says, "it's essentially all collected, solidified, gift-wrapped, and shipped to special repositories in the U.S." He smiles. We finally ask him why nothing's happening, we don't hear a sound. "It's shut down for a while," says the commander crisply, "for annual maintenance. Routine."

Later, at lunch in the mess hall, a young lieutenant wants to know about the tour up on Nukie Poo. "What did they tell you this time?" he asks. "It's shut down," I say knowledgeably; "annual maintenance." "Hoss-shit," he says. "It's down and it's going to stay down. They're dismantling the mother now, shipping her back to the States piece by piece.

It's hairy. The insulation containing chlorides, around the reactor piping, is wet. It means it's causing corrosion. It's also cheaper to burn fossil, Uncle Sugar has just found out." When we get home, we will learn that he is right.

Outside, the lieutenant commander who's showed us around PM-3A comes running up out of breath; he wants to correct a small point. The burnable poison in the system is stainless-steel-clad tetraboron carbide. Someone asks him if they're gift-wrapping that, too, and sending it stateside, along with the whole plant. He reddens and mutters that it's all scuttlebutt.

There is a conversation about food over lunch of fried liver, mashed potatoes, buttered carrots, celery sticks, and chocolate cake. "Of course it's a substitute for sex," says a submarine commander who's wintered over. He's here, by the way, because the navy's got more submarine skippers than submarines, and besides, he says, they're used to lone-wolfing it. "Food's the only pleasure you get out here, besides work satisfaction," he adds. "In a couple of months you become very very conscious of the chow, and you start getting bitchy if it doesn't come up to specs. The cooks are the real movers out here, good cook can make or break an expedition or a winter camp."

A quote on food, from Edward Wilson's diary, 1902: "Dreams of ball-suppers, but one shouts at waiters who won't bring a plate of anything; or one finds the beef is only ashes; or a pot of honey has been poured on a sawdust floor. One very rarely gets a feed in one's sleep. Occasionally, one does; one night, I ate the whole of a large cake in the hall of Westal, and was horribly ashamed when I realized it had been put there to go in for drawing-room tea, and everyone was asking where it had gone. These dreams are vivid — I remember them now, though it is two months ago. One night, Sir David Gill, at the Cape, was examining me in divinity and I told him I had just come back from the farthest south and was frightfully hungry, so he got a huge roast sirloin and insisted on filling me up before he examined me." Sir Douglas Mawson, the Australian Antarctic explorer: "Lying in the sleeping bag I dreamt that I visited a confectioner's shop. All the wares that were displayed measured feet in diameter. I purchased an enormous delicacy just as one would buy a bun under ordinary circumstances. I remember paying the money over the counter, but something happened, before I received what I had chosen. When I realized the omission I was out in the street and being greatly disappointed went back to the shop, but found the door shut, and 'Early Closing' written on it." Food's got to be the draw, says our NSF press aide coyly. What else would make a man lead such a moral life, having intercourse only with science and Nature?

Even in the short time I've been here, I find myself anxiously awaiting meals, and I'm not sure whether it's the activity that's made me genuinely ravenous, or whether it's a replacement, or whether it's just the social setting of a banquet hall where we go to laugh, talk, and plan our day.

Most of the meals are like last night's feast. Huge, split lobster tails, all you could eat with bowls of melted butter — not those little eyecups full you get in a seafood restaurant — plus steak, cooked to order, rich, thick soups, two kinds to choose from, potato casserole, green beans, salad, cake and ice cream, all white and rich. There's a commander in charge of the kitchen and he's standing behind the chow line every evening meal, flacking for the benefit of the visiting press. "Good old chowder from New England, fellas, potatoes from Idaho, them beans are from Wisconsin, steaks from Kansas City, and those lobsters, mmm-mm, they ought to get us in the papers back home, right?" "Say," says a galley slave standing under a picture of a bulldog in a sailor suit captioned, TAKE ALL YOU WANT BUT EAT ALL YOU TAKE, "say, you guys ought to come down here more often, we usually get fishcakes and steamed beans."

19

Wintering Over

Once your ships started north and the pack has closed
behind them, there is nothing else you can do. You are there to
stay, whether you like it or not, for eight months at least, and
all the resources of the world, were they brought to play, could
not liberate you sooner. . . . Having made your bed, you must
lie in it and take what crumbs of comfort there are.
— ADMIRAL RICHARD E. BYRD

The unique combinations of people will necessitate individual
adaptation to the close living environment as well as the physical environment. Survival should be a collective concern. The
close living conditions obviously make it mandatory that individuals be able to get along well with one another. You must be
tolerant of the idiosyncrasies of others while, at the same time,
not be overly sensitive about yourself. Your emotional composure
at work and play affects the whole station team.
— NSF *Antarctic Survival Manual*

In the winter of 1898, a Belgian Antarctic expedition,
nineteen men aboard the *Belgica* under the command of
Lieutenant Adrien de Gerlache, penetrated the pack ice in
the Bellingshausen Sea, were frozen in, and drifted thus for
thirteen months, no radios, no electrical power, until the
summer thaw freed them. Aboard the 250-ton former Norwegian sealer were Roald Amundsen as first mate and Dr.
Frederick A. Cook, an American surgeon-explorer, who was
later to be disgraced and branded a humbug for his claim of
having reached the North Pole first.*

* A surgeon with the Peary Antarctic Expedition of 1891–1892, Cook later
led an expedition to climb Mount McKinley, claiming success in 1906. Then,
as leader of his own Arctic expedition, he claimed to have reached the North
Pole on April 21, 1908, nearly a year earlier than Peary, and his book, *My*

Except for an occasional whaler, the *Belgica* expedition was the first to explore the Antarctic in fifty-five years, and though it never landed on the continent and reached no further than 71° 24' S., it added valuable data to the meteorology of the Antarctic Circle. But more than that, the *Belgica* expedition was the first ever to winter over in the Antarctic, and thus has given today's behavioral scientists studying the effects of polar isolation on humans a remarkable account of man's amazing adaptability to the stresses of prolonged darkness, cold, and sameness.

The hero of the ordeal was undoubtedly Cook, who, despite his later tarnished career, won the respect and devotion of captain and crew. He nursed ailing seamen and scientists, buoyed their downed spirits during the long, frigid sunless months, and advised on ice navigation.

"It is not too much to say that Cook was the most popular man of the expedition," Amundsen remarked when the ordeal was over, "and he deserved it. From morning to night he was occupied with his many patients, and when the sun returned it happened not infrequently that, after a strenuous day's work, the doctor sacrificed his night's sleep to go hunting seals and penguins in order to provide the fresh meat that was so greatly needed by all. Cook was incontestably the leading spirit in this work, and gained such honour among the members of the expedition that I think it just to mention it."

Cook's diary notes paint a vivid picture of Antarctic night and boredom, of death and survival:

Attainment of the Pole (1909), sold widely. It was subsequently charged that both of his claims, that of ascending Mount McKinley and discovery of the North Pole, were fradulent. Imprisoned in 1923 for a violation of the United States postal laws via association with a fraudulent oil transaction, he was released in 1930, then pardoned in 1940 by President Franklin Roosevelt.

March 21. Today, we are dissatisfied with the food. We have complained intermittently for a long time, but now everyone seems bent on having his say as to the badness of our provisions. We have tried penguins and cormorants but the majority have voted them unpalatable. . . . We are held by the increasing grip of the too-affectionate pack. We are imprisoned in an endless sea of ice, and find our horizon monotonous. We have told all the tales, real and imagined, to which we are equal. Time weighs heavily upon us as the darkness slowly advances. The despairing storms and the increasing cold call for some new fuel to keep the lowering fires of our bodies ablaze. I have taken the trouble to make a personal canvass of every man of the *Belgica* today to find out the greatest complaints and the greatest longings of each. The results of this inquiry was certainly a lesson in curious human fancies. In the cabin, the foremost wants are for home news and feminine society. We are hungry for letters from mothers, sisters and other men's sisters, and what we would not give for a peep at a pretty woman. Racovitza reminds us daily that he will write a book describing life in the ladyless south, and we have all agreed we will contribute. In the fo'c'sle, the men are less sentimental and less inclined to poetry. They desire first some substantials for their stomach, fresh food such as beefsteaks, vegetables and fruits. Two or three in lone, dark corners and in tears, slyly admit that a few moments with the girl of their hearts would be more to their liking. They would like fresh foods but they long for freedom from the lonely pack and the congeniality of a world of feminine charm. Our hatred is all heaped on one class of men. They are the manufacturers and inventors of the various kinds of canned and preserved meats. Our general name for embalmed beef is *Kydbolla*. If these meatpackers could be found anywhere within reach, they would become food for the giant petrels very quickly. In this one sentiment we are of one accord. . . .

I must hasten to add that our food does not lack variety. Its quality is good and it is perhaps all that could be desired under the circumstances. But men in the monotone of polar regions develop flighty longings. We have, for breakfast, cereals such as cornmeal, crushed oats, hominy, good freshly-baked biscuits, oleomargarine, marmalade and coffee. Our supply of sugar is low and the provision of milk is almost exhausted. . . . For dinner, we have soups of various kinds, canned meats, preserves and potatoes and macaroni, with a dessert of fruit pudding. Our supper consists of fish, cheese and an occasional conglomeration of macaroni, pemmican and tinned meats. . . . No one seemed to eat the penguin steaks with any kind of relish. . . . But somehow we've stored away quite a little stack of it. It is rather difficult to describe its taste and appearance. We have absolutely no meat with which to compare it. The penguin as an animal seems to be made up of equal proportions of mammal, fish and fowl. If it is possible to imagine a piece of beef, an odoriferous codfish and canvasback duck roasted in a pot, with blood and codliver-oil for sauce, the illustration would be complete. . . .

March 28. It is another day of clear, white silence. At sunrise and sunset, the twilights are almost becoming more and more marked. It is, tonight, an intense, purple-blue, and through it we see a star. Arctowski puts down the mysterious purple as a reflection of the shadows from the pack ice which at this time is a deep ultramarine blue, but to most of us is still a puzzle. . . . We all have big ambitions but I fear our efforts will be dwarfed when the gloomy, dayless night settles down over us. . . .

April 9. It is the birthday of King Leopold of the Belgians today. That we might better mark the king's birthday and remember it as a period of great rejoicing, and to arouse our sleeping regard for women, we have instituted a beauty contest. For several days, there has been electioneering and pointing out the special merits of the women of our choice. The pick has been made from the illustrations in a Paris journal, and nearly 500 pictures were selected, representing all kinds of poses in dress and undress, and anatomical parts of women noted as types of beauty.

Easter Sunday. But how different is our lot to that of the usual Easter worshiper. The seasons are here reversed. We have not behind us the winter storms and cold discomforts. We have not before us the evident joys of the coming summer. Sweet smelling flowers, green fields, pretty girls in new bonnets and the hundreds of things which go to make up the accustomed pleasures of Easter are all far-removed from us, and we are on the verge of what promises to be the worst winter on record. The faint delights of summer are behind. The desperation, the despondency, the mystery of the unknown, impenetrable darkness with its ceaseless frost is on the horizon. Hellish storms with icy vapors are almost

163

constantly sweeping over us. There is not a rock or anything suggestive of land within many hundreds of miles and there is not a tree or flowering plant within thousands. Nearly all of the circumference of the globe is between us and our loved ones at home. . . . We try hard to arouse a buoyant spirit and each has taken it upon himself to bring out the bright side of the one nearest to him. But our efforts are poorly rewarded, for after superficial laughter we sink into a lethargy which becomes more and more normal to us as the winter and the night advance. Someone has said we want only our home surroundings, some loving women, fresh food, a few flowers and our lot would be happy. I believe this, but I also believe it is just these which are all that are required to make hell agreeable to the average man.

April 25. Tonight, the temperature was almost minus 28 degrees. The difficulty of keeping the teeth from chattering, the eyes from quivering or the instruments from shaking can be more easily imagined than explained. Danco came in after making his sights, with a frosted foot and with a piece of skin torn from his eye and frozen to the metal of the eyepiece of his instrument. Lecointe lost some of his eyelashes and a bit of his ear was white. . . . It is an almost daily occurrence to have men come to me with fingers burnt, as they express it, by contact with pieces of cold metal. One sailor who was at work between decks nailing up cases placed two nails in his mouth. He snatched them out quickly, bringing out bits of his tongue and lip and leaving ugly wounds which were in character exactly like the injuries of a hot iron. The sailors who have metallic pegs in their boots claim that ice caps form under their feet.

May 16. The long night began at twelve o'clock last night. We did not know this until this afternoon. At four o'clock, Lecointe got an observation by two stars. According to a careful calculation, the captain announces the melancholy news that there will be no more day, no more sun for seventy days if our position remains about the same. If we drift north, the night will be shorter, if south, it will be longer. . . . The cold whiteness has now been succeeded by a colder blackness. . . . The curtain of blackness which has fallen over the outer world of icy desolation has also descended upon the inner world of our souls. Around the tables, in the laboratory and in the forecastle, men are sitting about saddened and dejected, lost in dreams of melancholy from which now and then someone arouses with an empty attempt at enthusiasm. For a brief moment, some try to break the spell by jokes told perhaps for the 50th time. Others grind out a cheerful philosophy, but all efforts to infuse bright hopes fail. Each man is intent on being left alone to take what comfort he can from memories of happier days, though such effort usually leaves him more hopelessly depressed and oppressed by the sense of utter desertion and loneliness.

May 20. It is the fifth day of the long night, and it seems long, very long, since we have felt the heat of the sun. . . . We have had little complaints and some insignificant injuries — bruises, cuts, strains and frostbites, but there has been little of which to make a medical note. Since entering the pack, our spirits have not improved. Quantities of food which we have consumed have slowly decreased, and our relish for food has also slowly but steadily failed. There was a time when each man enjoyed some special dish and by distributing these favorites at different times it was possible to have some one every day. Now, we are tired of everything. . . . Everybody having any connection with the preparation of food is heaped with some criticism. Some of this is merited, but most of it is the natural outcome of our despairing isolation from accustomed comforts. . . . This part of the life of polar explorers is usually suppressed in the narratives. An almost monotonous discontent occurs in every expedition through the polar night. It is natural that this should be so. For when men are compelled to see one another's faces, encounter the few good and many bad traits of character for weeks, months or years without any outer influence to direct the mind, they are apt to remember only the rough edges which rub against their own bumps of misconduct. If we could only get away from each other for a few hours at a time, we might learn to see a new side and take a fresh interest in our comrades. But this is not possible. The truth is that we are, at this moment, as tired of each other's company as we are of the cold monotony of the black night and of the unpalatable sameness of the food. Now and then we experience affectionate moody spells, and we try to inspire each other with a sort of superficial effervescence of good cheer, but such moods are short-lived. Physically and mentally and perhaps morally, then, we are depressed, and from my past experience in the Arctic I know that this depression will increase with the advance of the night. . . . Physically, we are losing strength, though our weight remains nearly the same, with a slight increase in some. All seem puffy about the ankles and eyes. The muscles which were hard earlier are now soft. We are pale, and the skin is unusually oily. The hair grows rapidly, and the skin about the nails has a tendency to creep over them, seemingly to protect them from the cold. The heart action is failing in force, and is decidedly irregular. About half of the men complain of insomnia and headaches. Many are dizzy and uncomfortable about the head. Others are sleepy at all times, although they sleep nine hours. There is one serious case at hand. That is Danco. He has an old heart lesion, a leak of one of the valves which has been followed up by an enlargement of the heart and a thickening of its walls.

May 27. There is nothing new to write about, nothing to excite fresh interest. I can think of nothing more disheartening and more destructive to human energy than this dense, unbroken blackness of the long, polar night.

May 31. The regular routine of our work is tiresome in the extreme. . . . We strain the truth to introduce stories of home, and of faraway future projects, hoping to infuse a new cheer, but it all fails miserably. We are under the spell of the black Antarctic night. And we are cold, cheerless and inactive. We have aged ten years in 30 days.

June 1. It is now difficult to get out of warm beds in the morning. There is no dawn. Nothing to mark the usual division of night and morning. Our appetites are growing smaller and smaller, and the little food which is consumed gives much trouble. Oh, for that heavenly ball of fire, not for the heat but for the light, the hope of life.

June 5. Today, we have to record the darkest page in our log, the death of our beloved comrade, Danco. It has not been unexpected, but the awful blank left is keenly felt and the sudden gloom of despair thus thrown over the entire party is impossible of description.

June 7. We have made a bag of sailcloth and into it the remains of Danco have been sewn. This morning we searched the crevasses for an opening which might serve as a grave. We found no place sufficiently open, but with axes and chisels we cut a hole through the ice in a recent lead about 100 yards from the

the bark. Owing to the depressing effect upon the party, we found it necessary to place the body outside on the ice on a sledge the day after the death.

June 8. The melancholy death and the melancholy burial of Danco have brought over us a spell of despondency which we seem unable to conquer. . . . We are constantly picturing to ourselves the form of our late companion floating about in a standing position with the weights to his feet, under the frozen surface and perhaps under the *Belgica.*

June 19. It is dark, dark, dark. Dark at noon, dark at midnight, dark every hour of the day. The darkness grows daily a little deeper, and the night soaks hourly a little more color from our blood. Most of us in the cabin have grown decidedly gray, though few are over 30. There is an absence of jest and cheer.

June 26. One of the sailors brought with him from Europe a beautiful young kitten. This kitten was named Nansen and steadily grew in our affections. . . . The long night brought out all the bad qualities of his ancestors. For nearly a month, he was in a kind of stupor, eating very little and sleeping much. If we tried to arouse him, he displayed considerable anger. His temperament changed from a good, lively creature to one of growling discontent. His mind wandered, and we believe his soul, too. A day or two ago, his life departed. We had showered him with our affection but the long darkness had made him turn against us.

The sun reappeared in late July, prompting Cook to declare ecstatically:

"How that great, golden ball of cold fire incites the spirits to expressions of joy and gratitude, how it sets the tongue to pleasurable utterances and the vocal cords to music. We have suddenly found tonic in the air, an inspiration in the scenic splendors of the sea ice and a cheerfulness in each other's companionship which makes the death-dealing depression of the night a thing of the past."

NSF has not told me in advance that they would be here, and I am somewhat stirred by the irony, even though I have grown accustomed to, indeed I even expect, those twists that make a good news story. Like the TV cameraman who stops on his way home from work at the scene of an accident to shoot some film, only to discover the victim is his own daughter. This is not as dramatic, but it is enough. I am sitting in the mess hall at McMurdo with two psychiatrists from Harvard, who are here to study the effects of extreme cold on the human psyche. At least I had not called them before, when I was rewriting my own clips, and their work is a little more deep, I am thankful.

Drs. Michael Popkin and Verner Stillner are interested in the biomedical aspects of human adaptation to South Polar stresses, and they're looking at the twenty-two men who have spent the last winter at that isolated station. Their work, they explain, is an attempt to understand the physiological and psychological factors responsible for a number of strange things that happen to men in prolonged isolation, such as alteration in sleep patterns, the "drifty" and staring states, depression, irritability, loss of enthusiasm, difficulty concentrating, and memory gaps.

They are checking into whether physiological factors, such as thyroid function and vitamin B-1 deficiency, are at work in creating the cluster of features in men who winter over, and they hope to get some answers from the blood and serum they have been drawing from the Pole people. Data has suggested, they tell us, that there are physiological changes, as well as psychological ones, in isolation. But what isn't clear is what these mean, and they're trying to define some baselines. Men at Pole, for instance, eat a heavy caloric diet, and they have access to vitamins. Their food is frozen, so it does not lose nutritive value. Therefore, if peculiar behavior is related to some deficiency, just how does this occur? One of the suggestions is that as a person consumes more cholesterol, his need for B-1 increases. Also, high consumption of alcohol might prevent the body from utilizing the vitamin properly.

Dr. Howard G. Muchmore, a specialist in infections at the University of Oklahoma College of Medicine, is also here in an effort to determine whether men's immunity to infection shifts during periods of isolation. Since 1957, he says, when the USARP program started, little attention has been paid to people. This is sad, he says, because the place is an ideal laboratory. But it's starting, and there's only a little data, and a lot of it comes from him. Dr. Muchmore wants to know, among other things, whether men are less resistant to infection when they leave the ice and go back to civilization. Is there a change in their immune balance that makes them more susceptible later? He says he wouldn't be here if he didn't think there was. Men who winter over at Pole, he explains, are selected for their good health, and they are young. The oldest to winter was forty-six. And they stay healthy when they get there. Such things as sore throats are exceedingly minimal. There is no sick call except for injuries. But a few days after that first plane comes in in the spring, they come down with stuff. Some 75 percent will have respiratory difficulties in a month. A return to civilization is followed by infections, in all of them, of one sort or another. Muchmore says he's trying to look at the state of health as a disease so he can learn more about immunity. It's possible that the people who winter over lose white blood cells that fight infection, because there is no infection to battle.

The information the psychiatrists and other medical specialists are gathering here will, it is hoped, be useful in constructing a fuller picture of certain aspects of human adaptation to extreme environments. It should also help them obtain more precise estimates in planning for human factors in future terrestrial and extraterrestrial explorations and provide significant data relating to the prediction of impending breakdown of men under stress. Massachusetts General Hospital psychiatrists (Popkin and Stillner work there also) have, in fact, been studying the different forms of stress that occur in polar regions and in ghettos, and the sort that occurred in the concentration camps of Nazi Germany. Dr. Chester M. Pierce, who has visited here on the ice several times, has focused on stress in the Antarctic and in the ghetto. His studies and the work of others on men living in space has enabled him to identify the traits which he believes to be common to every situation of extreme stress. These include dependency, forced socialization, spatial isolation, time elasticity, noise extremes, boredom, anxiety, sociological and biological dysrhythm, fears of abandonment, panic, and hopelessness.

He has theorized that these traits must also characterize the "mundane," everyday extreme environment, such as in the urban ghetto: "To my way of thinking, mundane stress is much more awesome than exotic stress such as that encountered in the polar desert. Mundane stress is subtle, cumulative, and incessant. People expect it automatically and accept it as unremarkable." While status and material compensation may accrue to men who venture into space or to polar regions, he says, life in the ghetto earns no such rewards. In space, under the sea or at the South Pole, men are aware that should anything go wrong, massive forces are poised to attempt their rescue. The ghetto dweller nurtures no such hope.

Experts generally agree that it is not the long polar night and the bitter cold that are the most important stresses causing maladjustment problems. The most serious difficulty appears to be adjusting to the enforced intimacy of a closed, isolated group for the long, dark winter. To be successful in such an environment, a person must have a combination of inner and outer sensitivities. He or she must have social awareness and understanding, or at least tolerance of others, and the ability to deal with one's own feelings. "The extrovert is ruled out from going to Pole," says Stillner. "The flash in the pan, the life-of-the-party guy, he does poorly there. He's all right at the outset but becomes intolerable at the end, and everyone wants to kill him. The best person is not necessarily an introvert, but one with fewer hobbies, versatile, someone who tells himself he must accommodate to the place and can be gratified by his job."

The ability to withdraw emotionally into one's self, on occasion, is of great value, observes another polar expert, Captain R. E. Strange of the Philadelphia Naval Hospital's Neuropsychiatry Service. In the small stations, opportunities are few for actual physical isolation from others, and it is vital for people to be able to retreat into a private world to heal the stresses of continuous group living.

The monotony of the environment and the absence of usual sources of satisfaction are the other significant problems of adjustment, Dr. Strange points out. Stimulation is essential to human beings, and variation in stimulation is essential for normal function. When the stations begin their winter of isolation, everything about the environment becomes remarkably the same, minute by minute, day to day, month to month, and depression and boredom are inevitable. Coupled with the monotony is the absence of the usual satisfactions, sexual, social, recreational, and academic. Substitute activities, says Dr. Strange, are essential for successful adjustment. From a psychiatric viewpoint, it is interesting that among the winter-overs, those who do best enjoy such unsophisticated and somewhat superficial social activities as bull sessions, food, and movies. Unfortunately, this type of activity usually includes drinking alcohol, and may progress to its abuse.

Dr. Strange admits that psychiatrists' ability to screen out individuals for proclivities to alcohol abuse and predicting potential for either alcoholic dependence or pathological release of impulse control under its influence is limited. The problem, however, must regularly concern the psychiatric examiner since any potential drinking problem can become worse on the ice and may well endanger the very survival of an isolated station.

It is also obvious that individuals with any homosexual problems be screened out of the group going to Antarctica. Any persons with effeminate mannerisms, says Dr. Strange, must also be disqualified. He adds that it is his impression that many of the difficulties experienced at one station were closely related to the homosexual threat created by obvious effeminate mannerisms and behavior in a member of the station crew.

One of the most important assets in the difficult business of adjusting, says Dr. Strange, is a sense of humor. Closely related is a sense of proportion, which enables a person to retain objectivity and to differentiate important from unimportant issues. One characteristic of isolated groups, in fact, is just such an impairment of a sense of proportion. As isolation continues, perception of what is important and what is unimportant depends increasingly on local emotional issues rather than on the usual values of the outside world.

FROM: The Commanding Officer, McMurdo Station
FAMILYGRAM 1-DF DET ALFA
Dear Friends and Relatives:

On February 22nd, the last Navy LC-130 Hercules took off from the Williams Field skiway. It circled the airfield, then flew low over McMurdo Station, dipping its wings. It was apparent to all on the ground who were following the silver bird that its maneuvers were irregular and had a certain meaning. This meaning was clear but impossible to comprehend, for since we arrived in October, planes have been flying in and out with great regularity.

When it disappeared in the North, we all knew it would not return for many months. Now, all of a sudden, the job was ours and ours alone — to close Williams Field and the unneeded buildings and facilities of McMurdo for winter, to maintain the base and to open the complex and be ready for next summer's operating season in Antarctica.

The Navy and civilian community size declined rapidly during the last weeks of February until all who remained on this second most significant day of our tour of duty in Det Alfa were 130 people anxious to commence wintering-over. The mixture here at McMurdo is 117 Navy, 13 civilians. There are two women scientists wintering-over, a first. Dr. Mary Alice McWhinnie of De Paul University is along with her four research assistants. They are studying annual variations in diverse metabolic phenomena of low temperature invertebrate animals, quite a mouthful of scientific jargon to describe an afternoon fishing trip or scenic science cruise on Winter Quarters Bay. Sister Mary Odile Cahoon of St. Scholastica College in Duluth, also a biologist, is the other woman wintering over. Two of the civilians are exchange scientists, one from Russia and the other from Poland. Three others are employees of Holmes and Narver, Inc.

With us on this great white continent, at other U.S. stations, are 21 (13 Navy and four civilians) at the South Pole, nine civilians at Palmer and four at Siple. Our only link with these isolated souls is through voice radio, and then only when atmospheric conditions permit.

Since the summer tourists left, there has been much work to do just in preparing the station for winter. One of the biggest jobs is simply sealing the buildings to keep out snow.

Every door, window and roof and wall penetration, even tiny cracks, must be sealed. Wide cloth tape, often stapled across cracks, is used as the primary means of sealing. Large tin cans are used to cover stove chimneys and building exhausts. After closure, many of the berthing as well as business structures are pulled by tractor from Williams Field downtown location to high atop man-made snow-mounds on the outskirts of town. This is done to keep them from being buried by snow-drifts. Most buildings which constitute this village on the Ross Ice Shelf are built on sled-type runners, similar to skis.

Edges of roadways, trails and footpaths must be identified with red and green flags on six-foot bamboo poles while these borders can still be seen. The outside lighting system requires a thorough checkout before 24-hour continual darkness arrives. Miles of water piping must have properly working heat-tape protection or the liquid in the lines, freshwater, salt and sewage, will freeze in minutes. These tasks must be accomplished before "It" comes.

Skua gulls, seals and penguins are all gone. Nights have grown to about 14 hours duration now. At high noon, the sun is barely visible over the hilltops. Our comrades at South Pole Station are already in continuous Antarctic night. The sun permanently disappeared from view there on March 21st.

Temperatures are steadily going down here at McMurdo. One can expect to hear minus 15 to 20 degrees F. along with the current wind chill temperature (often minus 50 to minus 60) on the morning weather report broadcast on AFAN Radio. At minus 20 degrees F. with 20 knots of wind, the chill temperature is minus 80 degrees. Fully clothed, one now becomes aware of the cold, and exposed skin will be frost-bitten in minutes.

A highly successful event occurred on March 9th when

members of the Public Works Department and the Nuclear Power Plant launched their annual Seabee Ball. The Chief Petty Officer's Club was gayly decorated for the occasion, and a splendid buffet of all kinds of eats and nibbles provided an ideal setting.

The annual event took on historic significance when, for the first time in the 19-year-history of Det Alfa, the Seabees crowned a female as their queen. Sister Mary Odile Cahoon was chosen to reign over the royal events of the evening, which included honors being paid to the oldest and youngest Seabee, live entertainment, theatrical interludes, and a pie-eating contest.

Amidst all this activity, we've not forgotten about our small but active component of the Det Alfa team isolated at the very bottom of the world. AFAN commenced daily live broadcasting to the Pole on the sixth of March. Through the ingenuity of the highly competent radiomen and electronics technicians at both ends of this network, AFAN transmits music, news, weather reports and entertainment to the South Pole Station via shortwave frequency. South Pole receives our broadcast, runs it through a frequency converter and rebroadcasts simultaneously through a homemade AM transmitter to all the under-snow nooks and crannies of the South Pole Station.

South Pole Station produced the very first new daddy of the winter-over season when, on March 26th, CE2 Chuck Nicholson became the proud father of a baby son. Two days later, through the cooperation of a stateside amateur radio station, the indignant cries of his infant son were clearly heard throughout the communications building at the South Pole.

All in all, Det Alfa remains busy as a long-tailed cat in a room full of rocking chairs. Our days are filled with down-right hard work and later tempered with wholesome relaxation. Bowling, karate, movies, amateur photography, amateur radio and college courses in mathematics, sociology, English and German are but a few of the activities and interests we share. Keeping thoroughly busy is the proper antidote to the frustration and loneliness of isolation, which at times overcomes each of us. The can-do spirit of the officers and men assigned to the most arduous peacetime duty the Navy has to offer has reaffirmed my faith in the ingenuity and adaptability of Navymen, and in particular, your husbands, sons and loved ones I have the good fortune to have serving in my command.

Nate Derya, Chief Hospital Corpsman, talking:

No way, no fucking way would I ever do it again. It was a year out of my life, really it was. I would not ever do it again. No, never. Bloody well never. Never will I do it again. No. And if you want to know why, it's simple. I like girls. I like my wife. No, thank you, it's just too long. I did it because other people did it and because I figured myself for a loner and it was a good place to get away. People who had been and didn't like it told me, they warned me, they said no way is it a place for someone who just wants to get away from people. They told me I'd be better off running off to some big city because then nobody would give a shit about me, people avoid one another in cities like the plague, everyone's so suspicious they just leave you alone, you know?

They'd tell me, you don't want to go down over a winter. Summer support is nice, maybe get a run into Chee Chee for some nookie now and again. But not to spend a winter. But I'd say, oh, I can do it if you can, I'll go, I'll see what it's like. Well, I went down, and I wouldn't do it again, rather take

176

eight-ten in the slammer. When I got off that plane at Mc-Murdo, I had this washcloth in my hand that had been wetted down, someone said, go ahead, carry it outside, and so like an asshole I did that, and it bloody froze, stuck to my fingers and I tore the skin getting it off. And I looked around, and I said, "God-damn."

Nothing. It was just white, all white. Desolate. There's a couple Quonset huts here near this so-called airstrip. A few miles over there is McMurdo and I looked at that, it's a fucking shit-house in distress is what it looks like, and I said, "Oh my Jesus."

Well, I stuck it out for one winter, and I only got depressed once, right in the beginning, when the last plane took off. First two or three days, man, I wanted to go home, but then, you know, you say, well, I'm here so I got to do it. We kept ourselves pretty busy in the dispensary, taking care of the malingerers, they'd come in looking for casts and splints for boils and warts, you know, and I'd fix 'em up every so often when the doc is at the flicks. Painted the place, put up paneling, retyped the health records, anything to take your mind off it. I didn't like the dark, either. All that black, coalsack city.

I got along with just about everyone, even though I hated it, and the thing I got most out of the experience was that I saved money. Adventure? Not one that I'd care to do again. They couldn't pay me enough money to go down there again.

My wife and I got four kids to take care of, and as far as I know everything was okay when I was down there. I told her fifteen years ago, "Look, this is my life, this Navy, and I'm going to stick it through for twenty. You like it or you ship out. . . ."

As far as women were concerned, there were a few there during the summer season; they got along pretty well with the guys, some better than others, if you get my meaning. There's the big stares, you know, when they walk into the mess hall, and everybody knows who's banging who, and they'd all say, hey, goodie, a woman, a woman, and they'd follow 'em around with their eyes, hungry, you know. We had a tour come in from the Lindblad *Explorer,* into Mc-Murdo. They brought all these women off of the ship to look around and see the officers, and we chiefs were tour guides. They were dressed in greens, but man, they sure smelled pretty. You know, one of the things you lose on the ice, along with your hard-on, is the sense of smell, no trees and flowers and so on, but man, they brought it all back, better than the botanical gardens in Christchurch. Oh yes, they did fraternize, there was a little of that, yes, there was.

Things are changing, though. They brought some women down last year to work in the kitchen or something, and one of them picked up a boyfriend and she told the skipper, "We want to live together. On the ice." Well, the old man had a fucking hemorrhage, and I don't know how they finally settled that one. Strange, isn't it? That's a social . . . It's accepted here now, living together, but down on the ice, it's still a no-no and they're so far behind the times, it's like the Fifties.

You know, that psychiatric screening we give, it's not worth diddly-doo. Very exacting, you know, supposed to screen out the faggots and the boozers. Look at these here questions they give you, you got to write your name and you give the answers that come closest to describing your opinion about things. Rate your answers, you know, like agree moderately, agree slightly, agree strongly, disagree lightly, moderately, strongly. Look at these. "One of the worst things about a Deep Freeze assignment is the long time I'll spend away from my family. The most important thing about a job is the money you make. I prefer to work outdoors. In choos-

178

ing a woman I prefer one who is interested in art and paint-
ing. I would rather teach a drama class than a physics class.
Most of the men who go to the Antarctic will wish they had
stayed in the United States. I have never done any heavy
drinking. I would like to stay in the Antarctic longer than
now planned. Life usually hands me a raw deal. A person is
better off if he doesn't trust anyone. I never worry about my
looks. I would certainly be found if I am lost in the Antarctic. The Antarctic will be an exciting adventure. I like to
compete with people. I like to drive fast. If someone does
something nice for me, I usually wonder if there is a hidden
reason." Look at that shit, a hundred and thirty-three of
them, all begging to be lied about. You know, one time on
the ice, they started these communal psych tests, one was a
buddy test, you know, requiring us to choose the men we
liked best and least and so on, and you had to do that on a
ballot. Well, man, we had guys grab-assing around with that
one, I'll tell you. Put down things like, I like Charly's ass
'cause it's fatter than Sandy's, or we hate the XO 'cause he'd
rather fight than switch, you know, funny things like that.
Well, the shrink got so pissed he stopped it.

When I went in for my psychiatric screening, before I got
to the ice, the shrink sits me down and he says, hey, how do
you feel about going on the ice? I said, well, you know, what
can I say, I mean I've been to Vietnam, and then he says,
well, how'd you like to go back to Nam, like I had a choice,
right? And I said, well, the Navy is my life and if they tell me
to go I'll go, that's all, and then he asks me what would I do if
all the troops are drinking too much, and I told him, well, I'd
try to keep 'em out of trouble and things. I lied my ass off, I
wouldn't go back to Nam, I'd jump ship first, and if the
troops were drinking too much, I'd be in shit-faced with 'em
myself, every bloody time.

179

FROM: The Commanding Officer, McMurdo Station
FAMILYGRAM 2-DF DET ALFA
Dear Friends and Relatives:

The month started in McMurdo with the grand opening of the "Winter Inn," Antarctica's finest restaurant. The opening marks the initiation of restaurant style serving in the mess hall which we will enjoy throughout the winter season. Monday through Saturday, the evening meal is served at your table with a choice of five entrees from a menu which is changed each week.

On the 24th of April, the sun set for the winter, starting the long Antarctic night for McMurdo residents. At 1:30 in the afternoon, all hands mustered outside in the minus 51 wind-chill temperature for a ceremony as the U.S. flag was lowered for the final time until the sun rises again on August 20. The commanding officer presented the flag, which has flown all summer over McMurdo Station, to DK-1 Jesse Wenzel, the DET ALFA winter-over sailor of the year.

The majority of the work being done now is inside. But it never fails, when least expected, an outside trouble-call arises. Most of this work is done with one man holding a flashlight. Another popular method is shining the headlights of a truck on the work area.

In a small way, I hope this Familygram has given you a brief insight into the life of your loved one while he courageously endures the many hardships of life on a continent that was not meant for man to inhabit.

I am continuously impressed and immensely proud, by the daily examples I witness, of people here making a genuine effort to be each other's keeper.

From the rough log of Jon Olsen, Commanding, North Base, U.S. Antarctic Service (Field Representative, U.S. Dept. of the Interior):

SEPT. 1. As I start this new book, I wonder what events its pages will record. Poised as we are on the edge of the unknown, both geographically and figuratively, it is an impressive experience to write the first lines in a book which may chronicle great achievement or great disaster. The stage is set for either in this austere and forbidding region. I pray that all will go well with all of us here at the North Base and with all of us who are striving along parallel lines at the South Base.

SEPT. 7. Had a talk with Chalmers this morning and somewhat surprised at some of the things he said. He said he would refuse to go on trail if O'Callahan were to lead the party. Fortunately, then, O'Callahan has not been selected to lead any parties. His early temperamental flareups here and his constant moodiness and his anti-American and anti-British talk, as well as his personal habits, have made him enemies. It is too bad that men cannot seem to learn to live peacefully in a polar camp. All seems well on the surface and suddenly someone who has been holding in will come to me with the wildest tales and rumors. Too bad. I have done everything possible to make North Base a democratic friendly organization.

OCT. 17. O'Callahan went up to cache this a.m. with a load and stayed *all day*, for lunch and dinner. He is getting terribly moody. I cannot say that I have much faith in his particular brand of Irishman. He is a good man with the dogs and on the trail, but I guess the enforced inactivity is getting to him. I cannot fully trust a man who early in our stay here had to be lashed into a strait-jacket after drinking ethyl alcohol. What a life.

I feel that one of the 24 of us should never have wintered in Antarctica. Three others would have been better off at McMurdo. The Officer in Charge was a young man who had had no previous experience in dealing with others.

He went through quite a learning process after arriving on station, which at times put quite a strain on his men and on others. This carried on into the dark period and was still evident when we were ready to leave. His relationships with his men were extremely poor and they did not respect him or his authority as they should. Isolation was particularly difficult for him.

The senior Navy radioman-electrician also had problems of isolated duty which manifested themselves in the performance of his duties. He was qualified to handle shipboard equipment but was unable to adapt his experience and training to our power at the station. He was neglectful of his duties, and would avoid the usual electrical jobs that any electrician could do. This developed because he was becoming more and more careless. He nearly killed himself on two occasions when handling live circuits. These things reduced his efficiency.

Mr. Charles Hammill, who was in charge of seismology, was also a problem. He was well qualified, but was what you might call a crybaby in that he continually complained about anything and everything that wasn't to his liking. Most of his complaints were without justification. The rest of us could accept or put up with the things he complained about, and this acceptance of our lot worked on him and put him in quite an emotional state. At various times we had to talk to him at great length to calm him down. Things like working conditions, money and sleeping bothered him a great deal.

Finally, the shock of learning what others thought of him

turned him completely around. Our problem child became a full member of the wintering-over party, accepted by all. I would be happy to winter with him again.

Mr. Michael Lorne was the only member who should not have wintered-over at Pole, or even sent to the Antarctic. He had very little self-discipline and was next to being an alcoholic. These two traits did not show up for some time, otherwise he might have been replaced before the last aircraft left us. He was a pathetic case.

Dr. Greg Sparke is a psychiatrist who wintered over with the Australian Antarctic Division:

The thirteen or fourteen men who were going on the expedition needed a doctor, and in Australia, when you finish your internship, in lieu of draft you could perform national service of some sort. You could go to the Aboriginal settlements, for a year or two, or go as an expedition surgeon to some place or other. It seemed a pretty good idea to me, and I figured I could save a lot of money. I wanted to special in psychiatry, and had in fact been accepted by the Institute of Psychiatry in London, and I asked them in London if they could put that off a bit because I could do with the cash.

I didn't like the bush or the heat and I didn't want to go into the Flying Doctors or some such as that. Well, the group I went down with was topheavy with people getting their Ph.D.s and doing their theses — that's what a lot of them go for, you know; that was their strong motivation. It was great for professional advancement in basic research; people can come back and become one of the world's few authorities on some esoteric subject, like radio physics. Some guys were just there because they were going to get married and they could save three or four thousand, you know.

I was the doctor, but I was also the catering officer, the biologist, the ornithologist, and, in those days, believe me, I didn't know the difference between a penguin and a seal. One of the most boring things we had to do down there was just count. It was terribly boring but it was, I suppose, terribly important. Just counting. They gave me charts and books and said those are elephant seals, those are penguins, just count them every time you see one. Also got to pick some lice out of the little buggers, counted those, too. Did some seal branding, banded penguins, collected gray-headed albatross. One guy I know went down on a grant to sample parasites on emperors. All you had to do was kill the penguin, lay him out and as the body cooled, all the parasites'd flee, and you just picked 'em up and put 'em in formalin. Another guy was interested in blood pressures of bull elephant seals. How do you do it? Well, we decided to anesthetize the beasties with rectal heroin, then do a cutdown into the brachial artery. You just can't wrap a sphygmometer around 'em, you know. Cherry-Jarrard said that since they were so sluggish on the ice it was quite easy to introduce things rectally into 'em when they were just lying about. What he was trying to insert and how he found out I'll never know. But, that was Cherry's observation, not mine. Well, what we did was creep up on the buggers, with a pump and a long length of hose full of smack, and whammo. That was really shooting up. . . .

Some funny things do happen to you. Your overall mental state changes. You become egocentric. Everyone used to ask me afterward didn't I feel isolated, and I didn't. You feel the rest of the world is isolated from you. It's the old story that when you're lost on the trail, it's the camp that's lost, not you. You become the psychological center. You also become mildly paranoid. Headquarters never answered our cables quick enough. They never showed any awareness of our problems. You lose a sense of perspective. I recall one of the guys really getting furious that one of the table-setters had put on the table a bottle of catsup that was nearly empty. He shouted and ranted, how can you do this to me? I can look back and say now that he was making a big federal issue out of the catsup. But at the time, I agreed with him, damn it, I'd say, well fancy that, a half-bottle indeed.

You get irritated at little habits, the way a guy laughs, talks, coughs, holds his knife and fork. Nearest we had to a guy being really disliked was this poor fellow who was accident-prone. Started when we left Melbourne, had his expensive Nikon stolen. He was also a violin player, and he forgot his bow on the train, arrived in Antarctica without the bow, thank God. Lost his pants once, went off to take a shit someplace and forgot to put 'em on again. Once sat on a birthday cake, his. He ran over a foot, someone else's, you know, with a tractor, broke an arm, lost a tooth, every fucking thing you can imagine happened to this poor bugger. And the awful thing was that we hated him for it. It was like getting tied up in an endless traffic jam at suppertime, and when you finally pass the guy whose poor car has broken down and caused it, you curse at him and shake your fist and wish he'd drop dead.

There'd be a few fights, common in an Aussie pub, though, so we didn't mind that all that much. The scientist-nonscientist split became decidedly hot one time. We had this big long messroom table, and they cut in in half so each group could have their own place to sit. One other guy locked himself in the darkroom for four months, show up every so often like the Phantom of the Opera. As I say, I wish I were not so much the participant-observer because you tend to lose your objectivity that way, and I would have been able to get a lot more out of the goings-on. . . .

It's fine, I suppose, to send fourteen slobs down there, and it may be fine, too, to send fourteen compulsively neat people. We're always asked what psychological qualities should be looked for in compatible people, and the answer is nothing extraordinary. Just so long as they all are slobs, or all don't smoke or all do. This neatness thing, when you're living in close quarters with others who aren't, it can be a problem. Or the swearing. I had trouble with one chap, a decent sort but he was a Salvation Army type, felt all swearing was horrid, and he got a lot of grief from the rest of us. If he ever heard a fuck or a shit, why he'd get so uptight he'd start to preach, and that made it all the worse, he got more fucks and shits back than he had bargained for.

But despite all that vulgarity, you know, there was not one single instance that I can recall, at least with our group, where people discussed their own sexual behavior. People just jerked off as they pleased, talked a lot about other people's sex life but not their own. If a guy said he missed his wife, he wouldn't be apt to say he was looking forward to a good screw when he got home. That sort of talk came out on the ship, heading home at last, and on ship you got more and more horny in anticipation of what you could do. Back on the ice, you were less so. It wasn't a conscious effort to be celibate; there's just nothing sexually stimulating there, at least not when we were there. Guys in various stages of beard growth, steadily growing uglier the more you see of them. I'm not aware, though statistically there must have been, of any gay guys, and we didn't seem to have any of that prison substitute-homosexuality syndrome. I suppose if there were two gay guys there that would be all right, keep it to even numbers, you know.

With Sea Daddy, Stormalong John, and another sailor they call Minute Maid because his only Antarctic duty before this was at Palmer Station:

186

"The hard part about it," says Minute Maid, sipping his coffee, "is when you come back to the world, to the hustle and bustle. Down here, once you get into the winter, you just get into a routine and it's nice and slow. Comin' off the ice can be rougher, to my way of thinkin', than goin' on. Like, you know what one of the first things that just hits at you is when you get off here? It's the shrill sounds that a woman makes. You get to really notice her voice, that shrill kind of piercing voice. And you notice the hardness of the pavements, and the different smells, and the traffic noises."

"Yeah," says Sea Daddy, "there's no red lights here, no traffic like that, no nothin', and you're on your own, that's why I like it, it's real fine."

"Different at Palmer than here, though," says Minute Maid. "This here place's a metropolis; down at Palmer we had ten, eleven of us."

"Whooee, beach party place, man," laughs Sea Daddy, showing white teeth through his black beard. "How'd you guys stand the fuckin' heat?"

"Buried myself in my work," says Minute Maid. "Mechanic and equipment operator, but you wouldn't know nothin' about that shit, Daddy; I do more accidentally than you do on purpose. Let me tell you, there was only but four Seabees in the whole place, so you sort of did just about everything that came up, like a lot of projects. We got a little bit of everything from building to utilities, which is plumbing. And I didn't volunteer for it, neither, not like that asshole, Daddy over there, and I just came up for orders. When they came in they had the words 'Deep Freeze' on there, you know? I called the detailer, which is the mechanic chief, Buddy Dew, and I talked to him and he says, well, he's been down there and he says he thinks it's a good thing for me, and I ought to go down one time anyway. I says, thanks a lot, you fat fuck, I could really care what you think of the place, I don't want to go, no way. But they shipped my ass down anyway."

"I had thirteen seasons down and three winters-over," Sea Daddy says proudly, thumping the table three times. "I own the fuckin' place. Pole, Byrd, McMurdo, name it, men. I was there when Crazy Charlie was down."

Stormalong John comes alive at Charlie's name, smiles wistfully, shakes his head. "Oh Jesus, Crazy Charlie. Used to get a little drunk down there, paint a face on the back of his head, didn't know whether he was comin' or goin'. Pasted a battleship on the top of his head and went to sleep like that at night. Crazy stuff like that to get morale goin', that's why they called him Crazy Charlie."

"Yeah, lots of laughs in those days," says Sea Daddy. "It's changed now. Place is becomin' Skirt City. Used to get lots of things in the old days. It's all over now, Navy's gettin' out in a couple years once we get Pole built, I'm gettin' out. Used to be like when you wintered over you got a promotion, sometimes got a first duty choice, sometimes got somethin' named after you. Now they're siftin' so many people in and out, it's like a Ford plant down here, not what they call . . . used to call, exotic duty, you know."

"I'll say one thing, though," says Minute Maid. "Everyone who asked for their first choice while down there this year got it. Palmer is good that way. Only thing is I didn't ask to go there in the first place, and I didn't think it was so great, duty or not. One year, right? Nine months before that I got Vietnam. Separated from my wife for a year then, right? I really didn't care that much for it. Now I'm down here. This time, all the guys were tellin' me that when I get the screenin', you know, all I got to do is run in there and kiss the first guy I see, and they'll let me out. Well, I didn't exactly do that, but when the shrink asks me how I felt about goin' onto the ice, I tell him anybody goes to the Antarctic and winters over is a nut. And you know what he says? He says, you're all right, get your gear together, buddy. Well, I got down there, and I didn't think too much about it until my ship, *Hero,* pulls out. Last one to leave, you know, pulls out in April and that's it, no more for a long time.

"Well, I hated it, but it really wasn't too bad, lowest it got was ten below, highest was fifty-five. But you still got all your Antarctic differences, changing winds that blow in circles, the isolation. They kept us busy, just busy. Only thing was I got tired of seeing the same guys all the time. Only two buildings at Palmer. To get away from the guys you had to go on a hike or some such. Like this one guy and I we went out onto a glacier with our sleeping bags and slept up there, just to break the monotony. But you know, I wouldn't winter over again. This is fine for a few months here at McMurdo, but I wouldn't winter over again. I've asked for summer support and I'll be goin' down a few more times, and there is an advantage of sorts, you know. You get to meet different people from other countries and you never find any hostility. Everybody is human down here. And there's somethin' about the Antarctic that you just can't describe. It has its own . . . environment or somethin'. I can't get the right words. . . . But it's just . . . somethin'. . . ."

Stormalong John says, "Let me say something about that. Last year I was out in the Dry Valleys at Vanda, and there was nobody around, nobody. I couldn't see a soul. The helo left and went over to somewhere else for a few hours and I couldn't see a soul. In my whole life, I never been in a situation like that, where you feel like it's the cleanest, nicest place in the world. But I think I've had enough, too; I've put in four times, given 'em three winters. And I put in for twenty choices of duty, too, and I got none of 'em. Last time, before this one, I got orders for Cape Hatteras, and I just had left one year of isolated duty at Pole, so they sent me to Cape

Hatteras, must have figured I needed a rest. But that place. Nearest dime store is fifty miles away and that's in the so-called States. Base was fallin' apart, they wanted it repaired, and there I was with a ulcer tour starin' me in the face, and I just got done with one ulcer tour in the Antarctic. Finished up the Cape Hatteras tour, and come back here, and figured that was the least of two evils. I don't really mind it, though. The wintering over is really the best part of it. Once you get the summer support people and most of the scientists the hell out, then it's good duty. During the winter you don't have fifteen, twenty bosses trying to tell you how to run a job, from the skipper on down."

"Yeah," says Sea Daddy. "More damned tourists comin' down, plus scientists, tellin' you what to do, tryin' to do five hundred things when they should be doin' one, or maybe none, lookin' at some of these ding-dongs."

"I'll give you a good example," says Stormalong John. "Sea Daddy's talkin' about tourists. Now, at South Pole Station, that's probably the biggest tourist attraction down here, not that there's anythin' there but what, like I say, the Bees are puttin' in. In 1964, we had about twenty-five Congressmen come down there. And water, as you know, in the Antarctic is scarce, and at Pole you got to shovel snow into a melter, pump it, and filter it. Well, they got flush toilets out there, under the ice in the living quarters. And people who have to shovel that snow, they're aware of the water problem, naturally. So they take it easy. You got a urinal over here and two commodes. And none of our people will take a leak in that commode and flush it. You use the urinal. Well, I walk in there and here's four Congressmen, the pride and joy of Washington, you know, takin' a leak in the toilet and flushin' it, and there goes five gallons of water right down the old tube, and they thought it was great fun takin' a leak, you know, at the South Pole and flushin' it down. I got a little indignant at that and I told them, hey, you just don't go around doin' that out here, use the damned urinal. You want to flush it, you go up there and fill five, ten, fifteen gallons of water into that tank, which is going to take you fifty to one hundred pounds of snow. These people just aren't realistic. It's a big lark down here. I've seen Congressmen get out at the Pole and stand on their hands and put their feet up against the flagpole, the leaders of our country?

"You know, everyone thinks that when the last airplane goes out you're going to be real depressed, but let me tell you that after you've had to put up all summer long with all the . . ."

"Bullshit," says Sea Daddy.

". . . planes, flyin' twenty-four hours a day, the noise, workin' two shifts, up twenty-six hours in a row. One time, we had three planes sittin' on the ice at Pole at one time, we'd get out there and unload one, and another would pull up and you'd unload that, it's fuckin' Pensacola Naval. So, two hundred fifty flights to either refuel or unload and you're so sick of these damn things you're glad when they leave you alone, so you can get down to doin' your own job and on a set schedule.

"It's better, like I say, in the winter. But, about halfway through, things start to happen, like you may be topside throwin' snow, and one time I turned out the lights and started lookin' out there, just standin' and lookin' and it's so pitch black, and I thought, why you dumb sonofabitch, what are you doin' here anyway? You got to be crazy. Periodically, you'll do that. Everybody'll sit there and all of a sudden someone will say, hey, what the hell am I doin' here? I must be fuckin' nuts. But all in all, I liked it. It ain't such a bad place. You're more or less your own boss, particularly at the outlying stations, and if you want to try something new they'll let you, build somethin' or try an experiment. If it works, great, if it doesn't, well, WTF. There's just no place in the service that you have that except on the ice. There's no place to go, but there's freedom.

"You either like it or you don't. And if you're winterin' in and you don't like it, well, man, you're in trouble.

"I was up at Pole when they locked up the first guy they ever locked up in the Antarctic. We built a brig and shoved his ass in it. He was with the weather people, an ex-Air Force guy, and he seemed like a real nice fella during the summer. Well, the day the last plane left he did a one-eight. He became a problem. Drinking, liar, a thief. Finally, one night they put him on medication, and he stayed on it and he seemed to do pretty good. Well, then he said the hell with it and he went bananas. When he first started up like that, the OIC says we're going to build a brig, and this guy got the message, he knew it was for him. They held that over him for a while, and he stuck straight. But, just when we got to where we had six to eight weeks left before we got relieved, he flipped again, and he got hold of some booze and some medicine, and he just went snaky. He decked the medical officer, and he decked me when I jumped in, and he run out and got a fire ax and started heavin' that around. Well, we finally got hold of him and quieted him down, and I told the watch that if anything happened don't mess around with this dude, just hit the fire bell. Well, I'm in the sack and this alarm goes off, and it was him, out on a rampage again. We finally found him hidin' out in the club, and there were twenty of us, and we gave him a choice, beat his ass off or he goes into the brig peacefully. Well, he says he's going to call his lawyer in New York, going to sue the OIC, me, the whole fuckin' Navy, goin' to contact his lawyer with a ham radio, he says.

"Well, we canned him for three days, and we sent a message out when we locked this dude up, and this was the first word, our message, that the admiral back in Christchurch had that we had a problem. He gets this message that we done locked up a civilian at Pole Station, and he went right up through the overhead. Well, he sent a message to McMurdo, told 'em to tell us to unlock this dude, we don't confine nobody, but nobody, much less a civilian, turn him loose or it's our asses. Well, the OIC, he starts sweatin', he's got twenty years in, and he says to me, hey, what do you make for base pay 'cause I think I'm goin' to be busted to chief after this is over.

"So, we let his ass out and put locks on all our doors, and he's out, roaming around the corridors night and mornin', and we stayed away from him as far as we could. We put up with that six weeks, scared shitless. Nothin' came of it that I know; they yanked six weeks off his pay. I think we would have killed him if he started in on us again during that six weeks. There was also this other civilian at Byrd Station, just started walkin' and just took off one night."

"That guy was so depressed," says Sea Daddy, "we never found a trace of him. Found the dog, but not him. We had some guys like that fella up at Pole, but after a while they straightened out. You do get a little downhearted when the planes go out, and I missed all the football. I enjoyed it, though, all in all; I met a lot of people, and even though it's changed I still like it."

Stormalong chuckles. "What you mean is you had a racket, right, Daddy?"

"Yeah, my job was mostly keepin' the runways clean, and the roads, haulin' cargo, unloadin' ships. When I first come down, Christ, we had to go out twenty miles on the ice to offload the ships. Now those ships just walk right in here. Easy stuff now. When I first got here, I had the feeling, Holy Christ, I'm stuck down at the bottom of the world, right with the devil. But after a while I get used to it. Kept busy, and ten years ago, like I say, you worked your butt off; even the

officers got out there and busted ass, runnin' front-end load-
ers and all that stuff. Now it's civilized here, lot of new buildings, like this big hotel they got here now. Before we lived in
them Jamesways. They were much better, too. You had the
canvas, and you'd put snow around them to keep them warm,
and you sleep good in there. I liked the outlying stations,
nobody to bother your ass. Like Byrd, that was under the
ice, too, and you could go down into those tunnels and hide
out. But you got to stay over one winter to find out what it's
really like here. A few days'll tell you nothin'. You got to be
here for a while."

"You know," says Minute Maid, "every guy comes down
for a winter finds out the good and the bad things about
himself. You know, like you might have a friend, he says, why
you're a no good sonofabitch, and you'll say to him, what the
hell are you talkin' about? But after you're there for a while,
you maybe find out what a really rotten bastard you are. You
really do. And you try straightenin' it out, too; that's the
good thing that comes with it all. I think everyone comes out
a better man, even though they don't like it there."

"Lookit," says Sea Daddy. "If you don't hear a bitchin'
sailor, why he ain't happy, man. You're always goin' to get
guys sayin' they hate the place, but after they're there a
while, they get it on okay. Now look at McMurdo. We just
got this thing in one of the clubs, they call it a pornoviewer.
You know, they show these films of chicks on the screen, and
they got music playin' with it, and it's a real horny show. We
got movies, four clubs, stag films, people bring 'em down,
coupla guys made their own in Chee, regular home movies;
they're in them themselves. You get to talk to home on the
ham; they can hook you up for ten cents."

"Sure, there's plenty to do," says Stormalong. "Different
strokes for different folks, as they say. Some guys like country
western, some like rock, build models, drink. Variety. The

drinkin' depends on your CO. Some guys, if you have one beer, they think you got a drinkin' problem. But if the CO sits down with the troops and tips a few, well, then you don't have a drinkin' problem. The first year at Pole, it was mainly First Class, no chiefs out there. Between the enlisted people, we had one hundred thirty-six years of Navy experience. Our OIC was a doctor and he had been in the Navy all of five months. And he got this Dear John from his girlfriend, and even though he used to drink with us during the summer, when he got that letter he all of a sudden got religion. No drinking. Nobody, no time, no how, nowhere. No. Usually, you'd knock off at noon, go over to the club and have one, 'fore lunch, you know. In every Navy station in the world the club opens at eleven-thirty. Want a beer, Navy figures you're mature, go on. But no, this pissant wasn't goin' to jeopardize his twenty-five-thousand-dollar education on a ten-cent beer. Sort of pissed the troops off. Said, hey, call McMurdo, skipper, call Byrd, see what they do? He says no, he don't care what they're doin' out there, there's no booze here. Period. Well, we said, we have our rights, too, but he says nobody drinks. Well, this went on for a month. Thursday or Friday morning, I'm over to the shop pumpin' water and the builder comes in. This is about eight-thirty in the morning, and he says, piss on him, I'm goin' over to the club and get me a beer. Says let's go over and get drunk. I say, that sounds good, so I secured the pump and me and him went over to the club. Pretty soon, someone sticks his head in the door and it's the equipment operator. Says, what are you doin'? and we tell him, come on in, babe, and get drunk. Then somebody else shows up, and we send him over to get Herbie the cook, and Herbie's at his stove, chow all over, and he says, Goddammit I'm comin' too, 'cause you got to know that Herbie the cook, best cook in the Antarctic when he was sober, likes a drink, and he'll get drunk in a heartbeat. So now we got everyone at a party, and noontime rolls around and the OIC goes over to the galley to get some chow and there ain't nobody there, and chow's burnin' on the stove, no cook, no nothin'. He hits the club and everyone is in there gettin' with the program. He sticks his head in, looks around with this shit-eatin' look on his face, and walks right out. Party went on and on, all day Friday, all day Saturday and Sunday, and when we went back to work Monday nary a word was said, and after that anytime we wanted a drink at noontime we just went ahead and got one.

"But the funny part of it was when the reliefs come in, and that's somethin' to see, when they come in. Scared, don't know where they're at, in a state of shock, they are. Well, you're so glad to see these guys you start a party. The admiral come out this one time on the first plane and stayed overnight, and we're in the club havin' our party. These new guys have altitude sickness, you know, and they're tired and not climatized and they're just sittin' around sort of stunned lookin' at these here animals. Well, the admiral is out there talkin' to the OIC, and our cook, Herbie, has got a beanie on. We built him this propeller on top, and he's really blowed out of his mind on them vodka freezes he used to whip up; he did that with snow and a eggbeater and they'll send you higher than helium. Well, Herbie walks over to the admiral and he says, hey admiral, have a drink. The admiral says, no thanks. And you know what that crazy-ass Herbie does? He pours one right over the admiral's head, right over the rear admiral's head, it's dripping right down his parka. Well, the admiral, he's a good shit, no one like him that I know, and he says to the OIC, ah, doctor, I uh think you ought to secure this here little party. And the OIC says, admiral, I ain't never secured one of their parties and I can't start now."

Stormalong John laughs hard, and Minute Maid asks him about the time they built this cage, for the benefit of the relief party, and they put this guy in it, and when the plane comes in there it is waiting for them.

"Oh Jesus, we used to do that shit all the time for the reliefs, scared the piss out of 'em. One time in sixty-nine our foreman came dressed as Mickey Mouse, made this plaster of paris Mickey Mouse suit, a beautiful thing. When the first plane drops down, there's the reliefs on board, eyes buggin' out, and there's ol' Myron standin' out there with this suit on, wavin' the plane to the fuel pit. Another year we ran up weather balloons, up about two hundred feet, strung a big sign between 'em, WATCH YOUR ASS. The best thing we did, though, was get out there with nothin' on, just your bunny boots, and you'd stand there, wavin' bottles of booze, and they'd just about shit, think we'd all gone Asiatic."

Stormalong John pulls out a card and waves it. It reads, "This is to certify that Stormalong John Wheeler, being of sufficient courage and questionable sanity, is a member of South Pole 200 Degree Club. Temperature: —108 F. Nutus Extremis."

"We started this club, and we built the first steam bath out there in sixty-four. The OIC, being a doctor, he's not familiar with Seabees, and they'll do anything. So we decided we're goin' to build a steam bath. Took a fifty-five-gallon drum, cut two-thirds of it off, stuck some holes in her, welded in some fittings, put in some electric hot water tank heating elements, and a float valve in there with a water line comin' into it so it maintained its own level, and we wired that up to a thermostat and took a piece of sheet metal and cut a hole out of it and set that on top of this, and we run a pipe out into this room we built under the ice at Pole. In July, we decided to commission her, and we called the OIC up and said, doc, we goin' to fire up the steam bath. By this time, he's ready for anything, but all he says — he's shakin' his head and stayin' in his quarters a lot — he says, it won't work. So we told him, oh yeah, that's what they told Orville, and we set the thermostat at one hundred eighteen, and we're in there in our skivvies, about twenty minutes. Somebody says, let's go out and roll in the snow. So we opened the door and run upstairs, and that night at Pole it was a record cold, one hundred twelve point five below. And that ain't includin' any wind-chill factor, either, like they do at McMurdo in them familygrams to let the folks back home figure it's a lot colder than it is. That's straight cold, I don't know what it is with wind. Well, we rolled around out there for a few minutes, and it wasn't too bad; you couldn't feel it at the beginning. When they took our pictures, you couldn't see nothin', only this blob of steam your body's throwin' off. Breaks the monotony. It's entertainment.

"Always somethin' goin' on. One time we had this Second Class radioman named Juker, a black guy, and everyone liked him so much we bugged McMurdo, where he was supposed to stay, to let him winter with us at Pole. He didn't much want that, but he came along. Well, at our midwinter party, we told him we were goin' to lynch him, told him we were goin' to build a cross, fire it, and hang him off of it. And we made this tremendous cross of burlap and rags and wet it down with DFA, diesel fuel, and we burn this cross. Old Juker, he's out there watchin' and scared shitless, and he's takin' pictures of the scene, said he was goin' to fix our asses with the evidence later. I think he believed we was goin' to string him up.

"The troops were always doin' something to ol' Juke. One time, we had these two big water tanks, and I got busy one day and painted 'em titty pink. Took a basketball, cut it in half and epoxied them on the front of one of the tanks, took erasers off a couple pencils and stuck those on like nipples. Then I took a can of black paint, took off my shoes and socks, dipped my feet in the paint, and go up a ladder, and with the ladder and some ropes I strung over some pulleys, I run these footprints up the tank and down the side and I paint these big red lips around one of the nipples, and I run the footprints over to Juker's bunk, and then over to the OIC's quarters. Well, the OIC he gets up and sees the paint and he goes right for ol' Juke, says, Juke, you're the only black man up here, I know it was you; lookit them prints.''

Sea Daddy is roaring with laughter.

"You got to do that stuff to keep from goin' crazy sometimes. The biggest time we had was when Walt Disney showed up with Cardinal Spellman. Came down one Christmas, to Pole, the first time he ever come. That year we had what they called the Snow Mine. Dug a tunnel all the way down, like about two hundred feet long under the ice, and every fifteen feet there's a naked broad's picture. The OIC we had said, hey men, we got to get rid of all this shit, the Cardinal's comin' in. I said, no way will we get rid of this here tit and clit show of ours. Well, down at the end of the mine is our best picture, the biggest cunt you ever see, that big, I swear, I tell you you could have fell right into it. Well, the Card, he gets the biggest boot out of that, I'll tell you. He made me take him down there, he did. He's laughin' his ass off, gettin' a lot of chuckles, and he says, hey Sea Daddy, you boys been real busy, ain't you? He was a real good shit.''

"That was like another time,'' says Stormalong, "the chaplain comes in and looks at all these nudies on the walls and gets indignant and wants 'em all down. So we figured, okay, we'll take 'em down. We went around cuttin' all these jock shots out of those muscle mags, all these bulging guys in little briefs, and we hang these up, and when the chaplain comes back in we're all standin' around pattin' each other on the ass, and he made us take them down, and we put our women back up. Shrink did ask me one time what I'd do if I ever found a faggot in the station, and I told him I'd hide the dude, man, hide him and feed him, let him out when I need him."

"Hey, first time I went down," says Sea Daddy, "I had to go take my physical and it was a female doctor, the first one I ever seen, she's up in Boston. And she was a hot shit, I'll tell you, about forty and she knew all the angles. I was in the club one night and I got a little drunk and she used to come in and get drunk with us. So she says to me one night when she's shit-faced with me, say, Daddy, how you goin' to like it on the ice? I said, oh no, Miss Coyne, I ain't goin' to that Goddam ice, no way, lady, ma'am. And she says, why? And I said, 'cause I hitchhike to California every night, that's why. And she looks at me and she says, I don't care if you beat your meat without missin' a beat, you're goin' to that friggin' ice. She was a good shit. She came down to McMurdo once to see us, and she said, hey Daddy, how do you like the ice? I told her better'n I figured, I froze a hard-on one night and it's been with me for sixteen weeks now. She laughed, and you couldn't bust her for nothin', knew it all."

"That's one place they don't need women," says Stormalong. "One time they had this USARP there and she was goin' out in the field with her husband, and we issued 'em survival tent and sleeping bags, and she says, whoa there, I ain't sleepin' in no bag. So VX had to come up to one of the barracks, take a bed apart and put it in a helo, fly it out. They should told her to screw off."

"Yeah," says Sea Daddy, "like last year, we had to go to this buildin', tear it apart because we got this female officer, first one in there for the summer, had to fix up a whole new thing for her. Partition her off, get her away from the guys; it's a real pain in the ass. Like we got fifty-five-gallon drums to piss in, and half-gallon drums to stick under you when you need a shit, and now it's all these flushes and Kotex machines. We had a bunch of women here this past year, Holy Christ, had to change everything around to suit 'em, and if you make a eyeball at 'em — it's the least we can get after the work we do for them broads — Christ, you'll get your ass up to mast. There's a couple of them that are down here that are all right. They know they don't belong here, and they're all right. Most of the time they're just a pain in the ass.

"And speakin' of ass, I'd like to pack theirs, that's the most fun I have down here, packin' ass. Guy gets off a plane, and you tear off all his clothes, swoop 'em right off, and he's standin' naked as a hen in a meat house, freezin' his stones off and wonderin' what's happenin' next. We got a hole ready in the snow, and we bury him, ass and all, right up to his neck. I used to be out there all the time, sittin' up on my front-end loader, waitin' for 'em, with all my troops in back just waitin' for the signal to charge. All them nice tender gear that'd never been here before. It's the initiation. We get the word who's on the planes who never had their asses packed, and we'd grab 'em, officers and all, dig a hole and just jam 'em in, man. It was better in the old days, though; we'd dump coffee on 'em and Coke, and we'd piss on their heads, but now all we do is toss 'em in the hole, for a few minutes. But all that's changin' too, and they're takin' a dim view of that. I want to pack some female ass before I go out, though; just got to do it. Couple came off the plane the other day, but they got hustled out because they knew what was comin' since I was out there, sittin' up on my front-end loader with these animals leerin' in back. No sense fightin', we tell the boys, more you fight longer you'll stay in the snow, so just lie back and take it. One night we had a party and we had the Kiwis over to help us unload the planes, and they love parties, you know, and they helped us, we packed one hundred eighteen asses that night, world record, ought to be in Guinness. Man, we had some good times."

"Yup we did," says Stormalong. "Last time I was at Pole we reversed the holidays, that way we got 'em twice. We'd have Valentine's Day in August, somethin' like that, a hundred-eighty-degree turns, you know. And Ground Hog Day, we'd have that in December. That way we'd have an excuse to have two parties, one on the real holiday, one on Antarctic Time. Some of the parties in midwinter, that's when you're over the hump, Hump Night they called it, halfway home. Everyone's got to think up somethin' different to do. One night, this kid jumps up and runs over to the galley and gets a big Number Ten can of molasses. And another guy runs over to the barracks and gets a couple pillows, and we all take our clothes off and take a big paintbrush and paint each other head to foot with molasses, and we break the pillows over us. And we go into the bar and sit on the stools, get drunk, and everybody's lookin' at us and scratchin' their heads.

"After we get cleaned up, we said, hey, that was fun, let's do somethin' else. So the corpsman, he runs over to Sick Bay and gets some tincture of violet crystals, and we dump that into this whirlpool bath, stir it all up and we shaved our heads right down to the scalp, and we took our clothes off again and pile into the tub, dunk under, get out and dry off, then do it again until we were all purple. So we go back into the club, climb up on the stools, naked like that, all purple, gettin' drunk, and they're all lookin' at us and scratchin' their heads again. We had our dog, Marsala, and she's sittin' there lookin' at us, too, and she ain't never seen nothin' like this, you know. Well, Herbie says, she's just jealous 'cause she ain't purple, so we fix that in a heartbeat, and throw ol' Marsala's ass into the bath, too, only purple husky in the world, I bet.

"And, my God, it took a week to get all that tincture off us. We hung onto it just long enough for the reliefs, though, and when they come in we took Fat Sam, all purple, and set him naked on the shitbowl in the head, just his white cap on, and we'd send the reliefs one by one into the head to see the Ice King sittin' on his throne. They like to shit, I'll tell you.

"But you know, you really get to feel like you own the place after a while, you've put so much into it. One time, after I left Pole, I was sent to Pensacola and I'm down there thinkin', I wonder what it's like at Pole right now. So, I talked to the old lady one night, I was comin' due for orders again soon, and she says, what are you goin' to do? I says, well, I'm thinkin' about goin' back down on the ice. And she looks at me and she says, what are you, squirrel? But she's the kind, you know, Navy's my career, it puts bread and butter on her table and a roof over her head, so she don't feel it's her place to tell me how to run my life.

"So I'm back out here, and about eighty-five percent of the people winter over now are draftees. Well, they just don't have that feelin' about wantin' to go down like I do and do a good job. Some of them do, but most don't. When I visited Pole again, I sat down in the galley and I just wanted to cry. Like I see a year's work that we did that went right down the tubes. It was in good condition when we was there. Three crews after us didn't do nothin'. They did exactly what they had to do to exist, no effort to improve the place. They had all this gear I couldn't figure. Look, you've got people sittin' back there in Washington, and they dream up a prototype, they call it, put it into the Antarctic, and the more complicated it is the better. But they don't have to come down here and maintain it. Used to have what we called the KISS System. Which means, Keep It Simple, Stupid. They've done away with that. Forget the lessons of the past, like of the Eskimos. Take a Eskimo. He gets his ass lost stumblin' around in the boonies. He runs into two buildings. An igloo and a metal shack. That ol' Eskimo, he goes in the igloo.

Knows that metal is a good conductor of cold, sucks up the cold just like that. But what do they do here now? Do they take a lesson from the Eskimos? No. They build a building outta steel, lot of them. And they wonder why they got problems tryin' to heat it? Plus they bring the heat in through the roof. Now, any grade school kid'll tell you that heat rises. Your deck is twenty degrees, the overhead is one hundred. Well, you're not living on the overhead, you're down here. I'm on the whippin' post constantly and so is my crew because this buildin' is too cold. Why you silly sonsofbitches, I tell the brass, you built it outta steel and you didn't insulate it right. The guy that designed this thing is sittin' in D.C. with his striped-ass and he ain't never seen the Antarctic. Jesus Christ. And he's sittin' there designin' buildings for this place. Give me the old Jamesways anytime. Canvas, burlap, pack some snow around 'em and you've got the best insulation in the world. We had nine, ten guys in 'em at McMurdo, heaters on both ends, and shit, you lived like a king. Wanted to get your beer cold, just stick it under the floorboards. Even wintered over like that and it never bothered me.

"Biggest disappointment down here is that incinerator building over there. They spent Christ I don't know how much, over a million bucks. You know what we're usin' it for? You'll shit when I tell you. They're storin' vehicles in it, and stuff we got off the goddam ship, acetylene bottles and all that stuff."

"More waste down here than you imagine," agrees Sea Daddy. "I told the admiral one day, I says, you know what I'm goin' to do when I retire? I says, I'm comin' down here with seven ships and divin' equipment, and I'm takin' all that junk off the bottom. Be a millionaire in three months. Christ, we got two D-9s down there, I think I run 'em but once. Only thing they saved off of 'em was the winches. Took 'em out on the ice and bing, right down."

"I swear, there are assholes runnin' the show," says Stormalong. "Lookit, one of the best conductors is copper, for electricity, heat or cold. The worst thing to work on under the conditions down here is copper. And copper and saltwater don't get along worth a damn. So what do they do? They run copper line all the way from the ocean up to the top of Nukie Poo Hill, then they run it all the way down again. We spent all one summer, day and night, workin' on that line. Well, I thought up the idea of, hey, let's use fiberglass, it gets stronger as it gets colder, it's not affected by salt and so on. But I had to fight like hell to get 'em to do it. We did it, and there's no maintenance problem now. And, you know, these are scientists down here, makin' these decisions. Maybe they know how to tell one rock from another, but they sure as shit . . ."

20

Distaff

MCMURDO SOUND, Antarctica (AP) — Spring is in the air down here and the men of Operation Deep Freeze 1957 are grooming their beards. Women are coming.

They are two stewardesses on a Pan American Airlines flight scheduled to arrive here today — the first women ever to visit the base.

The men plan a contest for the benefit of the two women. Those with the blackest, the reddest, the longest and the sexiest beards will win prizes.

I agree with Sir Edmund Hillary that the peak is too difficult for women to climb. Men are more powerful and speedier than women, and without the Sherpas we would have never scaled it.
    — JUNKO TABEI, first woman to climb Mount Everest.

Somehow, I don't think it'll be knitting.
    — LT. ANN E. COYER, first Navy woman assigned to Antarctica, when asked what she planned to take up on the ice.

Women are here on the ice of this overwhelmingly male continent, but so few in number that journalists must still write stories about their presence. It is somewhat like covering a physician who plays in a dance band, or a garbage collector who turns author.

They have trickled in and out of here, generally on brief visits, ever since 1935 when Mrs. Klarius Mikkelsen, a whaling skipper's wife, became the first to set foot on the continent. The first women to winter over were Edith Ronne, wife of Captain Finn Ronne, the Norwegian-born U.S. naval explorer who made thirteen trips to polar regions, and Jennie Darlington, wife of Harry Darlington, chief pilot for

Ronne's 1947–194 Antarctic Expedition. (In her book, *My Antarctic Honeymoon,* Mrs. Darlington announced that she and her husband conceived a child while there. She also mentioned an ultimatum handed out prior to the decision that she would accompany the party: "We the undersigned feel that it would jeopardize our physical condition and mental balance if the Ronne Expedition, consisting of twenty men, were to be accompanied by one or more females. Therefore, we agree to form a united front to block that possibility. We are all prepared to leave the expedition in Valparaiso as a group if one or more women accompany it." Seven men signed the petition. Earlier, her husband had told her desperately, "Jennie, please understand. It's just that there are some things that women don't do. They don't become Pope or President, or go down to the Antarctic.")

The handful who are here now have come as scientist and lab technician, secretary, kitchen help, and field assistant. For the first time in nineteen years of Operation Deep Freeze, a WAVE has been assigned to the Support Force as head of the administrative department, and two U.S. women scientists have wintered over at McMurdo, the first to do so.

But no woman has ever wintered at the South Pole, and the first females to visit the spot only did so on November 11, 1969. Escorted by Rear Admiral David F. Welch, six women — Lois Jones, Eileen McSaveney, Kay Lindsay, Terry Lee Tickhill, and Pam Young of Ohio State University's geochemical department, and Jean Pearson, of the Detroit *News* — made a historic landing at the bottom of the world. However, to avoid any future argument as to which reached the Pole first the six joined hands and marched together down the ramp of the Hercules to the circle of flags that marks the spot.

Jan Boyd is twenty-one, and a secretary for Holmes &
Narver. She is a vibrant woman, and she talks excitedly about
her six months at McMurdo:

I was more than a secretary, I really was. I mean, you can't
figure you're going to go down there and sit and type, because you're not. You're gonna . . . unload a helo every once
in a while, drive a truck. If I had said, look, all I'm going to
do is sit here and type messages, well, that's not right, not
when I'm fully capable of driving one of those trucks, and I
did. All the time I was there I was a scheduled duty driver,
and you have to understand that I enjoyed this kind of thing.
There's something exciting about it.

I do think there was a feeling among some that I was a
little odd, individualistic, maybe. You know, I like to do odd
things. And I have an odd liking to drive trucks. Enjoyed it
and it got me out of the office. They were real big, heavy
trucks, and maybe this is not the thing that your ordinary
American woman might enjoy. It's kinda hard to explain.

I think people tended to put too much emphasis on the
fact that there were women there. I was treated very well,
though, and as far as working was concerned, I was treated as
an equal, no question about that. And the last thing I wanted
to do was take advantage of the fact that all these guys enjoyed helping me out. Once in a while you got tested, in a
way, like there was this one minor incident about halfway
through the season when the icebreakers had come in. It was
a Sunday afternoon and I had a few hours off and I was
walking the length of McMurdo to take a picture of an icebreaker. There was this group of sailor types or Coast Guard
types, maybe my age or a little younger, and I thought they
had been drinking. And I was coming up the road and there
was no way I could turn around. They said hello to me, and I
said hello, but they were testing me. They all wanted my

address, they wanted me to go into the club. Well, I really didn't want to sit around and drink all afternoon, I had to go back to work, and I think they were testing me. Here was this girl, who is reasonably good-looking, running around in a red parka, let's all see what we can get her to do. Well, I wasn't, you know, going to have anything to do with it. I took the job and my place down there too seriously. This is what I think they didn't realize; I didn't react the way they expected. Like, I said, you know, I just came out here to take some pictures, and I sit down, put my telephoto lens on, take a picture, and they'd ask me, where are you from, what do you do, you want to go out when you get back to the States, and I'd go, no, I don't know you, like that. It all went well, nobody was mad or anything like that, but that was the one time I felt I was tested.

No, I was not buddy-buddy with everyone. I spoke to everybody, and the people I didn't like, I just stayed away from. I made a point of not getting too close to any one individual. Like at McMurdo, there were about six hundred people, about a dozen women. I felt it was an honor to be there, and anything that, in the loosest sense, might reflect on anybody that was responsible for getting me there, I wouldn't do. I might have been secretly kind of drawn to one individual, but I would not let myself show that. In the States, I'd be very open. If I was interested in someone, I'd make it obvious that I was. But you can't do that there. . . . We'd go to the club, a little bantering, a little joking, ringing the bells. I don't think I bought a drink for myself the whole time I was there. I bought a drink for a guy once, he was out of money. . . . I made it a point to talk, but not getting into any close conversation, nor did I stick to any one person for any length of time. It sounds so callous the way I'm putting this, but you really can't. I mean, if I had wanted to let myself go I could have, but it wouldn't have proven a thing. . . .

I loved my work down there. Think of this, the big passenger flights. A lot of what we did was cargo, and we might run two or three people out to a station, and bring two or three people back, and the hardest thing for me to do was to locate three people who had gone three different ways when the flight time's been changed. And you'd get on the phone, you'd drive around the base, you'd get everybody you could think of until you rounded 'em all up.

But what's really neat is when you have forty passengers, forty. You have to spread the word that a flight's been changed. You tell one of 'em he's supposed to be here at a certain time, and it just flashes around the station, and they all arrive with all their baggage, and you've already arranged to have the manhaul come, and it pulls up in front of the building, and you say, okay, get on the truck, and I'd check 'em off, call names, you know, line 'em up, you know, throw 'em on the truck, close the door and tell the driver to go. And I . . . this sounds terrible, I know . . . I *enjoyed* that. Here I was, ushering forty people around, into the truck, you know, roundin' 'em up, count heads, throw 'em on the truck. . . . And I don't know why I enjoyed it. I would look forward to these big flights. . . . They were like a bunch of sheep, and I just herded them around. I had a little clipboard, all these names, and I'd take roll, into the truck, this huge truck like a semi. Not a tour-guide kind of thing or anything like that, it was very official, these people had a flight and I had to manifest them, and I'd give them a speech, make sure they had everything, and they're all happy 'cause they're going home, they're not mad at me, even when the flight is a little late. . . .

Mary Alice McWhinnie has made several trips to Antarctica to study the mechanism of low-temperature adaptation. A Ph.D. biologist from De Paul University, she has been working with krill and was one of the first two U.S. women ever to winter over.

Wintering over was very beneficial to my work. Summer down there is heavy traffic and I was so glad to see that last flight go out. You can't do the kind of detailed work we do during the summertime. I'll take thirty-second readings for five minutes, then one at ten, and it takes me fifteen minutes to do a whole run, and then I start in and do it again. After I've finished, I've done it for two hundred and five hours, through the day and the night, and around and around. I could never do that, with that kind of intense application, under summer conditions. . . .

No, I didn't mind the winter, though I think it did begin to wear on some people. It's much harder on the men; they must go out and dig ice holes and fish holes for us to provide a steady supply of fresh animals for our work. I'm a night owl and it didn't bother me at all, and I'd say to myself, where in the world can you go out in the morning, noon, and night and the Southern Cross is forever overhead? Just magnificent. And when the moon would come into a full phase it was like a fairyland. Just beautiful. I don't think it ever got monotonous for me. It is especially hard, of course, on married men. Concern for their families and so on. There are a lot of diversionary recreation interests that should sustain them, and I think it did sustain most. There will, however, always be that group who can't stand it wherever they go, but they are very few in number. I must say I didn't sleep for two months, but so what? You expect that.

Being a woman didn't present any special problems, but it could, I suppose. I think they have to be very, very careful who they send down there, very careful. I had been accustomed to living with large groups of men on the *Eltanin* on other trips down, ninety-eight always aboard and rarely more than two women. I just feel that a woman must treat all of them, always, with the same high esteem and respect. No woman can have a particular interest in this or that person, otherwise it could lead to utter bloodshed.

And I ask myself, how is it that I love a hundred and twenty-seven men? That, to me, is the real secret of making a thing like a winter-over go. Very quickly, the lower level ranks, whatever they may be, builders or ET's, if they're excluded as important persons, you're just going to intensify their feelings of isolation. They must be as important as the commanding officer. They have to be approached as equals all the way, absolutely.

In some ways, I suppose the men did give more attention because I am a woman, but generally I think not. I used to say, now, please, I'm no different than the other guy, I have walked into your world and I can't disturb it. You have your job to do and I have men in my party. My photographer was outstanding, and that's why I have slides already of the research, barely get it up on a graph and it's already on a slide. And the men who cut holes in the ice and the men who got my instruments working properly, wonderful. But I like to believe they'd give this to anybody. It did become evident that in the minds of some of them was the idea that possibly I didn't belong there. But, this was a mistake on their part, they decided ultimately; this was really all right. And they said this quite freely. And I'd say, look, I know I've walked into your private world and if you pay no attention to me I would understand, fully.

Whatever the success might have been last summer, when there were a large number of girls there, it was not the howling success people thought. Through the winter, I think, the truth emerged. A lot of young girls, for reasons that are psychologically too complex, string a guy along, ride him into the ground, do a lot of things, and there was a lot of that in the summer, an awful lot, and it embittered many of them wintering over. It's terribly dangerous, really.

And I'm not sure, now, that there is a place for a woman unless she remembers that she's there to do a job. If she does this and doesn't decide to live all other aspects of her femininity, then she belongs there. But when she becomes too human . . . And I wouldn't say I was cold; I don't think anyone there could say that, or would say it. . . . But, you just have to have a deep respect for the man's feelings, for his feelings, and his, and his and his. The woman has much more responsibility than the man in situations like that. . . .

Yes, I'd winter over again, both for the work and for what I feel I might be able to contribute to lessen the dreariness that seems to set in on some people. It is natural for that to happen, though, for their wives are home, or their girl friends, or the opportunity to date. I would like to think that the women there do make some contribution to keeping their spirits bouncy and their outlook healthy.

We would go to the Acey-Deucey Club every other Thursday night because these three fellows would play their guitar and they'd say, hey, why don't you guys come. Well, there would be a bell go off whenever we'd walk in, and I'd say, what's that crazy bell? Well, that was to announce to the group who may or may not have noticed that two ladies had just walked in, and therefore watch the language. And I said, I don't hear anything, I really don't, you guys are free and you just live as you want, don't feel badly that we come and go. I think they relaxed later. For instance, several came over and they'd say, this is the enlisted man's club, and they appreciated that we didn't think we were too good to go into their place. Apparently many of the USARP women during the summer go to the Chief's or the Officers' Club. But there's the difficulty. They'll say, I'm going to pick for me the top. That man in the engineroom is just as important to me as the guy sitting up on the bridge. Anything else is dead wrong, for each contributes to our support. I wrote several a letter to that effect three, four weeks after we got there. I had been getting this sense of, you know, I'm nobody, or something like, you call this support of science but all I see is the laundry machine seven days a week, that kind of thing. They were grateful for the letters. . . .

Once, I was walking alone, and it was dark, and I could hear someone coming at me. So I said, excuse me, but who are you? And the voice replied, it's Bryan, don't be afraid. I said, I'm not afraid, I just wanted to know which one of the family you were. And that's what it was, really, a truly harmonious group. But I can see where it would be very dangerous to pay too much attention to one person. . . .

I remember when I went on the ship the first time in 1962, it seemed that it took some time for Admiral Tyree to adjust to this whole business. And I took a young student along with me, a very careful and wonderful girl, but one day I was coming out of my cabin and I see a machete go by in someone's hands and he's going after another guy, and I said, oh my God, I hope that guy makes it. Well, he did but I never went to sleep on that cruise because little Ellie was playing this one against that one and they were practically killing each other, and would you believe it, a year later they found her dead on a street in Valparaiso. And I said it's no real surprise to me because I've never seen anybody play men against men like that. Men in isolation can tell a lot of things. Say I'm nice to you, really nice, and to you and to him and all the other guys. They can tell if it's perfunctory, that you're saying, I'd rather be with him.

It was a very positive experience for me, and you learn some things, like there is no human being who isn't a bit of an angel. You'll see it in everyone if you'll just give it the time; you've got to give it the time. I used to come back from the lab at two or three or five in the morning and I'd always go into the dining room for coffee because I can't go to bed without coffee, and there'd always be a few guys around, and I'd want to just go and chat with them. I never saw more pictures of wives and kids than then; these men need someone to reflect their enthusiasm.

I can't say that I missed much while I was there. If anything it was probably the instant cutoff from the persons you work with, your family. My mother is seventy-nine, and two years ago we knew she had terminal cancer. But she was so well that on New Year's Eve in Chicago, at a party, Mom was dancing. Eleven days after I left she collapsed. She was in the hospital, not expected to live. Well, they were very careful to sift the information for me, but soon you'd have to catch the drift. She had been going in to the hospital every Friday for blood, and they were simply holding that from me. But beyond that, missing my family, I was busy, I think, learning about the soul of a lot of people.

There was Greg. Only met him in January when I arrived, and he was the biology lab manager, the senior representative for Holmes & Narver, twenty-six years old. We worked quite closely together, and at night I always went back to the lab after dinner. A group of men would sit in the next lab, playing guitar, drums, and sax, and Greg was one of them, learning guitar. Then they'd disappear over to General Services to tape-record their performance. Greg would come into the lab often, have a cigarette and a cup of coffee. The night that he disappeared I was working at my bench, using a syringe that was faulty. And I said, I'll go tell Greg. Well, he had his parka on and we sat for about an hour, just chatting, and he talked about his days in the desert which he loved so much, about tomorrow and how he was going to talk to the NSF rep in New Zealand, Alice was coming down to New Zealand and they'd be married, and about his guitar, he wasn't good enough, had to practice more. We talked about just everything.

And he looked at the clock and said, oh, it's ten-fifteen, I have to go. And I stayed in the lab until eleven-thirty and then decided to go home. Well, there had been a truck parked outside when I arrived and now it was gone. Okay, that meant he was gone, and I kicked myself again and again afterward that I didn't ask him where he was going. But then, I never asked anyone where they were going, it was really none of my business. And had he told me, I still wouldn't have done anything about it. He had gotten so accustomed to jumping into a truck and driving somewhere without calling the firehouse. . . .

No one could accept it, the accident that killed him, his truck off the road, and I couldn't find any of his closest friends for twelve hours after it happened. I looked for them. I walked to the field center, to the Acey-Deucey, to the garage, to Special Services. I thought, oh my God, have they been so depressed that they did something foolish?

For days afterward, no one was evidently sad, but everyone was silent. No one had much to say, just nod a greeting at each other. The CO and the XO thought it would be proper to close the club and have no movies that night. And I said, what do one hundred twenty-nine people do when they do nothing? Maybe better they do something. So they reversed the decision, but not very many went to the show or the club. It was so quiet for three or four weeks. It hit hard, very hard. The winter and the darkness and being closed in made it worse. And it didn't seem wise to make any announcement about where Greg would rest, and that began to bother them. They'd say things like, I suppose he's frozen somewhere, and I would say, yes, with the greatest respect and care. And then out of the blue, someone said, you know, I really liked that kid. . . .

A conversation with Sister Mary Odile Cahoon, who win-
tered over with Dr. McWhinnie. I tell her that before she
came down on the ice, I was talking to a group of workmen
and they said a couple of women were going to winter over,
and one of them said, "Hey, wait a minute, one of them's a
nun." And someone said, "So what; she's a woman, ain't
she?"

(Laughs) Well, I don't know, because neither Mary Alice
or I were subjected to anything but very nice relationships.
So it wasn't . . . There was a young woman who went down
and I guess there was some trouble. In fact, they kept her
isolated from the group that had wintered over. Tensions do
run high. . . . I had been used to working predominantly
with men at Argonne summers, and being older than most
of the men down there, there was more of a relationship
similar to one with an older sister, or a maiden aunt sort of
thing. There wasn't a problem, certainly, and I don't think
we made it any more difficult for the men, as two women. I
think if there were young girls there over a winter it would
have been more of a strain on the fellows. In the bar, the
men were always very cordial about asking us over, and they
were careful about letting us know if they thought it was
going to be kinda rough. They were very considerate. I remember that at one of the All-Hands parties, at sundown
and midwinter and at sunrise again, at one of those there
was going to be a skit of some sort, and one of the officers
told me that he thought maybe I ought to go to the powder
room or something during it. My feeling is that they should
be able to do whatever it was they were going to do, whatever would fit in, and my being there shouldn't inhibit
them. I also appreciated being warned.

Women's place on the ice?

It's a hard thing to get at. If women are in science, and science is there, then women need to go there as scientists. And yet, I can see a problem in wintering over. I know that some of the young scientists who would like to stay over feel discriminated against. But the isolation is such a long period, and it cannot be an indiscriminate thing, this selection of women.

My feeling about, say, straight exploration, is that I would suspect it is partly a male attribute, that drive to conquer the elements, overcoming the cold, the wind, and so on. And, speaking for myself, I don't feel that challenge. By that, I don't feel I have to go out and prove that I can survive on a camping trip. But, I do feel the inner sort of exploration of science, and that's not bound up with just physical endurance. It could very well be that there are women who do feel they want to be involved in endurance of the physical sort. But I would suspect it is primarily a man's thing.

Has being a nun helped in any way, on the ice?

Well, first off I don't find there is any conflict between my religious life and science. If, as members of a religious community, we have to run institutions of higher education, then we have to be professionally with it. . . . We have to be as much a scientist, if we are scientists, as any other scientist. I find that I must be active professionally, and for me biology isn't just teaching it. It must also include research, and I must be involved, totally.

In many ways, though, being a nun has helped. I don't, for one thing, have the distractions of family, the responsibility, all of the financial things, housing and food and so on, are taken care of. It frees up my time tremendously. The support of the community is a factor, too, because a single person might have a good deal of freedom but be very lonely. But even with all of this, there are distractions in a college setting; teaching does get to be kind of minor because you have administrative duties and this committee to work with and that one. But down on the ice, there are no committees, no distractions, you can work as much as you want. . . .

On occasion, you'd suddenly be aware of . . . You'd be restless, and there was nothing to do to relieve it. You couldn't go off in a car and drive someplace; you couldn't go on a shopping spree because maybe the ship's store wasn't open. Yes, we got those feelings but we usually had enough work, grinding out research, and our minds were very active. Movies every night, too, a pretty good library, some sports, the clubs were open, always available for those looking for that sort of thing. There was always something, but it was closed in, no question there. Like, the meals were tremendous, but you couldn't decide, well, I'll go someplace else tonight for supper. There just wasn't any other place. Sometimes, this would kind of come in on you. . . .

There were enough people, one hundred twenty-nine. And maybe community living helped me there, too. I'm used to going to the dining room with the same people. It's similar in a way, Navy living. I found it surprisingly very much like what I've been used to at the school. Used to having to put up with regulations for the whole crowd, that everything can't work individually because there are too many people. I was struck with the way the men helped each other and were really nice to each other, and I thought this was very much like the community spirit, and it had never before occurred to me that the Navy might be like a religious community. When someone was down, you'd always find someone there trying to help him out, he's really uptight and about to do something not too bright, and there's someone helping.

Professionally, the advantage of being there is obvious. But it's also done other things for me, I think. At home, if you feel tension, you can go for a ride, or find somebody, do anything to distract yourself. Down there, because there aren't all these distractions, you have to work out all these tensions that come along. You either work them out or you say, okay, so I'm tense today, and you go about your work. You get to face yourself more, I think, on the ice, instead of distracting yourself. You know what you can deal with. I think it was a wonderful experience. The thing I didn't know how I'd cope with was the darkness, and I didn't know how it would be. But now, looking back on it, I can say it was a time of peace and quiet and beauty. I really much preferred it over the sunlight. I found the twenty-four hours of light extremely tiring. Noisy in the summertime, the coming and going of planes and so on. With that constant light you'd work through a day, go to supper, and then it's broad daylight, so you go back to the lab and work some more, and you think, this is nonsense, and you go up to housing and everybody is sitting around in broad daylight, and who goes to bed in daylight? You get up next morning tireder than when you went to bed. But the darkness. There was a kind of reflectiveness that came with it, and I appreciated it. . . .

Jerry and Elena Marty work for Holmes & Narver, Inc.; he in the company's headquarters in Anaheim and as resident construction engineer in Antarctica, she as a secretary. They have just finished a six-month tour together on the ice, one of the few husband-and-wife teams to do so. Jerry has a B.S. degree in industrial technology from Wisconsin State University, and Antarctica was a place he'd always wanted to visit.

"I'm from a small country town," he says, "and the school I went to had nine students. It was a one-room school, and we walked to it, and I used to lie on the floor next to an old stove that we'd throw chunks of wood into, and I'd read books like *Dash to the South Pole,* and I'd read and reread *Call of the Wild,* and I always thought it'd be terrific to go to the South Pole or the North Pole. I read all about Byrd and Siple, and I'd say that someday I'm going to go there. My parents, of course, never believed me. When I was a sophomore in college I started writing letters, to NSF and to Holmes & Narver, and when I graduated I landed the job in Anaheim. Finally got down on the ice as a general field assistant in 1969, worked at Byrd Station."

Elena says, "One of the things that first attracted me to Jerry when I met him was that he had been to Antarctica. It's funny that something like that should have appealed to me, but, you know, here was this person who had pursued something enough to get there, and that really attracted me."

They are a handsome young couple, dressed modishly again at last now that the experience is over.

Elena: When we first got down there, I was not really prepared for the way things were. There was, for instance, this thing that I really wanted to look pretty instead of just grungy old Antarctica, and I really wish I had brought some nicer clothes. What I did was bring my old jeans, no new pants and so on, but I wish I had. I suppose that after a while, I really wanted to have an identity. I wanted to be Elena, you know, feminine, right? I wanted to wear a little makeup, not necessarily for someone else, I just wanted to make myself feel pretty. I did try to do that as time went by, but it just wasn't fulfilling enough. That was one of the big impressions it left on me down there. Two and a half months and it wasn't bad, but after that, you get into the third and the fourth month, around Christmastime, and it just starts to really bear down. You could actually lose your physical identity. I mean, at the beginning you're flattered by all the attention that you're getting, people see a parka with long hair rather than short flowing out, a girl, you know. But after a while they're used to seeing you around, and you start to yearn for a little more identity. I'm sure a man would feel the same way.

Jerry: I don't think I had any confrontations with myself in terms of identity, in terms of wanting to be better dressed. There are some articles of clothing I would like to have brought along, and I will next time. I will admit that a small percentage of the time I'm tired of being dirty, untrimmed hair, the same clothes day in and day out, the only change of wardrobe when I washed my jeans. I had a new shirt, and I changed that every two weeks, and that's not uncommon in construction. To put on a new shirt with a pair of jeans that had just been washed . . . I guess I did feel different when I did that, maybe my personality resurfaced to what it ought to be.

Elena: It was a welcome relief when we got to New Zealand. I spent nearly two and a half hours in the bathroom. It's a difficult situation down on the ice. There are so many men, and when a woman comes on, all heads turn. I mean, you really can't do much without being noticed. You walk into a bar and it's like Christmas. We didn't go into the clubs too often, primarily because we really wanted some time to ourselves. But when we did go it was like everybody was buying us drinks. It really did boost morale to have Jan, the other girl from Holmes & Narver, there. Just our presence, not necessarily our personalities, just the presence of women seems to boost morale tremendously.

Jerry: But I think the reason it boosts morale is because men who are in isolation, away from the opposite sex, are subconsciously trying to assure themselves that they can still carry on an intelligent, meaningful discussion with a female. If they've been there two months, three months, and they see a woman, regardless of her marital status, her position on the ice, well, they go to that individual and they're seeking that reassurance that they can yet communicate with a female. What happens is that you go into the mess hall, a social gathering of any kind. Strangers will come up and start talking to the girls, to Elena, and they'll rattle on endlessly and aimlessly about nothing. I think it's simply that they're struggling, trying to reassure themselves that when they get home they'll still be able to talk to their girl friends, their wives, their mothers. And if there are two people, or more, and one is talking to Elena and I'm present, the other individual will talk to me, reassure me that he can still carry on a conversation in a group setting and not just talk about the things that two men would talk about if they were confined for six months. He'll talk about topics of the day, changes in his home state and so on. . . . I do think there was excessive acknowledgment of me. I could not go anywhere without . . . I was a derivative of her purpose in terms of morale boosting, I picked up the overflow.

Elena: The men were always wanting to talk about their families. They were definitely relating to the fact that I was a woman; they were trying to put themselves into a social frame.

Jerry: It just got to the point where we would actually avoid contact with crowds, not so much because we didn't want to talk to people or that we weren't interested in their views or that we were introverts. But it was such a burden. I couldn't just sit down and talk with one person. People would come up and put their hand on my shoulder and say, boy, it's really great for you to have your wife here. That was always the opening statement, and from that point on I knew I had that person talking to me for a long time, if I wanted. I found I couldn't put up a . . . pseudointerested display after a while. These people never changed. There was always *x* number of people, and they converged on us everywhere we went, and after a while there was only so much to talk about.

Elena: And, you know, there really wasn't anyplace to go to get away. The only place you could go was your quarters and those were such that . . . There was a very small lounge area with a couch and it was really cold there. It wasn't conducive to relaxing or to writing a letter, not at all a getaway. For the first month and a half I was screaming for privacy. You could hear the guy across the hall breathing, and you can imagine what that did to our marital relationship.

Jerry: And when we were eating. We had the crowds converge on us because we were married, and there was always a problem with my sitting down with Elena, alone. I never could do that and actually talk just to her at dinner. Long tables and twelve chairs to a side, the person next to you talking about his scientific experiments, someone else talking about home, and everybody at the table wanting to talk to a woman.

Elena: I think, though, that we handled it pretty well as a married couple. But I think there could be situations where you just weren't so tolerant and you shut these people out. Mostly everybody there is single, and the fact that we wanted to be alone might have caused some trouble. I did try to distribute myself as evenly as possible on those social occasions, when we'd go to one of the clubs, and I did enjoy everybody. Those people that I did feel an intense dislike for, I just avoided. There were a couple of situations when a fellow would drink too much, just as in any bar. I've learned, though, that a girl staying away and keeping to herself in a bar might be more noticeable to a drunk, especially if you're the only girl in the place. He's going to want to know why you haven't come around to see him. . . . Everybody was more than happy to escort me to make sure I was being treated with respect, though, and I must say there never were any overtures made. I was quite surprised at that, to be perfectly honest. I was really treated like a lady.

Jerry: I think that goes back to the fact that the reason people were kind to you was that self-identity thing they were struggling to retain. They could still be human beings. They didn't really see you but the people they loved back home.

Elena: That's possible. But also, you know, the more I was treated like a lady the more I wanted to act like one. Like some of the bad words that I had learned. I just found myself not saying them there. It was much easier being a real genuine feminine lady. I got more that way as time went on, too. Although, in those clothes I didn't really feel very feminine. I worked in Jerry's office with the construction crews and those guys can become a little foul-mouthed, though I'm sure they held back quite a bit for me. They used to call me Construction Momma. . . . Jerry and I found that being isolated like that, a situation that could make or break a marriage, definitely brought us closer together. It made me, for instance, a little more understanding of Jerry's work and his ideas. Seeing how he works, being right there with him; a lot of wives can't do that sort of thing.

Jerry: We did become closer, we did learn to understand one another, and we became more tolerant of each other's goals and desires. We really learned that you do need time away, together, away from home, and you learn things about each other. We've been married three years, and I learned things about Elena that just astounded me, things I had never known before, and that I probably wouldn't learn in the next ten years. They're all about how she acts under pressure, about her anxieties, even her politics. If you can tolerate the pressures, recognize the demands, you can learn on the ice. But if you don't recognize them, you'll give up, and this is where you'll lose, if you're married and together there, your tie. And you're ready for a divorce in three weeks.

Elena: I noticed, for instance, that when Jerry is under pressure he doesn't blow up like a lot of people do. He is very patient. There were several circumstances where people would be very trying and I could just tell that these people were just grating on him. Well, he'd sit there so patiently and explain. I can't believe the leadership ability that I saw in him. It's something that I knew in the back of my mind was there, but I did learn a lot about how to deal with him on certain planes.

Jerry: We wouldn't recommend doing it for twelve months straight. Now that we're through, we'll demand our own time separate from the other. I don't think it could last for more than six months.

Elena: We worked closely together on the ice. I was his secretary, but I don't think I could handle that back home at the company. Like Jerry says, we have to have our own time away from each other. While he's at work, I'll be at home now; I won't be going back to the company. We did learn, on the ice, the importance of having private time. One of the things that Jerry laid down the law about was that when we fought I was not to raise my voice, I was not to cry. Let's see, Jerry, what else did you restrict me to? I did break out crying a couple of times, in the confines of my office, though, when everybody was out, and I did raise my voice. Antarctica is sort of restricting in that way, I suppose, and a husband-wife thing like crying, and yelling and screaming at one another, that's all normal at home. . . . But these things aren't done there.

Jerry: Another thing is we enjoy drinking wine together, and sometimes we enjoy drinking a lot of wine together. We agreed before we went down that the consumption of wine would be minimal because of the job and because we'd probably raise our voices when we were talking in our room, and we'd probably be heard throughout the barracks. But, you know, all the rules and regulations you establish before you leave really aren't that important, and when you get there it's a whole new game.

Elena: One of the things was . . . I'm a very affectionate person, and I would always reach for Jerry's hand, no matter what. I never thought anything about it, even when we were wearing those big gloves, I'd want to hold his hand, that's all. It's just a habit. Jerry would get so mad. He'd say everyone around here is denied this, why should I be demonstrating the fact that we're married and he has his wife with him and so on and can show her affection. Maybe he had a point.

Jerry: I desperately wanted to hold her hand, to become affectionate, but I just felt it was probably the wrong place. I think a couple should recognize that if they go as husband and wife, and they are as affectionate there as they are in everyday life, I think this could cause a few problems after a few months in Antarctica. After the third or fourth month, morale starts to dip a little bit. I have the opportunity to hold my wife's hand, Mr. X doesn't, so I feel I shouldn't.

Elena: The place is different, there's no question about that. It was really terrible, in fact, at times. McMurdo is large, but it gets so small, like a town, and gossip travels from one end to the other, men worse than women in some ways. They rumor and gossip, and it got so bad that whenever I heard something about someone, I'd figure right away that it was nothing but overemphasis. Some of the single girls had more of a problem than the married ones, I'd suspect. If they were seen in the company of someone, people would automatically assume something was going on, and they'd start talking. There were two girl messcooks hired by the Navy, there was Jan, two girls with the Dry Valley drilling project. I had hoped for a little more camaraderie, but there was none. I hoped the single girls would all get together and talk, but I was really surprised that they didn't. Nothing, absolutely nothing. Maybe it was the caste system. . . . One thing I didn't notice while on the ice was the amount of prejudice I was up against. It wasn't until people started leaving that they'd pour out their hearts, tell me exactly how they felt about women's presence, and how that opinion had changed for some of them. They'd say they really enjoyed my company, that they had always thought women had no place there. They said it with profuse thanks for my being there, and they'd say I had boosted morale, and their minds had been changed, and that maybe women did fit in. . . . They didn't really see too much of what I was doing as a worker. They had more occasion to meet me on a social level, and if I could do my job and still be a social person, well, they liked that. In my fantasies, you know, I used to wonder if I could have gone along with Scott or Amundsen on those expeditions, and I do believe a woman could do such things, of course. I myself couldn't. But I know some women who could and who would if they weren't held down, trained not to do something instead of trained to do it. And if they were given the opportunity to go on these treks, they'd make their own facilities. There's too much emphasis on that business of facilities. You hear a lot of people argue that, well, it's a lot easier for a man to go out there, you know, dig a hole in the snow and go to the bathroom or something. A woman would just make do, and she's just as imaginative. So, no, I don't feel that exploring is purely a male endeavor.

Jerry: I most definitely think an explorer in the eighteen hundreds and the nineteen hundreds could have been a female. I've seen Elena put up with things, like when there weren't bathroom facilities. She just went outside and used an old coffee can. But it's more than that, of course. Dig into history; in the covered wagon days, for instance, when the man got shot off the driver's seat, it was the woman who took the thing into town, and with the kids. I think we could go out now and get women, even old women, to lead a women's expedition to the South Pole, and they'd do all right. I would have no qualms about following a woman leader on an expedition.

Elena: I think that one of the next hurdles, in Antarctica, is putting women in positions that are not necessarily associated with women. Like, Jan and I went down as secretaries, and I know I found myself doing a lot more administrative work, and I saw her doing a lot more than some people who were down there. They could have been functioning as secretaries, and we could have done a lot more, too. But, we were women, and women are shoved into secretarial positions. One of the situations that came up, going to the Pole. When the time came for us to petition to visit the Pole, they didn't want to let us go. We were special, we were girls, we were different. They didn't want us out of the nest at McMurdo, and we would argue that we were the same as everyone else that gets to go, how come? It was almost insulting. We were treated as females, which was lower. I've been a secretary for a number of years, but I feel I can extend myself further. On the ice, I would often be given responsibilities, and often those would be taken away from me by someone who wanted to prove himself. I was low on the totem pole, and I'd get trampled on. Hello, hello, I'd feel like saying, please notice me.

21

The Pole

And yet even today we hear people ask in surprise: What is
the use of these voyages of exploration? What good do they do
us? Little brains, I always answer to myself, have only room for
thoughts of bread and butter.

— AMUNDSEN

We stampede noisily from a lecture on the fossil tetrapods of
Coalsack Bluff and the theory of continental drift. We flee
from the mind-twisting prose read to us from the hallowed
pages of *Science* journal: "Nearly horizontal beds of the Bea-
con Supergroup rest on a pre-Devonian erosion surface that
was cut across a metasedimentary and metavolcanic basement
intruded by Ordovician granitic rocks." We dash, shouting
our glee, to our barracks for our survival kits, uncaring that
someone has just found a small dicynodont and several skeletons of *Thrinaxodon* and they want us to write it up.

Going to the Pole at last, and I do not give a damn at this
moment, really, about what they are doing there, building
their station, studying atmospheric particulates, or taking
their photometer measurements that indicate the boundaries
of the auroral oval are much wider if subvisual auroras are
included.

I simply want to go, so fiercely that I am trembling as I
pull on my trousers, heavy with liner, and the cloddish
thermal boots of rubber. So it's been discovered, who cares? I
want to go anyway; would anyone not who has come this far,
to the farthest faraway place? I do not want this to be an
opportunity that cannot be regained once lost, and the rea-

son is no more complicated than nourishment for a craving mind, and some ego-tripping. It has little to do with self-discovery. No Yaqui Indian's questing for a beneficial spot, no Jerry Rubin plunge into rebirthing with est. The pleasure I am after right now — and I am sure I will know this most emphatically when it is over — won't be for life, only for curiosity, for a quick jump of the nervous system. Thank God for the boredom, the rewriting, and the summer shrinks, for the lectures on ionic movement in the Dry Valleys and glacial deposits and lateral moraines. They are the foils, not to be taken seriously in themselves, that set off the excitement and make it more delicious. Live and enjoy and do different things, and I am sorry, Tolstoy, but at this moment, as I clump heavily in baggy clothes, weighted down with survival bag, toward the big-bellied LC-130 sitting there on its skis, fat and silver-gleaming, orange tail sticking up high over the blue ice, black-tipped nose pointing south, I am sorry, but the sole meaning of life is not to serve humanity, not now anyway. Perfection of my moral nature can wait, too, until the tryst is over.

We pile inside — and it is drab and bare, in sharp contrast to the bright shine of the outside fuselage — and settle ourselves facing each other across the aisle in canvas-mesh hammocks strung against the bulkheads. The pilot drops in to say hello. It is the gray-haired crew-cut man from Skyland. He grins and tells us we're in good hands when we fly with All-State, that's what they called him in college. He warns us it's going to be a little drafty; this here crate isn't one of the newer LC-130R models, which have, we might like to know, greater range and endurance and an increased allowable takeoff gross weight. This is a 130F, but, he adds, WTF, right? All-State also says he's sorry, but it'll be very noisy, and though they can't supply all of us with helmets, the loadmaster, who's already passing it around, will get us some stuff to deaden the sound. For a minute I think it's pills he's giving out, but the large jar contains wax, in the shape of little pellets. We jam these in our ears. "We come a long way, ain't we, baby?" chuckles the loadmaster. Dacey Higgins wonders why they just can't give us swimmers' earplugs; they'd fit better and they aren't apt to melt in there and then freeze up when we hit the ice. "Infection, man," shouts the loadmaster as All-State revs up his four engines. The loadmaster has braced himself against the door. "It ain't clean, man, we'd have to sterilize every fuckin' plug every fuckin' trip." "What a kick in the ass," says Dacey. Before he came down he had to make one of his regular visits to Sick Bay, get the wax buildup plucked out so he could hear straight. "Now," he says, "fuckin' Navy's puttin' it back in after they pay to get it out, sonofabitch."

Into the air at last, propellers sputtering and billowing steam. It is breezy and chilly because the loadmaster is having difficulty keeping the door closed. Every so often it pulls loose a crack and he has to lean against it, closing it at last, with a crate to hold it shut and tied with a piece of rope to make sure. We glance warily at it, and at each other across the aisle, making desperate hand signals because of the wax plugs.

It'll be about as many flying miles as from Boston to Chicago, but slower than commercial, at about 23,000 feet. After a few minutes we are unstrapped and on our knees, peering out of portholes down at the sunlit white flatness of the Ross Ice Shelf rolling by below. As vast as France is that snowplain, 200 feet thick now beneath us, more than 1,500 feet deep farther inland where it welds to the base of the Transantarctic Mountains, over which we will fly. Ross was stopped by it, Shackleton and Amundsen and Scott marched across it, and on it now a dozen or so USARP glaciologists and biologists are camped, trying to understand its motion and its history of change, studying the nature of the underlying organisms and the sedimentary processes of the sea floor, measuring the vertical motions caused by the tides beneath it. And somewhere in that shelf, hidden under many feet of snow or already swept into the sea with the glacier's creep, lie buried the collapsed tent of Scott's last camp and the frozen bodies of Scott and Wilson and Birdie Bowers.

Robert Falcon Scott's last expedition, aboard the *Terra Nova,* was a financially more modest enterprise than his *Discovery* journey. While its sledging and scientific equipment was first-rate, it was jammed and overloaded into a vessel, along with 65 men, that as Cherry-Garrard put it, was "picked up second-hand in the wooden-ship market, and faked up for the transport of ponies, dogs, motors and all the impedimenta of a polar expedition, to say nothing of the men who have to try and do scientific work inside them." The expedition's goals, however, were no less ambitious than *Discovery*'s. It had a larger scientific staff than had ever before been taken south, and the aim was to build on the successes the previous voyage had scored in research and exploration. The overriding goal, however, was to attain the Pole. Shackleton had come close, and there was personal rivalry between him and Scott. Other countries, too, were contemplating similar dashes, probably out of a growing awareness that Antarctica might be an exploitable resource.

But it was in England that the time was right for heroes, and there was an urgency to remedy what the London *Times* referred to as the "depressing materialism" of the age. It was the aftermath of Queen Victoria's reign, a time of increasing disillusionment with traditional moral values, of religious conviction challenged by insolent science. National pride was lost, some felt, and in an effort to regain it, fervent nationalists touted their jingoism and the belief that every-thing English was inherently superior.

In the temper of this time, Scott outlined the plan for his second expedition, announcing, "The Main object is to reach the South Pole, and to secure for the British Empire the honour of this achievement."

Edward Wilson, more scientist than explorer, tempered the sentiment in a letter to his father: "No one can say that it will only have been a Pole-hunt, though that, of course, is a sine qua non. We *must* get to the Pole; but we shall get more, too, and there will be no loopholes for error in means and methods if care in preparation can avoid them. I can promise you it is work worth anyone's time and care and I feel it is really a great opportunity. We want the scientific work to make the bagging of the Pole merely an item in the results."

It is highly unlikely, however, that Scott ever would have obtained financial backing for his expedition — particularly in the face of growing unemployment — had not his objec-tive been the Pole. His earlier attempts to play down the Pole quest in favor of scientific achievement gave way, ulti-mately, when he was confronted with a short-money situation and the strong will of the renowned explorer and president of the Royal Geographical Society, Sir Clements Markham, who was not one to let science stand in the way of glory.

Scott and the *Terra Nova* left England in June, 1910, ar-riving at McMurdo Sound in January. Unable to base again at Hut Point because of ice conditions, he built the Cape Evans shack, returning later to the first hut to stage the trek to the pole.

Scott's plan called for the use of three motor sledges, nine-teen Manchurian ponies, and thirty dogs for transport. A ton of sledging stores, fuel oil, and fodder for the horses was hauled to a depot to be used by the polar party on the way back from the Pole, 130 miles from Hut Point, on the Barrier. The cairn, marked by a flag on a bamboo pole, was called One-Ton Depot. Because of adverse weather and travel conditions, it was placed 36 miles from where it had been intended. Had the original plan been carried out, the subsequent tragedy might not have occurred.

On the polar journey itself, the sledges were to carry supplies as far across the Ice Shelf as possible, then the ponies and dogs to the foot of the Beardmore Glacier. From there, the dog teams would return to base and the ponies be killed for meat. It was Scott's attitude toward the dogs — a mixture of compassion, doubt about their ability to perform, and abhorrence at using them for food — that has drawn much criticism. "A dog must be either eating, asleep or interested," he wrote. "His eagerness to snatch at interest, to chain his attention to something, is almost pathetic. The monotony of marching kills him. This is the fearfullest difficulty for the dog-driver on a snow-plain without leading marks or objects in sight. The dog is almost human in its demand for living interest, yet fatally less than human in its inability to foresee." But it is another of his comments that is more telling of his rather stuffy, sometimes autocratic, manner of dealing with such matters, and in the end it may have cost him his life and those of the four others he chose to accompany him. "In my mind," he observed grandly, "no journey ever made with dogs can approach the height of that fine conception which is realized when a party of men go forth to face hardships, dangers and difficulties with their own unaided efforts and by days and weeks of hard physical labour, succeed in solving some problem of the unknown. Surely, in this case, the conquest is more nobly and splendidly won."

An admirable view, but from Hut Point to the South Pole

and back is 1,766 statute miles, a formidable enough walk even through fields of clover, but foolhardy when done, unaided, in bitter cold and stabbing, blinding blizzards, 600 miles of it uphill all the way over a chain of mountains and a glasslike glacier and in breath-shortening altitudes. Scott's goal and pluck were commendable, but his strategy — which did not include the support of animals that have more often than not proven themselves under such conditions — was faulty.

There was another obstacle in the way, Roald Amundsen, a professional polar explorer. Amundsen was the meticulous planner, with all the practical sense that Scott lacked. The Norwegian was ready to embark on an expedition to find the North Pole, aboard his Nansen-designed *Fram,* when he received word that Cook (and later Peary) had already discovered it. Unruffled, he announced to his crew that the new goal would be the South Pole, not the North. "Success," he remarked later, "is a woman who has to be won, not courted. You have to seize her and carry her off, not stand under her window with a mandolin." And regarding the purpose of the trip, Amundsen minced no words: "On this little detour, science will have to look after itself."

The news of Amundsen's switch in plans was not well received in England. The conquest of the South Pole was to have been Scott's show. The Norski, as Amundsen was referred to in the press, was not playing by the rules, and the so-called "ethics of record-breaking" were discussed fully. "The question has been raised," complained one scientific journal, "whether it is decent and permissible for two explorers to try to reach the same point at the same time from different bases and by different means."

Amundsen's answer was yes, and his plan was as efficient, despite its short notice, as Scott's was inept. His crew was mobile, numbering only twenty men and including some of Norway's best cross-country ski-runners and dog-drivers. There were the many dogs themselves, to be used for draft and food. (Each fifty pounds of edible meat in the carcass of a husky meant hundreds of pounds less to be carried and cached.) "I worked out the precise day on which I intended to kill each dog," said Amundsen, "as its usefulness for pulling supplies diminished and its usefulness as food increased." This schedule was adhered to, almost to the exact day.

Amundsen set up his base at the Bay of Whales, a neat indentation in the shelf, sixty miles farther south than Scott's base at McMurdo. Sixty tons of seal carcasses were prepared for the expedition, and some three tons of meat and other provisions were carried to three depots on the route to the Pole. Flags and snowbeacons plainly marked the way and, unlike Scott, whose party relied on woolen underclothing and windproof outer garments, Amundsen fell back on fur. He even used a new form of tent, more quickly erected and more windproof than the conventional one; its dark color also reduced the glare of light that interfered with sleep on the trail.

"I don't know what to think of Amundsen's chances," Scott commented as the two expeditions prepared to head south. "If he gets to the Pole, it must be before we do, as he is bound to travel fast with dogs, and pretty certain to start early. On this account, I decided at a very early date to act exactly as I should have done had he not existed. Any attempt to race must have wrecked my plan, besides which it doesn't appear the sort of thing one is out for. . . . After all, it is the work that counts, not the applause that follows."

Amundsen was on his way on August 20, 1911, in brilliant weather, with four sleds, thirteen dogs to each, enough food for four months and four men — Helmer Hanssen, Oscar Wisting, Sverre Hassel, and Olav Bjaaland. Four days later,

Scott and three teams of four men each shoved off onto the Barrier ice, with two dog teams, ten ponies (half of the original group was dead), and two motor sledges.

Amundsen's pull to the Pole was unbelievably easy, almost leisurely. One account maintains that the party actually rode on their sleds for the first hundred miles to the 80° S. depot, which they reached in four days. From there on to 85° S. they were towed behind the sleds on their skis, so well-conditioned were the dogs. The weather held up beautifully, no storms, the winds mostly light and easterly. Food depots were laid at every degree of their trip south. And on December 14, Amundsen was standing at the South Pole. As he described it: "At three in the afternoon, a simultaneous 'Halt!' rang out from the drivers. They had carefully examined their sledge-meters, and they all showed the full distance — our Pole by reckoning. The goal was reached, the journey ended. I cannot say — though I know it would sound much more effective — that the object of my life was attained. That would be romancing rather too bare-facedly. I had rather be honest and admit straight out that I have never known any man to be placed in such a diametrically opposite position to the goal of his desires as I was at that moment. The regions around the North Pole — well, yes, the North Pole itself — had attracted me from childhood, and here I was at the South Pole. Can anything more topsy-turvy be imagined? After we had halted we collected and congratulated each other. We had good grounds for mutual respect in what had been achieved, and I think that was just the feeling that was pressed in the firm and powerful grasps that were exchanged. After this, we proceeded to the greatest and most solemn act of the whole journey — the planting of our flag. Pride and affection shone in the five pairs of eyes that gazed upon the flag as it unfurled itself with a sharp crack, and waved over the Pole."

It was over, this chase after a symbol, and even the staid British journal *Nature* reported later, "The pursuance of the main aim of the expedition was a splendid example of efficiency in plan, equipment, transport, physical strength and skilled leadership. . . . There was the point of view of the explorers, differing somewhat from that often taken by persons of other nationalities, displaying an indifference to comfort and a resistance to fatigue that appears remarkable, while at the same time there is a general levity of spirits which, unless one reads between the lines, might mask the unshakeable determination which drove the united party of five straight to their goal. . . . The scientific results, with the exception of those on oceanography, are of trivial importance, but they yield some scraps of new information and help to confirm the important facts described by Captain Scott, Sir Ernest Shackleton and others."

Meanwhile, Scott, who had left his *Discovery* hut on November 3, was in trouble even before he got off the Barrier ice and onto the Beardmore. Thick snowstorms and poor running conditions had slowed his pace, and his party was starting to consume rations planned for the summit. On December 5, at a camp they called the Slough of Despond, they were struck by the fifth blizzard since starting out. It held them up for four days, and undoubtedly played a part in the disastrous finale. Wrote Scott in his diary: "The blows we have had hitherto have lacked the very fine powdery snow, that especial feature of the blizzard. Today we have it fully developed. After a minute or two in the open air, one is covered from head to foot. The temperature is high so that what falls or drives against one sticks. The ponies — head, tails, legs and all parts not protected by their rugs — are covered with ice; the animals are standing deep in snow. The sledges are almost covered, and huge drifts are above the tents. . . . We have had breakfast, rebuilt the walls, and are now again in our bags. One cannot see the next tent, let alone the land. What on earth does such weather mean at this time of year? It is more than our share of ill-fortune, I think, but the luck may turn yet."

Scott's party finally plodded up onto the Beardmore. All of the ponies had been shot, and the dogs sent back to base camp with supporting parties. At the last moment, Scott selected the four men who would accompany him to the Pole: his friend Wilson; Captain L. E. G. Oates of the 6th Inniskilling Dragoons; Lieutenant Bowers of the Royal India Marines, and Petty Officer Edgar Evans.

"I am one of the five to go to the Pole," wrote a jubilant Wilson in a letter to his wife, to be brought back to the ship by the support party. "So this may be the last you hear of me for another whole year. . . . I am glad for your sake that I am one of the five . . . all fit and strong and well, and only 148 more miles to go. It seems too good to be true that this long journey to the Pole should be realizing itself — we ought to be there in less than a fortnight now. Our five are all very nice together and we shall be a happy party."

On ski and afoot, buffeted by incessant wind and stung by minus twenty degree temperatures and unaware that Amundsen had already reached the prize and was sledging homeward, Scott's party manhauled their heavy sleds slowly, for weeks, across the polar plateau to heartbreak on January 16. Wrote Scott: "The worst has happened. We marched well in the morning and covered seven and a half miles. Noon sight showed us in latitude 89° 42′ S. and we started off in high spirits in the afternoon, feeling that tomorrow would see us at our destination. About the second hour of the march, Bowers' sharp eyes detected what he thought was a cairn. He was uneasy about it but argued that it must be a sastrugus. Half an hour later, he detected a black speck ahead. Soon we knew that this could not be a natural snow feature. We marched on, found that it was a black flag tied to a sledge bearer; nearby, the remains of a camp, sledge-tracks and ski tracks going and coming and the clear trace of dogs' paws — many dogs. This told us the whole story. The Norwegians have forestalled us and are first at the Pole. It is a terrible disappointment, and I am very sorry for my loyal companions. Many thoughts come and much discomfort have we had. Tomorrow we must march on to the Pole and then hasten home with all the speed we can compass. All the day-dreams must go; it will be a wearisome return."

The next day, Scott wrote:

"January 17. Camp 69. T —22°. The Pole. Yes, but under very different circumstances from those expected. We have had a horrible day . . . companions labouring on with cold feet and hands. We started at 7:30, none of us having slept much after the shock of our discovery. . . . We have been descending again, I think, but there looks to be a rise ahead; otherwise, there is very little that is different from the awful monotony of past days. Great God! This is an awful place and terrible enough for us to have laboured to it without the reward of priority. Well, it is something to have got here, and the wind may be our friend tomorrow. We have a fat polar hoosh [a thick soup] in spite of our chagrin, and feel confident inside. Added a small stick of chocolate and the queer taste of a cigarette brought by Wilson. Now for the run home and a desperate struggle to get the news through first. I wonder if we can do it."

A day later, the party's flagging morale sagged lower with the discovery of Amundsen's tent and the official record that five Norwegians had been at the spot. "The tent is fine," wrote Scott, "a small, compact affair supported by a single bamboo. A note from Amundsen, which I keep, asks me to forward a letter to King Haakon!" (The exclamation point seems to hint that Scott was annoyed at the Norwegian's audacity, but the request to forward was, in truth, in the event that Amundsen didn't make it home safely.)

Thoughts of being a loser, second-best, explanations on his return — these must have eaten at Scott, but he kept them well under control in his subsequent diary entries, and there is but a single wistful statement as he and his men headed down the windswept plateau: "Well, we have turned our back now on the goal of our ambition, and we must face our eight hundred miles of solid dragging and goodbye to most of the daydreams."

After that, Scott's journal paints a frightening picture of a hopeless pull over snow that had as much glide as desert sand, groaning sledges, overcast skies, shrieking blizzards that tore the tops off snow-dunes and hurled the dry powder into their eyes, lost tracks, desperate searches for their food depots, hunger, daily weakening, and the cold, always the cold and always far below zero, numbing, hardening, and cutting open their lips and noses. Scott records the first death, that of Evans: "I was first to reach the poor man and was shocked at his appearance. He was on his knees with clothing disarranged, hands uncovered and frostbitten, a wild look in his eyes. He died at 12:30 A.M. (Feb. 17). It is a terrible thing to lose a companion in this way, but calm reflection shows that there could not have been a better ending to the anxieties of the past week."

March 2. It fell below −40° and this morning it took 1½ hours to get our foot gear on. . . . The surface is simply awful. . . . We are in a very queer street since there is no doubt we cannot do the extra marches, and feel the cold horribly.

March 3. God help us, we can't keep up this pulling, that is certain. Amongst ourselves, we are unendingly cheerful, but what each man feels in his heart I can only guess.

March 4. Things look black, indeed. . . . A colder snap is bound to come again soon. I fear that Oates at least will weather such an event poorly. Providence to our aid! Shall we get there?

March 5. Regret to say going from bad to worse. . . . Went to bed on a cup of cocoa and pemmican, solid, with the chill off. The result is telling on all, but mainly on Oates whose feet are in a wretched condition. . . . We mean to see the game through with a proper spirit, but it is tough work to be pulling harder than we ever pulled in our lives for long hours, and to feel that the progress is so slow. One can only say, God help us, and plod on our way, weary, cold and very miserable, though outwardly cheerful. We talk of all sorts of subjects in the tent, not much of food now. . . .

March 6. For the first time during the journey, I overslept myself, more than an hour. . . . Pulling with all our might, for our lives, we could scarcely advance at a rate of a mile an hour. Then it grew thick and three times we had to get out of harness to search for our tracks. . . . Poor Oates is unable to pull, sits on the sledge when we are track-searching. . . . He grows more silent. . . .

March 16 or 17. Lost track of dates but think the last correct. Tragedy all along the line. Day before yesterday, Titus Oates said he couldn't go on. He proposed that we should leave him in his sleeping bag. That we could not do and induced him to go on. . . . In spite of its awful nature for him, he struggled on and we made a few miles. At night he was worse and we knew the end had come. Should this be found, I want these facts recorded. Oates' last thoughts were of his mother, but immediately before he took pride in thinking his regiment would be pleased with the bold way in which he met his death. We can testify to his bravery. . . . He woke in the morning, yesterday. It was blowing a blizzard. He said, I am just going outside and may be some time. He went out into the blizzard and we have not seen him since. . . . We knew that poor Oates was walking to his death, but though we tried to dissuade him, we knew it was the act of a brave man and an English gentleman. We all hope to meet the end with a similar spirit, and assuredly the end is not far. . . . I can only write at lunch and then only occasionally. The cold is intense, −40° at midday. . . . Though we continually talk of fetching through, I don't think any one of us believes it in his heart.

March 18. My right foot has gone. . . . Two days ago I was

the proud possessor of the best feet. These are the steps of my downfall. . . . Like an ass, I mixed a small spoonful of curry powder with my pemmican. It gave me a violent indigestion. I lay awake and in pain all night.

March 21. Got within 11 miles of depot [One-Ton]. Had to lay up all yesterday in severe blizzard. Today forlorn hope. Wilson and Bowers going to depot for fuel.

March 22–23. Blizzard as bad as ever. Wilson and Bowers unable to start. . . . Tomorrow last chance. No fuel and only one or two of food left. Must be near the end. Have decided it shall be natural. We shall march for the depot with or without our effects and die in our tracks. [Earlier, Scott had "practically ordered" Wilson to hand over the means of ending their troubles. "Wilson had no choice between doing so and our ransacking the medicine cases. We have 30 opium tablets apiece and he is left with a tube of morphine."]

March 29. Outside the door of the tent it remains a scene of whirling drift. I do not think we can hope for any better things now. We shall stick it out to the end, but we are getting weaker, of course, and the end cannot be far. It seems a pity, but I do not think I can write more. R. Scott.

Then, a last entry: "For God's sake, look after our people."

Eight months later, a search party, with Cherry-Garrard among them, found the tent just south of One-Ton, drifted over with snow. The tips of two pairs of ski sticks and the bamboo sledge mast protruded out of the snow. Cherry-Garrard has described the scene: "Two of us entered, through the funnel of the outer tent and through the bamboos on which was stretched the lining of the inner tent. There was some snow — not much — between the two linings. But inside we could see nothing — the snow had drifted out the light. There was nothing to do but dig the tent out. Soon we could see the outlines. There were three men here.

"Bowers and Wilson were sleeping in their bags. Scott had thrown back the flaps of his bag at the end. His left hand was stretched over Wilson, his lifelong friend. Beneath the head of his bag, between the bag and the floor-cloth, was the green wallet in which he carried his diary. The brown books of diary were inside: and on the floor were some letters. . . . Near Scott was a lamp formed from a tin and some lampwick off a finnesko. It had been used to burn the little methylated spirit which remained. I think that Scott used it to help him write up to the end. I feel sure that he died last — and once I had thought that he would not go so far as some of the others. We never realized how strong that man was, mentally and physically, until now."

Inside the tent also were some thirty pounds of geological specimens and several rolls of photographic film. "There was even a book which I had lent to Bill," said Cherry-Garrard, "and he had brought it back. Somehow, we learned that Amundsen had been to the Pole, and that they too had been to the Pole, and both items of news seemed to be of no importance whatever."

During the last few days, perhaps hours, of his life Scott wrote the letters which, along with his remarkable diary, tell the unhappy tale of failure, but failure with the honor he prized so dearly.

To his wife: "What lots and lots I could tell you of this journey. How much better has it been than lounging in too great comfort at home. What tales you would have had for the boy. But, oh, what a price to pay."

To Vice Admiral Sir Francis C. Bridgeman: "I fear we have shipped up. A close shave . . . I want to tell you I was not too old for this job. It was the younger men who went under first. . . .

To Mrs. Wilson: "If this letter reaches you, Bill and I will have gone out together. We are very near it now and I should like you to know how splendid he was at the end . . . never a word of blame to me for leading him into this mess."

To Sir James Barrie: "We are pegging out in a very comfortless spot. . . . I may not have proved a great explorer, but we have done the greatest march ever made and come very near to great success. . . ."

To the public: ". . . We are weak, writing is difficult, but for my own sake I do not regret this journey, which has shown that Englishmen can endure hardships, help one another, and meet death with as great a fortitude as ever in the past. We took risks, we knew we took them; things have come out against us, and therefore we have no cause for complaint, but bow to the will of Providence, determined still to do our best to the last. But if we have been willing to give our lives to this enterprise, which is for the honour of our country, I appeal to our countrymen to see that those who depend on us are properly cared for. Had we lived, I should have had a tale to tell of the hardihood, endurance and courage of my companions which would have stirred the heart of every Englishman. These rough notes and our dead bodies must tell the tale. . . ."

The search party never moved them. They simply took the bamboos of the tent away and the tent covered them. Over the bodies, they built a great cairn of snow, and fixed a cross, made out of skis, on it. On either side they set the two sledges, upright and dug in.

Below us now the brown mountain peaks, thrusting up through the snow that buries most of their bulk, and then we are over the Beardmore, 140 miles of glacier creeping down from the 9,000-foot-high Polar Plateau over the mountains, to the Ross Shelf behind us. How effortlessly the gleaming slanted glacier's crust glides by beneath us. I wonder how they would have felt, Scott and Amundsen and Shackleton, doing it this way, hearing All-State up in the cockpit saying that landing up here on the plateau is as easy as pie, when the weather's good. "What you got's really a twenty-thousand-foot runway with five thousand feet of overrun, and you got to be blind, man, really blacked out, to miss it. What you do is you hit them back skis across the top of the snow hills before you set the nose ski, else you'll hotdog her and it's all skua bait. But it's when you do a little hero, like settin' her down in a whiteout, that's interesting. What you do is you set your gadgets here, automatic descent at sixteen hundred, seventeen hundred a minute, and you just lay back in your seat there and light up a cigar and wait till you feel them skis hit, and you glide in on the ice, nice, nice."

The loadmaster is complaining how things are changing at Pole with the new construction project. "Used to be a real camp, real frontier," he says. "You're lucky you're going to get to see that before it goes down the tubes for good. This is the last year anyone's going to get into the old facility under the ice; next year it'll be Chrome Dome City. Shit, used to be when you first went down you got this here medal. That's a winter-over medal, buddy, and to get that you had to be here thirty days at least. Now, guy gets off a plane and whammo, they hand him one of these and goddam, that ain't right. All you got to do now is walk around down there and they nail one of these on you. All you got to do is cross sixty-south and you're entitled to it, don't even have to land on the continent. No, the only fun about comin' down anymore is Chee Chee. Clubs used to close at six and you had to wear a coat and tie unless you lived in the hotel where you're drinkin'. That's a class place, Chee Chee is. Now, they open till ten but you still got to get dressed up. And the women, man, I get spoiled every time I pull liberty there. To hell with the states, to hell with the ice, let me stay in Chee. Christ, girl picks you up, takes you home, feeds you, takes you to her sack, wakes you up in the morning, and here comes her old lady with eggs, man, how you want your eggs? Oh, mother.

Christ, you come back to the states, man, and you get yourself laid you got to get your own chow afterwards."

All-State's on the intercom, telling us we'll be landing at Pole in five minutes. "It's minus forty degrees down there," he says, "a good stiff wind, and remember it's nine thousand feet high, so don't take any breaths real fast, or walk fast. If you get sick, we got pills, and don't be afraid to ask for oxygen." He says he'll be taking off after we debark, and if all goes right he'll be back at sixteen hundred, 'fore we turn into snowmen.

We hit the ice with a jolt and a swish, and shudder along to a stop as the loadmaster kicks away the crate and cuts the rope holding the door with his sheath knife. All-State does not shut down his engines. Standard procedure here at Pole is to keep them running to prevent freeze-up. "This is the place," he says over the intercom, "Ninety-South, there ain't no more." I have a sudden need for someone to congratulate me, and I wish this were being covered on live TV for the folks back home.

We go clumsily out the hatch, dragging our bulky survival kits, and plant our footprints for man and mankind, and are immediately engulfed by a swarm of scientists who have been waiting for us, beards heavy with ice. They're all wearing sunglasses. Mine are stuffed in my pocket, and that is the first mistake, for I am suddenly blinded by the fierce sunlight glancing off the miles of white that surround us, and the sandlike snow that I do not flinch from quickly enough, grainy, dry snow whipped into my eyes by a slapping wind, stinging and drying them as a blotter dries ink. I am embarrassed, and raise a bearclaw in front of my smarting eyes, shielding them and my face that feels like it's been hit with a pail of cracked ice. I ask hurriedly, "Where's the Pole, where's the Pole?" "Over there," someone shouts and points, and I career off, head hunched in the wind, hauling my bag, trying to make it as fast as I can to the circle of flags fifty yards away, a blur of color through my dried-out eyes. The rapid move is also a mistake, and I have exerted myself in the rarefied air of this plateau I had forgotten was one, and I am unexpectedly thrown into a fearful, clawing panic. I gasp desperately for breath, suffocating incongruously out in the open, in the middle of miles of nothing. My heart is beating out of control now, adding to the fright, and all I can think of is, fuck the Pole, I want to get in somewhere.

A few yards away is a plywood shed engulfed in swirling snow, and I stumble toward that in steely cold, losing one of my gloves and feeling a sudden searing in one of my fingers as I yank open the door and step onto a landing from which a flight of stairs leads down deep beneath the ice to a dimly lit corridor. Hoarfrost, hard and thick and old, is on the plywood sides and on the back of the door, on the ceiling and the first few steps. Still struggling to breathe, I reach for a banister to steady myself, and in a few moments I am calm, my breathing and racing heart slowed to normal. I plan never to go out there again. Those guys, Scott and Amundsen, they had to be nuts.

I am still in place on the landing, nursing my frozen finger, when the door goes out and my group herds in, nearly knocking me down the stairs. "We'll go out later, when the wind dies," says Dr. Wirtz, the station scientific leader, "get you to the Poles later, you wouldn't want to miss them." "Them?" Right now I don't want to see even one. "Yeah," says Wirtz as we clump down the stairs, "we've got two." I hope he isn't going to give me any more nonsense about geomagnetic and magnetic. "No, it's just that there's one right outside the door that they call the Photographer's Pole, and several hundred yards away there's the actual Pole." The reason for all of this is that the ice cap is moving slowly, twenty meters a year to be exact, and the Photographer's Pole — that's the one with the flags around it that I caught a blur of while stumbling in here — has slid along with the cap. It was over the real Pole once. The actual Pole, of course, doesn't move; it's a geographical point. The new station being built a quarter-mile away, upstream, as Dr. Wirtz puts it, is also moving with the ice cap and should be over the actual Pole in about five years.

We walk and slide down the icy stairs, and end up about thirty feet below the ice that is crushing this old station, in faint light and in an eerie maze of frost-rimmed corridors that smell and feel like a walk-in meat refrigerator. We go past open and closed wooden doors, past stacks of crated food stored along the walls in the interlocking corridors, enough for three years, Wirtz says. Chow mein, he adds, he's sick of it. There's a Christmas tree with a sign, FAKE FIR, hanging where the star ought to be, and another sign that reads, PEOPLE'S PARK, KEEP OFF THE FUCKIN' GRASS, stuck in the floor. Down another corridor radiating off to the left, its sides shored up with plywood, is a lantern hanging from an ice-coated beam. It is beginning to look more like an abandoned coal mine, until Dr. Wirtz pulls open a door and invites us into The Club.

It is dark inside, and that is comforting to my eyes that are still hurting from the snow glare and the sharp snow dust. Hanging on the walls are six red lanterns, each positioned carefully to cast its scarlet beam directly on a color photo of a nude female, supine, prone, chair-straddling, and bicycle-kicking. Metal bases of used JATO bottles serve as ashtrays next to soft leather chairs set on platforms stepped off the floor in various parts of the room, each chair with a hassock. Through a door are visible a Ping-Pong table, a movie projector, a pool table under a picture of a penguin in earmuffs and scarf, a sign hanging around its neck, IF YOU THINK YOU GOT IT TOUGH TRY WINTERING OVER WITH AN EGG ON YOUR TOES.

But it is the bar in here, a mammoth oaken affair, with an enormous nude on the wall behind it, a mate of the one at the Ross Hilton back in McMurdo, that dominates the room. Lighted red and green lanterns hang over it from beams, their glow reflecting in the highly polished wood. On one end of the bar sits an open jar of peanut butter, a knife dug into the contents. On the other, a menorah. And over the menorah, framed and under glass, is encased a pair of pink bikini panties, an inscription over them, MISS SOUTH POLE'S SKIVVIES. Except for those, captioned as they are, there is no other visible reminder that this is really the South Pole. Sinking back in the soft leather, staring at the bar, its leather-covered stools and its illuminated nude backdrop, we are lulled by a stereo playing "Me and My Shadow" and listen, on and off, to Dr. Wirtz, who is telling us about the thermal pendulum probe that is melting its way down through the ice here to the rock beneath the cap, its sensors beaming back information on the age of the ice at various levels. Except for the panties and now Dr. Wirtz, it's hard to imagine that upstairs is a white world of storm-beaten ice that can drive a human being in on himself and force him to come to terms with what is out there. A fearful thought comes, as while sitting in a crowded theater or in a small bar beneath street level. Fire. It is the greatest fear here in Antarctica, particularly at Pole, as it has been since the early days. Fire and the short water supply. Production of water, says Wirtz, is the most arduous task here, time-consuming and back-breaking, and in that regard it's another example of how far we haven't progressed from when Scott lived in Antarctica. It is strangely reassuring that there is a bastion like this that Scott and Amundsen, whose names and pictures are on the outside entrance-shed, would have been comfortable with, to know that though the LC-130 has replaced the dog team there has been, up to now anyway, some limit on how far the modern world is allowed to trespass. It is upsetting, too, to dwell on the thought that this last stand against space-age intrusion could send us all, in case of fire, up and out there where the loss of even a cap or glove could mean death in a few hours.

We finish our rest and tour the station that, back in 1956, was being built by twenty-four Seabees. It was on top of the ice then, six aluminum and plywood huts of varied colors, connected by these tunnels, now buried under years of drifting snow. Dr. Paul Allman Siple was the scientific leader. Siple, then forty-eight, was Admiral Byrd's protégé. He had already spent more time on the ice than any other person, and when he left it for the sixth time in 1958 he had chalked up nearly six years of polar life. Siple first went to Antarctica as a nineteen-year-old Boy Scout with Byrd's first expedition after a year as a biology major at Allegheny College. Siple had twenty-one required merit badges and thirty-eight additional ones, and was "physically fit, morally straight and mentally awake," as he put it in the essay that won him the coveted trip to the ice with Byrd. He wrote that he had had five years of Sea Scouting experience and spent thirty-five weeks on camping trips and overnight hikes, and had done "at least four weeks of winter camping, spending the majority of the nights in shelters of my own making, in snowstorms and very inclement weather." From this experience, he said, "I feel somewhat prepared to withstand Antarctic conditions. I have passed my hiking merit badge and do considerable walking every day. In this respect, I am sure I could not be a detriment to the expedition."

Siple had also opened on a note that could not have helped but please the Admiral: "From my first observation of Commander Byrd, I have highly admired him and his work. Because of the scientific training and experience that I would receive from association with him and his companions, I hope to be the fortunate Scout to go on the Polar expedition. If there were no other merits to be derived except the close relationship with Commander Byrd, I would feel highly honored if chosen."

Siple spent twenty-two months between 1928 and 1930 on the continent that at the time was actually more mysterious than the sunlit side of the moon. He shoveled coal as a deckhand aboard the *City of New York,* he collected seals and penguins, he did taxidermy, he trained and handled dog teams. "He went South with us as a Boy Scout," said Byrd, "but he took his place as a man."

Siple was back in the Antarctic, as chief biologist with Byrd, on the 1933–1935 expedition. In 1939–1941, he made his third trip with Byrd, as a base leader and as a navigator on exploratory flights over the continent, and a fourth trip in 1946 with the Navy's cold-weather exercise, Operation High Jump. At Byrd's urging, Siple was given scientific command of the new Pole Station, the building of which Byrd saw as one to "tax all our ingenuity and will in itself be a great national achievement."

We walk the corridors for a while, huffing and puffing clouds of vapor, and it is difficult not to feel some remorse over the modern world come to Antarctica. The huts at Cape Evans and Hut Point and Cape Royds evoke a nostalgia for a romantic era long gone, and so, too, does this primitive camp that is being pressed out of shape by the ice above. What makes the sense of loss stronger here is that this station is still lived and worked in. I can see and hear the encroachment of the ice, as it creaks and buckles the old overhead beams and warps the plywood and curved metal walls that separate the huts. I have talked with the men who have stayed here, or read what they felt, and I know why they liked or hated it all. In a year, it will be abandoned, and the men will move into the carpeted and paneled rooms inside the aluminum dome that is going up a quarter-mile away. I was not a part of the abandonment of Scott's or Shackleton's huts, merely a pilgrim paying homage sixty years after the wake. But here, although I have not helped to build this comfortable old station, nor spent a winter here, the feeling is much like what I felt when urban renewers smashed down a Boston tenement I had lived in as a child. It was demolished to let the developers inflate the seventeen dollars a month rent my mother paid for the view of the Charles River and a subway line a block away to three hundred a month for a studio and six hundred for the works with pool. I've always wondered whether my favorite toy soldier, lost in that apartment when the building went down, got buried and is there still, under the asphalt or the grass or the pool. I think of it now, that soldier, lying prone with binoculars fixed to his eyes, as I step into the head and up to the urinal. Peeing, I figure I'm leaving something of me here, too, when this place is buried for good.

"Say," says Dacey Higgins, standing at the next urinal. "You see that toilet over there? Used to have it rigged up a few years ago, sign over it says, 'Lift cover to read Scott's last words.' When you did, there's a sign inside the cover, says, 'Cryonics, You Fucking USARPS, I'll Be Back.'"

The small mess hall is brightly lit, in sharp contrast to the corridors and The Club. It is a museum of nude art. Walls papered, every inch, with centerfolds and covers from every skin magazine on earth, ass shots, crotch shots, and boobs galore. The tops of the mess tables are similarly decorated, thick glass laid over, and it is somewhat unnerving as we dine on Rock Cornish hen with sherry sauce and lemon and apple pie to have to stare into clumps of pubic hair. Dacey makes the obvious remark about eating pussy, it's better than Cornish hen, and Dr. Wirtz, digging into a slab of pie, says, "There is a lot of oral gratification in here, isn't there?" When the men are ready to leave here, he says, "They'll tell you who they're going to screw in Christchurch, when, how many times and how." Wirtz doesn't think it's a good idea to keep women out of Pole Station. No wonder these guys have trouble relating when they get back home, he says. "They've been locked in a place like this for a year with nothing but stylized views of women, all boobs and snatch, and when they get out they see a female and she looks like she's from another planet, because she's got clothes on." The conversation turns to what it would be like if the situation that currently exists in Antarctica, a handful of women to hundreds of men, were reversed. "Now you're talking," says Dacey. "Don't kid yourself," says Dr. Wirtz; "you wouldn't like it. Just think, he says, of all that premenstrual tension clocking out in a hundred-thirty ladies, two, three guys caught in the middle of it; why it'd be holy hell every day of the month."

Good food and drink over, we are ready to go topside and look at the Pole, the real reason we came, after all. The panic is gone now, and so is the pain in my finger. Up the icy stairway and out the door, glasses still in my pocket, we are packed into a waiting tracked vehicle. "We'll get you to the real Pole first," says Wirtz, laughing, his breath actually crackling in the intense cold. "It's not as pretty as that shutterbug's delight over there, and we'll get to that while we're waiting for the plane to come pick us up."

We bump along, lumped together in a furry bundle in the back of the truck, and in a few minutes we are there. We climb out, flinching again in the dazzling sun that drenches the awesome snowscape that has unfolded all around us. We are standing on a massive disc, now bright white, now peacock blue, absolutely featureless in every direction we turn, no distant ranges, no hills, not a twig to mar it, the whole panorama capped by the cloudless dome of a lovely azure sky that fits neatly down over the high plateau. The place has been blown clean of haze and dust, and I feel as though I am walking through cerulean heavens, so clear is the reflection of the sky in the snow. I can sense the utter silence beneath the wind that pierces it, and for a moment the blue loveliness that absorbs us is forgotten, supplanted by the reality of a dreary nothingness, of a dead world where all directions are north, where it is always the heart of winter, where the ice does not pass away with the end of the long night, and where springtime's promise of resurrection is broken. For there will be no flash of robin's breast here, ever, nor bluebird's wing, no crocus or rosebud or earthworm in this spring without fever. Not even the ugly black skua, for nothing that lives can survive for long here where Nature has overplayed its role, except bundled and sheltered man. I am, at last, under the brass screw. I think of the tons of snow pressing down on the rock bed almost two miles below my rubber-booted feet, and wonder about its purpose. At home, in a New England winter, it seeps into the earth, protects the garden under a soft coverlet, and replenishes rivers and springs. But here, it lies heavy and unmelting, either God's big joke or His warehouse. It may be, too, that this world that does not change or move from the spot to which it is fixed by the daily rotation of the planet, has been put here to thwart those boring media prophets of weather, for it is a place where, thank God, they are not needed. No need for a TV personality who passes off U.S. Weather Bureau forecasts for his or her own, nor *Farmer's Almanac* in this place where winter is forever on the loose. No need for the Bang's Corners Bug Barometer that the UPI and AP chortle over every year out of Ohio, full of omens dark and heavy about the coming of winter weather, like woolly bear caterpillars black on both ends and bluebottles dopy and nearly dead, and hornets hanging their nests higher to keep from smothering in the drifts that are expected. They'd all be out of business here, after one report of winter in July.

There is a slender red-and-white-striped stick stuck in the snow to mark the precise bottom of the earth, and a low wooden sign staked next to it. We head for it, compelled to stand at the exact spot. "Geographic South Pole," proclaims the sign. "Ice Thickness Over 9,000 Ft. Elevation 9186 Ft. Aver. Temp. —57°F." This is the storied spot of human aspiration and mystery, where all the time differences in the world converge and one can set a watch to suit a whim, where to go anywhere from here you simply turn north, where you cannot walk a straight line and maintain the same direction unless your course is spiral. We walk around the stick several times so we can write later that we've walked around the world, several times. No one, thankfully, stands on his head. We have agreed that's too much like putting on a lei in Honolulu.

Now I feel the silence deepening, and sense the infinity, and the aloneness that is there even though someone is with me. I have felt less alone in a room by myself. The white monotony entrances me. It is suddenly monotonous no more, and I hear the tinkling of ice crystals blowing across the crusted snow. Overhead, the sky has changed its hue, powder blue near the horizon now and almost royal blue overhead. There is a halo sparkling around the rime-ringed sun. There are thoughts of south as I knew it, before coming here, of cotton fields and magnolia, of pleasant-scented southernwood and warm winds blowing softly. South, directly opposite to north on the left when one faces the setting sun, never to question that all through life, until this moment. South, the side of a church that is on the right hand of one who faces the altar. I wonder how you would build a cathedral here. There is music that I do not hear, Grieg and Sibelius and Mendelssohn's "Wedding March." There are lines by someone anonymous, of realms of purest alabaster white, wreathed in vast infinitude of light, a glittering azure world of crystal day.

But it is the horizon that is the restorer, not this mote sought by Shackleton and Scott and Amundsen. Not this artificial point of reference, but the visual limit of the plateau, encircling me and dropping off somewhere in the blue. It is out there, the real goal, unending. From here, at this vantage, I can see into the beyond, from this limit of earth I can see no limit. In the distant horizon is the search, and I feel as though I am standing in yesterday, looking into tomorrow.

Back at Amundsen-Scott Station, having our pictures taken under the orange and black barber pole topped by a mirrored glass ball. The ball was placed on the Photographer's Pole years ago for an experiment permitting a wide-angle reflected view of the sky so that halo photos could be made. But it had too many imperfections, and now it's an ornament.

While waiting for All-State to come back for us, we tour the new station that is abuilding, and we clamber over the base that will support the aluminum dome in a year. Amorphous bladders, full of fuel, lie bloated in the snow, and the area is cluttered with heavy equipment: tractors, trucks, bulldozers. I pick up a chunk of snow. It is clean and light and hollow-sounding when rapped with a knuckle. It can be sandpapered, it is so dry. I put a bit in my pocket to see how long it will last as a souvenir, and the LC-130 comes swishing in to gather us up.

When I was a boy, I had this book, a treasury of heroes and heroines, a record of high endeavor and strange adventures, and I would sit with it for hours in a rocking chair in front of an oil stove in my kitchen, letting the tales ease me into fantasy. I was John Paul Jones shouting he had not begun to fight, and King Arthur grasping the magic sword that none but the bravest might hold, and it was death for me, William Tell, if I missed, and death for my son if I shot too close. I had difficulty with Jeanne d'Arc drawing the arrow from her breast with the courage of a veteran, and with Molly Pitcher firing cannonballs squarely into British lines, mostly because I felt heroes were made to impress the girls, and in my fantasies there was always a girl, all bosom and thighs and in love with me.

I can fantasize, too, here on the ice as an adult, even though we can buy silver penguins in the Ship's Store, or listen to Navy DJ Al Bray break a world's record for continuous radio broadcasting, on for a steady 269 hours and five minutes at the mike of Station AFAN, or watch an Antarctic Basketball Association championship game between the VXE-6 Penguins and the Junior Officers. For despite the neutron monitors that chatter like machine guns as they trap and process cosmic rays and punch the data on tape, the plastic Christmas trees stuck in lifeless snow and the hitch-hiker we pass as we scout for thinning ice in a Trackmaster — the sign he holds aloft reads, "How About A Fucking Ride?" — despite technology, the ghosts of heroes are everywhere. They haunt us, and I am ever eager, along with all the rest, to believe that this isolated place is the last bastion of the existentialist prescript that we are what we make of ourselves.

Prodded by the ghosts and perhaps also as reaction against the convention that has come to a place we feel it has no right to be — or perhaps it is because we are amateurs — we all have an irresistibly strong urge to do our own special "hero thing." The individual feats are studied and often frivolous, like pissing into Erebus's smoking crater or lying on the ice in bathing trunks. "I did the hero thing, you know," a young construction worker tells me. "At the Pole, I took off my gloves, unzipped my fly, and flashed it. Got frostbite, a real asshole." He uses the expression in an offhanded way, with a trace of deprecation, as though he does not want me to take him seriously, that it's all kid stuff, not hero. But what he really wants is for me to say, "Holy Jesus, this guy's got balls." And I do, and I mean it, for we all want to go down in legend and song, maybe even merchandised on T-shirts.

So the day before we go home, I climb with three others to the top of Observation Hill, over ancient cinder, lava, and crumbling rock and patches of snow and ice. I am the only one in thin dungarees and canvas mukluks instead of heavy windpants and rubber boots. To a mountaineer, this height is a hump, but I am an amateur and there is a saying here on the ice that the greater the amateur the greater the adventure. It is midnight and the sun is pouring down on us, and we are gasping and laughing uncontrollably and full of brandy. Exhilarated, I cling in high wind and icy cold to the weathered wooden cross, nine feet tall, that Cherry-Garrard helped drag up here sixty years ago and jam into the rocks on the crest in memory of daring men who knew this formidable height well, who gazed thankfully up at it each time they returned from hard pulls over windswept snows and through gloomy polar nights. The cross against which I lean now, with the cold wind whipping my face, has a worn inscription on it, the concluding lines from Tennyson's *Ulysses*: "To strive, to seek, to find, and not to yield."

The view from up here is grand. Below us sprawls Mc-Murdo with its huddle of fuel tanks and crude huts. In the clear distance are the somber mountains of the Transantarctic Range and the long, white shining slopes of swollen Erebus, its spew of steam etched in the slate-blue sky like a Wedgwood cameo. Out there, too, with the cross facing toward its icy solitude, is the Barrier on which Scott and his men died, their footprints and their bodies covered by wind-scoured snow, perhaps forever preserved in desolation. Holding onto the cross, I think of them lying in the stillness and the sunshine and the shadow. I think also of what made them come here — science, adventure, personal gain — and how those very reasons are what drive today's Antarcticans. All that is different is the time and the mode of travel.

And I can admire them all, Scott and the USARPs and the Sea Bees. It is difficult not to. No matter that each, at some time on the journey south, has brought a share of mediocrity and conformity and questionable motives and, as a result, has helped make this unconventional place almost like any other to which men and women have come in a pack. And no matter that few, if any, have come like Thoreau's woodchopper merely to wallow in wildness, seeking it for its own sake. A journey to Antarctica has never been a passage to freedom and purity of spirit, tempting as it is to think that it could be. But it is a different journey, one for which only a few are singled out, and there is more warmth and fellowship here than there probably is anywhere else on earth. I am sure of that now, staring out over the Barrier. There will always be weathermen in purple track shoes who will come to Antarctica, like the one I met back at Skyland. But it is Cherry-Garrard and not the weatherman who makes sense. "Courage, or ambition, or love of notoriety may take you to the Antarctic, or any other uncomfortable place in the world," said the man who helped set this cross against which I lean, "but it won't take you far inside without being found out."